Secret Identity Crisis

Secret Identity Crisis

Comic Books and the Unmasking of Cold War America

MATTHEW J. COSTELLO

continuum

NEW YORK • LONDON

2009

The Continuum International Publishing Group Inc
80 Maiden Lane, New York, NY 10038

The Continuum International Publishing Group Ltd
The Tower Building, 11 York Road, London SE1 7NX

www.continuumbooks.com

Library of Congress Cataloging-in-Publication Data

Costello, Matthew J. (Matthew John), 1963–
  Secret identity crisis : comic books and the unmasking of Cold War America / by Matthew J. Costello.
      p. cm.
  Includes bibliographical references and index.
  ISBN-13: 978-0-8264-2997-1 (hbk. : alk. paper)
  ISBN-10: 0-8264-2997-1 (hbk. : alk. paper)
  ISBN-13: 978-0-8264-2998-8 (pbk. : alk. paper)
  ISBN-10: 0-8264-2998-X (pbk. : alk. paper) 1. Comic books, strips, etc.—Social aspects—United States. 2. Comic books, strips, etc.—Political aspects—United States. 3. Cold War—Influence. I. Marvel Comics Group. II. Title.

  PN6725.C69 2009
  741.5'30973—dc22

                                    2008030564

Printed in the United States of America

9780826429407

Contents

Acknowledgments

IT IS COMMONPLACE TO NOTE that any academic work is a collaborative effort, and this is no exception. One of the joys of finishing such a project is finally thanking everyone who helped make it possible, and I have many thanks to offer. At Continuum, David Barker and his fellow editors were supportive and critical. Carol Pinkus of Marvel Comics helped secure permissions for the artwork that Marvel has graciously allowed me to reproduce in this book. Portions of chapter 6 were presented at the American Studies Association Annual Meeting in Atlanta, November, 2004.

At Saint Xavier University, a semester sabbatical and financial support from the Center for Educational Practice helped secure materials necessary for research (and yes, I bought comic books with your money). Conversations with colleagues, including Judy Hilmer, Michael Bathgate, and Karen Benjamin, and with several classes of students helped refine my thinking on several of the issues treated in this book. Nelson Hathcock has been particularly helpful, listening to me often, reading through several drafts, and offering insightful and graceful criticism. Carl Bonasera of All American Comics in Evergreen Park, Illinois, was a font of information and ideas, a knowledgeable analyst of the comic industry and the books. These colleagues gave their time and expertise to improve this project; any flaws are the product of my own limitations.

Finally, three generations of Costellos have helped make this book possible. My parents indulged my early fascination with superhero comics, although my father always wondered about the attraction of the "goddamned funny books." My wife, Cathy, has been a constant source of support, inspiration, and criticism; she has read several portions of the manuscript, offered astute criticism, and has graciously suppressed her embarrassment at the boxes of "research materials" in our basement. My sons, Ethan and Dylan, have been both a major inspiration and at times a welcome distraction. They are my true superheroes. I dedicate this book to my family, without whom it never would have come to be.

Introduction

PHYSICIST BRUCE BANNER, caught in the nuclear explosion of his experimental gamma bomb, is transformed into the rampaging green monster the Hulk. High school student Peter Parker, bitten by an irradiated spider, gains the powers of the spider and becomes Spider-Man. Reed Richards and his friends are caught in a belt of cosmic radiation while orbiting Earth in a spacecraft and are transformed into the Fantastic Four. Human teenagers develop superpowers through genetic mutations as a result of increased radiation in the atmosphere and are organized as the X-Men. Matt Murdock, blinded by an accident with radioactive waste as a child, develops superhuman senses and becomes Daredevil. While Stan Lee suggests he clung to the hackneyed idea of radioactivity in creating Marvel's stable of superheroes because of his limited imagination,[1] radiation and the bomb are nonetheless the big bang that spawned the "Marvel universe."

The Marvel superhero comic that came to dominate the comic book industry for most of the last five decades was born under the mushroom cloud of potential nuclear war that was a cornerstone of the four-decade bipolar division of the world between the United States and the USSR. These stories were consciously set in this world and reflected the changing culture of Cold War (and post-Cold War) America; they thus provide a very useful avenue through which to explore the political culture of the period.

Like other forms of popular entertainment, comic books tend to be very receptive to cultural trends, to reflect them, comment on them, and sometimes inaugurate them. The Marvel comics of the 1960s and 1970s were seen at the time by their readers as engaged with the contemporary political and social cultures and, as such, were widely read not only by adolescents, but by college

1

students and other adults. Stan Lee, the main writer and public face of Marvel comics, became a highly sought-after speaker. The letters pages of these comics reflected not only an engagement with the stories Marvel was telling, but also with the social and political issues of the day. In the 1970s and 1980s several creators of comics saw themselves as active social critics. In more recent years the popular and lucrative migration of many of these characters from the cultural ghetto of comic books to the highly profitable cinema suggests that these characters still touch some aspect of American cultural identity.

The American Self in the Cold War

This book examines the impact of the Cold War on American national identity as seen through the lens of superhero comic books. The first fifteen years of the Cold War were characterized by major transformations in the American political economy as the United States developed the national security apparatus to contain communism, and the delayed consumer demand of World War II and vast increases in productivity paved the way for unparalleled economic growth. Cultural change followed material change, as Americans became increasingly concerned with issues of identity, both national and personal. This was manifest particularly among youth in the 1960s, as people on the left and the right sought an authentic politics, leading them to join in the popular mobilizations associated on the right with the Young Americans for Freedom and on the left with the Students for a Democratic Society. During the 1950s, a myth of a unitary national identity was created, fostering what Godfrey Hodgeson has called the ideology of liberal consensus.[2] The tension between this consensual American identity and an increasingly unclear personal identity represented by this quest for authenticity became a major fault line along which Cold War culture fractured over the next three decades. As this consensus identity ruptured into conflict over civil rights, the Vietnam War, and Watergate, Americans were left mourning the loss of a common public identity that was more myth than reality. Retreating from the public sphere, Americans rejected the quest for public identity to focus on their private selves.

The collapse of the myth of consensus had deeper repercussions. Developed as support for the new Cold War political economy, the consensus myth had blended elements of the rhetoric of American identity in a new and vital way. These rhetorical elements defined America as a virtuous nation of autonomous individuals engaged in a divinely inspired progressive mission of moral uplift. These elements—freedom, progress, and providence—had been the core of any definition of the American self for well over a century and were the contours of the contested terrain that was the battle to define the American self. As the myth of consensual identity became increasingly hegemonic, these rhetorical elements became rigidly fixed into a specific configuration. Any challenge to the consensus thus undermined their rhetorical power. Thus, as the identity consensus dissolved into an identity crisis, Americans came to question the validity of these elements. The Cold War thus weakened the very language of community in America. As the continual reference to culture wars in political life over the last two decades attests, absent a legitimizing rhetoric of national identity, defining the American self became highly problematic.

The end of the Cold War was equally transformative. The national security state of the Cold War lost much of its raison d'être with the collapse of the Soviet Union. The Fordist industrial plant of integrated firms and organized labor had spawned a political economy that made labor, business, and the state partners in maintaining industrial output and providing social services. Under the impetus of global competition, that production structure gave way to leaner, more mobile firms, weaker unions, and a reduction in government regulation that created a less organized political economy, one in which ever more transactions took place at arm's length in the market, outside the integration of the firm. A more individualized economy generated a more individualized politics, with many citizens demanding smaller, less interventionist government by the 1980s. Attempts to reconstruct the myth of consensus failed in this new context, and both national and personal identity became increasingly contentious, reflecting that the effects of the cultural breakdown of the Cold War were even more profound than the mere dissonance between a myth of consensus and a more divisive reality. By the

1990s, culture wars and identity politics were the major arena of social and political contestation. The politicization of national identity was largely a product of the Cold War—both in attempts to gain support in the 1950s and the breakdown of that support through the 1970s. The extent of this breakdown was evident in the twenty-first century as the United States embarked on a new national security crusade, the so-called War on Terror. Not even the most deadly attack on American soil could generate sufficient galvanizing power to re-create and sustain a sense of national purpose. While support for the War on Terror was nigh universal in the aftermath of the terrorist attacks of September 11, 2001, within three years there was much popular questioning of counterterrorism policies, both international and domestic. Within five years the president who oversaw the War on Terror would have an approval rating in the low 30th percentile, and his war would be supported by only a minority of the public. The rhetorical elements of the American self have lost their power to describe the American reality and seem capable of being asserted descriptively only with irony. They have not lost their power as aspirations, however, and continue to inform expressions of hope. Absent the myopia of the Cold War consensus, it is possible that these rhetorical elements of freedom, progress, and virtue may continue to motivate people to action even though they are no longer seen as descriptive of the American reality.

Superhero Comic Books and the Cold War

Born just before World War II, comic books became the dominant medium of youth culture before the advent of television. The industry went into the doldrums in the 1950s, but emerged again in the 1960s with a broader readership extending to young adults, particularly college students. Poor management and increasing competition from television, movies, and video games saw the industry almost collapse in the 1980s and 1990s but stabilize at a lower level of readership. In the last few years, the highly successful migration of comic book characters to movie screens has created a new awareness of and interest in the medium. As a disposable commodity, comic books have generally operated on a slim profit margin, and thus the industry tends to be highly responsive to cultural trends among its readership. A medium with relatively wide circulation (at least for young and late adolescent males) during most of its history, and one that is highly responsive to cultural trends, the comic book provides a unique window into American popular culture.

Comic books, and particularly superhero comic books, are closely linked to warfare. Emerging first in the 1930s as an offshoot of pulp magazine publication, the earliest comic books reprinted comic strips from the Sunday papers. The first superhero comics—*Action Comics* featuring Superman—debuted in 1938, inaugurating what is commonly called the "golden age" of comic books as the new medium exploded into existence.[3] Superheroes soon became the dominant character in the form. The earliest Depression-era superheroes, particularly Superman, evinced a strong populist orientation, often directing their actions against corrupt businessmen and politicians. This changed with the attack on Pearl Harbor and the rise of the European conflict. Adopting the martial spirit, nationalist superheroes proliferated to combat the Axis powers. As many have noted, since it would be impossible to imagine the war if superheroes confronted these threats directly (could Superman not defeat the Nazis single-handedly in an afternoon?), the comics fought the war on the home front, against saboteurs, spies, and treasonous criminals. The proliferation of superheroes immediately prior to the war—and their early involvement in confronting the Nazi threat—signaled the prowar sympathies of comic creators. Perhaps most famous is the cover of the first issue of *Captain America*, in which the hero is depicted punching Adolf Hitler. This magazine, dated March (and released in February) 1941, predated the United States' entry into the war by nearly a year.

It was against the Nazis and the Japanese that the superhero comic came of age. Comic books proliferated after the United States entered into the war, and nearly all superheroes were engaged in fighting the Axis in some form. Gerard Jones suggests that the superhero comic represented a uniquely American exuberance that characterized the space between Great Depression and World War II:

Superheroes were . . . an expression of a rising American thrill.
All the queasiness of the Depression was about to be blown
away in a great and terrible battle, and as much as people
shook their heads about the horror of war, there was a hunger
for it, too. The war meant not survival and dirty compromise,
but utter triumph or utter despair. It meant unity of purpose
too, and the superheroes embodied that in their polychrome
simplicity: Superman, Captain America, and Wonder Woman
were the most distinct individuals imaginable, but at the same
time, each of them was all of us . . . America had won the
last war. Since then it had only grown in size, influence, and
industrial capacity. It had held itself back from world events as
fascism spread, but Roosevelt's voters knew how powerful the
country was. America was playing Clark Kent. It was time to rip
off the suit.[4]

Representing nationalist aspirations, the superhero comic was
also prone to jingoistic excesses. Ethnic stereotyping was common. The Japanese were generally portrayed as nearly subhuman;
the Germans were stentorian and easily fooled. Caricature and
stereotyping also typified the heroes: if the villains were physically
subhuman and totally immoral, the heroes became wooden, char-
acterless visions of virtue. Given the weakness of characters—both
heroes and villains—it is unsurprising that few superheroes survived the war; by the end of the 1940s the only superheroes still in
existence were Batman, Superman, and Wonder Woman.

As the superhero faded from the scene new genres emerged.
War, cowboy, romance, and jungle comics all became popular
after the war. Bradford Wright sees these books as "basically
affirm[ing] the triumphalist culture of postwar America. All
expressed moral certainty about American virtues, confidence
in the nation's institutions, and optimism for a new age of affluence."[5] William Savage, who views 1950s comic books as more
challenging than does Wright, still argues that "comic books
functioned to maintain (if not boost) morale in the face of a few
unthinkable things, including atomic war and/or Communist
takeover of the United States."[6]

The crime and horror comics that became the best-selling
genre were different, offering a macabre and perverse vision of
the heart of consensus America. The most famous of these—*Tales*

from the Crypt and *Vault of Horror*—were published by William Gaines at Entertaining Comics (originally Educational Comics, or EC). Gaines pushed the envelope of taste and decency, defying the conformist climate of postwar America. For instance, in an advertisement for contributors in *Writer's Digest*, he specifically requested "logical stories in which the villain tries to get away with murder—and probably does. . . . Virtue doesn't have to triumph over evil."[7] In the face of Cold War fears of the breakdown of the American family and the apparent rise in juvenile delinquency, comic books became a target. Comics were condemned by critics as a source of delinquency and a threat to morals. Several communities had public burnings of comic books in the late 1940s.[8] To preempt further action, the industry proposed to establish a self-censorship code in 1948, but this attempt failed to gain support from National Periodicals, the major producer of comic books. The furor over comics abated for a while, but was renewed with the publication of Fredric Wertham's *Seduction of the Innocent* in 1954. Wertham charged that comic books promoted teen violence, antiauthoritarian behavior, and homosexuality.[9] The outcry raised against comic books following the publication of Wertham's book led Estes Kefauver in 1955 to hold U.S. Senate hearings into the comic book industry.

Gaines's testimony at these hearings was a less than stellar defense of the industry. Perhaps most painful was an exchange between Gaines and Kefauver concerning the cover of *Crime Suspense Stories* 22, which showed a man holding the severed head of a woman and a bloody axe:

> **Kefauver:** Do you think that is in good taste?
>
> **Gaines:** Yes, sir: I do, for the cover of a horror comic. A cover in bad taste, for example, might be defined as holding the head a little higher so that the neck could be seen dripping blood from it and moving the body over a little further so that the neck of the body could be seen to be bloody.
>
> **Kefauver:** You have blood coming out of her mouth.
>
> **Gaines:** A little.
>
> **Kefauver:** There is blood on the ax. I think most adults are shocked by that.[10]

Fearing government regulation, the comics industry again moved to self-censorship, creating the Comics Magazine Association of America, which established the Comics Code for content and reviewed all stories, affixing its seal of approval to all published comic books.[11] This self-censorship, a form of Cold War control, affected the content of comics for several decades. It was revised in the early 1970s and all but abandoned in the early twenty-first century. Requiring that heroes always win, authority figures be respected, and disturbing imagery expunged, the Code put a halt to the kinds of art and storytelling that had propelled EC to prominence and led to a major decline in the quality of stories being told.[12] EC stopped publishing comics in 1956, retaining only its slick satirical magazine *Mad* while other publishers sought ways to conform to the new rules. Unsurprisingly, readership declined, several publishers collapsed, and the industry as a whole suffered major losses.

The comic book industry began to recover in 1956, when Julius Schwartz, editor of National Periodicals (later DC Comics), relaunched the Flash, a World War II-era superhero with a new costume. For aficionados, this is the event that inaugurated the "silver age" of comics, as a new era of superheroes was born, reviving the industry. The Flash was followed by a revived Green Lantern, and then by most of the stable of heroes from the war years. A highly successful superhero group magazine, the *Justice League of America*, would be the impetus for an even bigger industrywide transformation.

The Origin of Marvel Comics and the Marvel Method

In 1961, Martin Goodman, publisher of Atlas (formerly Timely, later Marvel Comics), asked his writer/editor/nephew Stan Lee to create a superhero group to compete with the Justice League.[13] At this time Atlas published a handful of monster and suspense magazines with no superheroes. Lee had been working in the industry for decades and was on the verge of quitting when the request was made. Deciding this was his swan song, Lee decided to take a chance. He and artist Jack Kirby produced a new kind of comic book, the *Fantastic Four*. Where superhero comics had previously employed simplistic plots, stock characters, and costumed action, Lee and Kirby put character and personality at the heart of the tale. Stories frequently emphasized the squabbling within this family that included Reed Richards, his fiancée Sue Storm, her brother Johnny, and their best friend Benjamin Grimm. Attempting to beat the Soviets in the space race, the four blast off in a rocket ship designed by Richards and flown by Grimm but are caught in a wave of cosmic radiation that causes them to crash and imbues them with spectacular powers. Richards can stretch his body into any shape, Sue Storm can become invisible and emit force fields, and Johnny Storm can burst into flame and become the Human Torch. The most brutal transformation is that of Grimm, whose body is changed into a moving pile of rocks that is human only in shape but also immensely strong. Many stories would focus on Grimm's distress at becoming a monster in exchange for his superhuman strength and Richard's guilt at having cost his best friend his humanity.

Over the next several years Lee and artists Jack Kirby, Steve Ditko, and others would create a stable of superheroes following the innovative style of the Fantastic Four. With Lee acting as head huckster, Atlas would rename itself Marvel and take its new style into the position of industry leader, displacing National. Lee's salesmanship led him to try to create an intimacy with the readers of Marvel magazines. He printed letters pages, referred to the writers and artists as a "bull pen" (as if they sat around the offices writing and drawing), and offered a page of personal notes on the activities of the comic writers and artists. He also included an editorial column each month, "Stan Lee's Soapbox," in which he offered the "Marvel Philosophy"—much as Hugh Hefner did with *Playboy*.

An important element in Marvel's success was the different method used to produce the stories. Comic books at this time were generally constructed from a script; a writer would produce a full script of the story, with dialogue and descriptions of action, which an artist would then render. At Marvel, however, owing largely to the quantity of scripts Lee was producing each month, a method developed in which the writer (generally Lee) would give a basic plot pitch to an artist, who would construct a visual story around the sketch, with notes for the writer on each page. The writer would take the drawn story and add dialogue to it.[14]

The result was a product in which the visual storytelling was equally important to the words, and where the visuals frequently drove the story. This method created strong, holistic products, creating a blend of words and art that was better than what had been achieved previously. It also caused some animosity. As Lee became increasingly popular as the face of Marvel Comics, many artists, most notably Kirby and Ditko, became embittered at the lack of credit they were given for creating many of these characters and memorable stories. Both would leave Marvel before the 1960s were over, and the rancor between them and Lee would never fully subside.

While the marketing ploys of Lee were clearly important to the commercial success of Marvel, it was the innovations in how comic book stories were told that catapulted the company from a second-tier follower to the position of comics industry leader. In addition to the stronger emphasis on visual storytelling, there were several innovations in the content of the stories produced by Marvel, including an emphasis on character, real-world settings, and narrative continuity.

Character and Antiheroes

The emphasis on character created a more sophisticated story line for the Marvel books than was typical of comics in general. Along with this was an emphasis on flawed heroes or antiheroes, of which Benjamin Grimm was the progenitor. Blessed with strength but cursed with ugliness, Grimm presents a paradigm of the Marvel hero who must pay a price for his power. The emphasis in Cold War culture on the politics of identity rendered this a timely development and led to its commercial success. Coming between the earlier James Dean and Marlon Brando and the later motorcycle riding Peter Fonda—named Captain America after the Marvel character in *Easy Rider*—young adult readers in the early 1960s were receptive to troubled, angst-ridden, and verbose characters whose very existence spoke to the questions of identity that were at the forefront of cultural debates. All Marvel heroes fell into this mode—whether Spider-Man, whose failure to use his power led to the death of his beloved uncle; the Hulk, whose great strength came with a loss of intelligence and an uncontrollable fury; or the Mighty Thor, who was condemned to live on

Earth rather than Asgard because of his lack of humility. There continued to be plenty of action, with spandex-clad heroes chasing spandex-clad villains, but the stories were frequently generated out of the character's angst and quest for redemption, and it was an ever-present element of the narrative.

New York and the Real World

The second innovation was to set these stories in the real world, generally New York. While the heroes from National were all set in cities that were modeled on New York (Metropolis, Gotham, Central City) none of them were actually *in* the real world. By placing its heroes in the real city Marvel created a closer link between the world of the superheroes and the world of the readers. The books were consciously set in the contemporary context; Marvel superheroes were in fact fighting the Cold War.[15] This would create extensive opportunities for direct cultural comment. In several of the earliest Iron Man stories, where the eponymous hero frequently confronts Soviet spies, Nikita Khrushchev appears as a character. (Over the years, real-world characters, from Lyndon Johnson and Richard Nixon to David Letterman—not to mention Stan Lee and Jack Kirby—would appear in Marvel comic books.) The early Marvel comics were set specifically in Cold War America and could not help but offer cultural commentary.

Continuity

Tying the real world and the real character emphases together is the extensive narrative continuity begun by Marvel; stories were constructed such that what happened in one issue affected what came after, and what happened in one title would affect all other titles. Thus there developed a (relatively) consistent history to the world that was created within the books (generally referred to as the "Marvel universe"). Some of this was pure salesmanship—if stories continued across books with guest stars, and what happened in one book affected others, people would feel compelled to buy more books. Still, this continuity creates a collection of stories that share referents, symbols, and a common cultural approach over a forty-year period.[16] This becomes something more specific than a genre; such continuity creates opportunities for marking changes in the meaning of cultural symbols more directly than within the broader structures of genre narratives. Richard Reynolds suggests that this structural continuity lends a mythopoeic power to the narratives.[17] This may go too far; but the continuity does provide an opportunity for close comparisons over time of the iconographic meaning given to characters, images, and events, providing a unique venue for cultural analysis. No other medium—save, perhaps, soap operas[18]—offers such an artifact for cultural studies. Comic books of the 1980s frequently refer back to their 1960s incarnations, could be read as self-conscious commentaries on those earlier stories, and were frequently written to be so read.[19]

The Political Economy of the Marvel Universe

The Marvel universe has expanded and contracted over the years, but there has been consistency at the core of its characters and what they depict. Not all characters represent the world around them in the same way, but they all do represent the outside world, the culture within which they exist. The Fantastic Four and Spider-Man represent the familial and social aspects of American culture, and, as noted above, the Fantastic Four is a functional—if troubled—family. At times, for instance, Sue Richards (née Storm) has been separated from her husband, thought about having an affair with another man, and given birth to an autistic child. Her hotheaded younger brother (the Human Torch) has been infatuated, been in love, and run away; the Thing (Benjamin Grimm) has been tormented by his desire to be free of his ugliness and his responsibility to his friends. Spider-Man was consistently concerned with the issues of adolescence: could Peter Parker get a job, the girl, free of the tormenting of the football hero?

Several books compose the core treatment of the political economy of the Marvel universe and will be the main focus of this study. At the center is the scientist-entrepreneur Tony Stark, who runs an electronics company that primarily manufactures weapons for the U.S. government. During a field inspection of one of these weapons in Vietnam, Tony Stark is wounded and captured by communist guerrillas. They force him to build them a weapon. With a piece of shrapnel moving toward his heart and certain death, Stark creates a suit of battle armor that will keep him alive and allow him to defeat his captors. He thus becomes the Marvel hero Iron Man.

With a huge private fortune and a genius for inventing weapons, Stark is well placed to become the benefactor of Marvel's anticommunist forces. He is both a founding member and financial backer of the supergroup the Avengers, which will include both Captain America (found floating in the Atlantic in *Avengers* 4) and the Hulk (at least initially). Stark is also the creator of the fantastic gadgets used by Marvel's superspy Nick Fury and a major supporter of the agency, the Supreme Headquarters International Espionage, Law-Enforcement Division (SHIELD). In his position as president and CEO of his own firm he will represent a vision of corporate capitalism that is highly individualistic. His centrality to the various aspects of Marvel's political economy renders him an important representative of both American business and anticommunism.

Captain America, clad in red, white, and blue stars and stripes, is a bearer of a vision of American democracy. Created on the eve of World War II to fight Nazis, he is offered as the embodiment of what is best about America. He is a member of the Avengers and works closely with SHIELD, linking him directly to American anticommunist activities. While Iron Man is the most ardent Cold Warrior of Marvel's characters, Captain America is the most ideological; he is, in fact, an avatar of American ideology and, thus, offers the most direct commentary on the character of Cold War America.

Also significant are Nick Fury and the Hulk. As head of SHIELD, Nick Fury is at the forefront of Cold War actions. He rarely takes on communists directly, but instead faces organizations that resemble a communist conspiracy. A noncommissioned officer in World War II (he also starred in the military book *Sergeant Fury and His Howling Commandoes*), he is promoted to colonel by the time he takes over the directorship of SHIELD. While popular in the 1960s, the character would not sustain a readership, and his comic book was canceled in the early 1970s. It would be revived for a short time in the 1980s, but Fury and SHIELD remain a fixture of Marvel's Cold War political economy, later featuring heavily in many other books.

The Hulk is only tangentially linked to the Marvel political economy. Created by a nuclear accident in a bomb test, he represents some of the anxiety about the bomb in the early 1960s. His earliest exploits involve avoiding capture by the U.S. military while fighting alien superbeings and communists seeking to capture American nuclear secrets. Because of the immeasurable strength of the Hulk, it was difficult to write stories for him that placed him in conflict with human beings. The Hulk thus rapidly moved out of the anticommunist realm to fight more powerful creatures. He became more significant in the 1970s and 1980s as the story of his character unfolded and his portrayal changed from that of victim of the rampaging power of a nuclear explosion to that of misunderstood creature with a distinct past.

Superhero Comics and National Identity

Superhero comic books offer an insightful yet underutilized window into the study of cultural change. While comic books have many genres—crime, horror, funny animal, teen romance, war, and western—the superhero comic has been the bread and butter of the industry since Superman first appeared in 1938. The popularity of the superhero is based on many things, not least of which is the wish-fulfillment fantasies of adolescent males. The superhero story has been seen to conform to several mythic types, making it a recognizable tale filled with social and cultural meaning. Reynolds has examined the genre as a modern mythos, conforming to elements of the monomyth,[20] and Peter Coogan sees the superhero as part of a twentieth-century version of a peculiarly American vision of heroism, as does Thomas Inge.[21] John Shelton Lawrence and Thomas Jewitt see the superhero as key to a uniquely American monomyth, although they give scant attention to comic books.[22] Several writers have focused specifically on the comic book as cultural product, much like any other form of popular culture: Ariel Dorfman and Armand Mattelart offered a famous analysis of Walt Disney comic books as purveyors of an imperialist culture.[23] Gary Engel has explored the iconography of Superman on the occasion of the superhero's fiftieth birthday,[24] and, more recently, Will Brooker has examined the iconography of Batman and its consumption not only in the United States but around the world.[25]

Three elements of the superhero comic render it a particularly revealing avenue for the exploration of national identity. These are the relevance of the heroic narrative to social values, the specific ideological content of the books as cultural artifacts, and the mechanism of the dual identity.

The Heroic Narrative

The heroic narrative describes a story of value and virtue, defines good and evil, and offers a guide to proper action by which redemption can be achieved. In so doing it defines for a culture that which is admired and that which is feared. Because the hero exemplifies the values of a society, his role is to defend those values, to maintain a given way of life against potential threats, or to redeem it from a threat realized. This renders the hero, as Reynolds has noted, essentially a conservative figure.[26] As a fantasy, the heroic narrative does not reflect the mundane elements of daily existence, does not describe how one empirically behaves, but instead offers a guide for what would constitute heroic action, virtuous behavior. Mike Alsford, while viewing the heroic tale in a psychological rather than political economic context, suggests that "being a hero has to do with *being in the world* in a certain way."[27] The villains in heroic fiction personify that which confronts the nation as a threat, the "other" against which the nation-as-hero must contend in order to maintain its existence, its virtue, its identity. Alsford notes that "the hero and the villain may be seen as aspects of the same tragic character, one who encounters a crisis of some sort or another and chooses to respond in a particular way."[28] By rendering the ideals of a nation in stark, Manichean terms, the heroic narrative offers an avenue through which one can access the core values of a society, the ideals that give that society an identity, and the "other" that society fears.

Often the heroic narrative renders these values as so timeless and objectively real that they transcend the very political economic organization of society. Because the hero follows a code of behavior that transcends laws and politics he is often outside the scope of the legal order. In Frank Zinneman's classic *High Noon*

(1952), Gary Cooper is the sheriff who has just married his lady (a Quaker, played by Grace Kelly) and turned in his badge when he hears that his nemesis, Frank Miller (Ian MacDonald), has been released from jail and is returning to Hadleyville. Admonished by the town, his friends, and his new wife to run away, he stays to face Miller. The majority of the film depicts his desperate attempt to find deputies in order to get the town to defend itself against the lawless violence of the anticipated Miller. At each point the town refuses to defend itself, and in the end the townspeople huddle in their homes in fear and dread. Why does Cooper stay? Whenever he is asked he responds in the same manner: "If I have to explain it you wouldn't understand." The code of behavior that governs the hero transcends the law, transcends the community. An inner-directed figure, the hero thus represents the values to which we aspire but often fail to achieve. The dark side, of course, is that the hero may see himself above the law and seek to remake the world in his own image. Jewitt and Lawrence thus see the American superhero as a redemptive figure, but one who has the potential to subvert the democratic ethos of the American community.[29] The hubris of the hero, often a major contributor to the hero's demise, is generally presented as the great temptation from which the hero must abstain.

While the heroic narrative in general offers a definition of social values, the superhero comic book has specific characteristics that render it particularly useful in the exploration of national identity. Each superhero has a specific story, a specific set of issues with which she deals. They thus reflect different aspects of a society, different ways to treat the values embodied in a culture. Not all superheroes will reflect the same aspects of cultural meaning. While at the core they all treat the subject of the "right action" (or, as defined by Stan Lee, "with great power must come . . . great responsibility"), the arenas for such action and the configuration of those various arenas to compose a social identity will vary. Thus, for instance, the Fantastic Four has generally focused on the meaning of family, and Spider-Man has generally focused on coping with adolescence. Similarly, Superman is often read as a story of an immigrant trying to fit into American society, and Batman is about the consequences of urban decay and familial breakdown. Will Brooker discusses the "branding" of superheroes, how their meanings are constructed by creators and readers in a discursive community, although always within the bounds of these meanings, rendering them variable but stable.[30]

Superheroes and Ideology

Umberto Eco has argued that the superhero comic is a very appropriate venue for cultural myths of late capitalism. Unlike traditional myths, the superhero comic does not tell a developing narrative but recounts a series of events that essentially disrupt time. All events are in the present, and the stories are mere reiterations of the same theme, offering the same redundant message. This iterative scheme, Eco suggests, serves the needs of contemporary industrial society, where constant social and economic change renders the sameness of the superhero story the only possible form of relaxation available to the consumer. Moreover, he contrasts the vastness of Superman's powers with the limited scope of his activity to suggest that the comic necessarily legitimizes private property and a narrow view of social conditions: "The plot must be static and must evade any development, because Superman *must* make virtue consist of many little activities on a small scale, never achieving total awareness."[31] Eco thus suggests that both in his mythopoeic role and the ideology it represents, Superman serves a pedagogic function that permits the reproduction of late capitalism.

The iterative redundancies that Eco saw as the key to the relevance of the superman myth in late capitalism changed in the 1960s as superhero comic books changed. The continuity of the Marvel comics brought a sense of linear time back to the books. The real-world setting placed them in a more defined, clearly Cold War, context. The books thus became less mythopoeic and more direct cultural commentaries.[32]

While creating greater continuity, the Marvel comics still offer much of the redundancy Eco sees as a key feature of the superhero narrative. These thematic redundancies continue to be a useful means of examining the changing meaning of the comic book stories and the heroes therein. In the following pages, the political and cultural changes of the late Cold War are linked to changes in the various thematic elements of the superhero narrative. This is not an isomorphic mapping of cultural trends onto a cultural artifact but an exploration to reveal how cultural ideas are translated into this format and the ways comic books have attempted to reconstruct American identity.

Dual Identity

For issues of identity, the superhero comic is particularly relevant. Identity is a key to the superhero story. Since Superman, superheroes have generally had dual identities—they have been both civilians and superheroes. The mechanism of the heroic dual identity did not originate with the superhero comic, but has become its most basic element. Gerard Jones has suggested that the dual identity was particularly appealing to immigrants:

> Secret identity stories always reverberated with the children of Jewish immigrants, of course, because they were so much about the wearing of the masks that enabled one to be an American, a Modern, a secular consumer, but still part of an ancient society, a link in an old chain, when safely among those who knew one's secret. The superheroes brought something to these stories that Zorro and the Scarlet Pimpernel never had, for their true identities, the men in colorful tights, were so elemental, so universal, so transcendent of the worlds that made them wear masks that they carried with them an unprecedented optimism about the value of one's inner reality. We all knew that Clark Kent was just a game played by Superman and that the only guy who mattered was that alien who showed up in Metropolis with no history and no parents.[33]

Generally justified as necessary to protect those around them from the actions of villains, secret identities have become the norm to the costumed hero. This duality has psychological and cultural implications that have been a major theme of, for instance, Batman comics. When cultural norms seem relatively certain, there are few major themes to be explored in this dual identity. When cultural meanings are contested, when norms shatter, the ambiguities inherent in the dual identity become highly relevant and the issue of identity becomes a major theme of the superhero story.

The dual identity serves several functions within the superhero comic book. For Reynolds, identity is bound up with costume, which functions as a "sign for the inward process of character development."[34] Costume, representing the identity of the hero, is frequently tied to the origin of the hero's powers and, thus, is closely linked to the identity of the hero as hero. It identifies the hero as such, and it provides an anchor for the treatment of that identity over time. The costume represents the basis of continuity, and changes in the costume signify developments to the character. Additionally, costumes create a community among those who wear them, setting them apart from others.[35] The maintenance of a civilian identity brings the costumed hero back into a realm in which the reader can identify with them.

Danny Fingeroth sees this duality functioning as a psychological element through which readers can identify with the hero and fulfill their adolescent fantasies of respect, commenting that "if only they (whoever your 'they' may be) knew the truth (whatever that truth may be) about me (whoever you believe yourself to be), they'd be sorry for the way they treat me."[36] More significantly, he suggests it offers a vision of "societal identity crisis" between public and private identity. While the hero may be beset by various problems and neuroses, superheroes always choose to serve others through good works. "This may be the key to the societal identity crises the heroes reflect," notes Fingeroth. "For the superhero, the answer to the contradictory needs is: 'Don't be selfish. Serve the community and the rest will fall into place. Who am I? I am the mechanism for perfecting and serving society. *And I know exactly what actions I must take to do that.*'"[37]

Functioning both narratively—in character development—and psychologically, the secret identity becomes a central element for cultural commentary. Fingeroth suggests that dual identities have become less significant; several characters, such as the Fantastic Four or the X-Men, no longer use them. Nonetheless, even where an identity is not secret, the public duty of the hero and the private role of the civilian remain in tension. There is still a conflict between the civilian husband and father Reed Richards and the costumed hero Mr. Fantastic, or the oppressed, persecuted mutant Scott Summers and the powerful X-Man Cyclops. The demands of "keeping the secret" add another layer of tension to the tale, but the dual identity remains a central narrative focus of the comic book superhero and a strategic location for cultural commentary.[38]

Narrative Components: Origins, Allies, and Villains

The tension between public and private made overt in the duality of the superhero makes comic books a particularly relevant artifact through which to explore the culture of national identity. This duality is central to the development of the characters, rendering the secret identity an element articulating changing visions of political identity. The context through which the dual identity of the hero is defined—the return of villains, changes in the supporting cast, the retellings of origins—all provide opportunities to compare cultural meanings across different periods within a highly controlled context.

One way that identity is treated is through retellings of the origin story. As writers and artists change, each seeks to put his stamp on the character; one way to do this is by retelling the origin. All are constrained by the threads of continuity, but within that continuity changes can be made, more background given, deeper biographies developed. The retelling of origin permits the incorporation of elements into the continuity that had been previously unexplained or unexplored. Changes to origins—the addition or subtraction of variables—signal new visions of the meaning of a character, and thus reveal changes in the culture which these characters reflect.

Along with origins, allies and sidekicks are important indicators of cultural meaning. Sidekicks and allies are an important reflection of the ideas, issues, and ideologies that pervade the popular psyche. Whether they are children or adults, government or civilian; whether they associate with the private identity or the superhero identity; whether they share the hero's ideas or challenge them—these are all vital questions that contribute to the cultural vision the allies of the hero present. The allies represent the greater cultural milieu within which the hero exists, and thus contribute to the social identity of the hero as well as providing a vision of the society in which he operates.

Even more significant than the allies are the villains. The villain represents that which the hero is not, the "other" against which the hero strives. By defining himself as *not the villain*, the hero situates himself culturally for the reader. Villains tend to recur in these stories, and which villains are prevalent and what they desire is a key element to the cultural representation in comic books. Reynolds has suggested that, for Batman, at least, it is the villain rather than the hero who is most important. The hero is, for Reynolds, a fixed identity, unmoving and unmovable. The villains, however, can change, present different threats, represent different elements against which the hero must react.[39] While this may go too far in reducing the cultural meaning of the hero, it is nonetheless true that which villains populate a given period and how they are portrayed are vital components to the cultural meaning of the books. Of the villains, certain characters achieve the level of nemesis, and most superheroes have one supreme nemesis. As Batman has the Joker and Superman has Lex Luthor, so too does Iron Man have the Mandarin, the Hulk has the Leader, Nick Fury and SHIELD have Hydra, and Captain America has the Red Skull. Each of these nemeses represent the most fundamental aspect of the cultural conflicts that pervade these books.

The Comic Industry

While affected by the waves of American popular political culture that buffeted the nation and comic books over the last four decades, a variety of other factors have influenced the trajectory of comic book narratives. The industry has faced a varied market that has seen dramatic declines in the last fifteen years. Marvel, for instance, was selling roughly 230,000 copies of each title per month in the late 1960s; by the mid-1990s this figure was closer to 80,000. Sales have risen again in recent years as interest in the medium has grown as a result of popular films based on comic book characters and the marketing of "graphic novels" in mainstream bookstores. By the end of the 1970s, however, readership had declined by nearly one-third, and a new marketing strategy developed. Rather than sell through general magazine vendors, supermarkets, and drugstores, comic book companies began selling through specialized retailers, known as the direct market. Under the previous distribution system the companies had overprinted each issue, sold on consignment, and repurchased any unsold books. With the direct market they sold directly to retailers with no returns; retailers kept the unsold books for resale as back issues to the collector's market. This change in distribution mirrored a changing audience. No longer the preferred medium for youth, comics were increasingly sold to an older audience. By the late 1980s the industry boomed with the emergence of a strong collector's market, with many nontraditional collectors seeking out comics as investment opportunities. When this market collapsed in the mid-1990s, only the older collectors were left, with the investment seekers entering only to purchase special issues. Today, the average comic book reader is no longer a teenage male but an adult male. Most youth who buy comics are second-generation readers, introduced to the medium by their fathers. The changing distribution system and audience have transformed the kinds of stories told and the depth of cultural representations, although the cultural representations have continued.

Another industry-influenced change in narratives has occurred with the rise of the market for "graphic novels." With the popular acceptance of some comic book art, such as that of Art Spiegelman or Harvey Pekar, the market for graphic novels has grown rapidly. Most bookstores today have a section for graphic novels alongside more traditional divisions such as mystery and self-help. Most graphic novels are reprinted monthly comic book stories collected into a single trade-paperback volume. This has generated a restriction on the story arcs in the monthly comic books that now must be of sufficient length to be republished as a stand-alone trade paperback. As a result, most story arcs run six or seven issues; tales that run longer are structured to be broken into volumes collecting six or seven issues. Thus, changes in marketing comic books have had repeated effects on the kinds of narratives the books contain.

Similarly, changes in editorial direction or in writers have generated changes in specific books. This has not had as profound an effect as one might expect. Comic book writers and editors have tended to come in generational cohorts, and thus the cultural impact on one writer tends to be the same on his cohort as well. For instance, Dennis O'Neil is often credited with bringing socially relevant issues into the comic book story lines with his run on *Green Lantern/Green Arrow*.[40] His experience with the New Left in 1960s is seen as a seminal influence on the comic book. Steve Engelhart, who scripted a series of socially relevant Captain America titles had similar formative experiences in the 1960s and brought similar concerns to his writing. Thus, the effects of any one writer or editor are minimized in the overall flow of the continuity.

Reading Comic Books

The mechanical conventions in reading a comic book are well known by regular readers but may not be obvious to those less immersed in the medium. There are generally three types of words in a comic book: spoken dialogue, internal monologues, and narration. Spoken dialogue is represented by word balloons with solid lines, and internal dialogue by thought balloons with jagged outlines. Narration by the editor, writer, or other third party (sometimes a character) is located in captioned text boxes. The standard comic book page contains six to nine panels of action, separated from one another by a blank space called a gutter. The first page is often a single-panel illustration, called a splash page. The page is read from left to right, and top to bottom. Dialogue within panels is also generally read from left to right, top to bottom. While these are the conventions of the medium, they are often altered for dramatic purpose. Within these conventions, the image possibilities are endless. Not only the action of the art but its style, inking, perspective, location in panels, size and type of panels, arrangement of panels on the page, and lettering all affect the meaning of the narrative. The visuals of the comic book can reinforce, alter, or undermine the apparent meaning of the words.

Because comic books use both words and images to convey meaning, the general relation between the two is for the image to convey the action of the words, to offer a visual narrative. To read a comic book requires attention to both image and word. This is sometimes difficult. As Roland Barthes notes, because of their stylized renderings, drawings embody a set of rules for conveying meaning—a code that needs to be understood—that more realistic images such as photographs do not. Understanding the code (which is not completely fixed and is open to multiple interpretations) is an essential aspect of reading comics. What happens in comic book images, the use of line, the arrangement of panels on a page, the presence or absence of a gutter can all suggest different meanings to different readers. These differences, however, are bounded. The words, to follow Barthes, anchor the way the image is interpreted. At times, however, the image will present a view of the text that differs from that coveyed by the words. This creates a space for a subtle irony as the denotative context of the narrative text is contradicted by the connotations of the visual text. Readers are often very conscious of these moments that disrupt their normal consumption of the texts, and they frequently become touchstones for later narrative development.[41]

The methodologies for interpreting the visual language of the comic book remain relatively underdeveloped.[42] Such interpretations tend to be more idiosyncratic than the readings of verbal narratives. Because my object in this book is to read the broad continuity, I tend to emphasize the narrative elements and overall trends in the visual representation. This permits me to avoid some of the pitfalls of idiosyncratic readings, as I examine the visual trends in broad terms, asking whether the contrasts between images are strong or weak, whether the lines are clearly defined or obscure, whether the colors are bright or dark. Sharp contrasts and clean lines tend to suggest a greater certainty to the messages being conveyed. Darker hues may invoke a more sinister setting than brighter colors. In addition to the general trends for each period, I do read specific representative pages for deeper meanings when of particular relevance. I focus on whether the images support the narrative or problematize it, and the manner in which the dialogue is placed into question. This is particularly important when the concern is with the certainty with which cultural values are articulated. These tighter, more specific readings are also more vulnerable to personal biases. This cannot be avoided, and I hope to convince the reader of my interpretation based on the broader context in which these readings are nested. In so doing I try to balance the reading of visual and narrative elements.

Some brief commentary on citations and sources should be offered. Comic book page numbering is often absent and generally inconsistent. As a consequence, I have not cited page numbers for specific quotes. The bulk of this study has been done using original books. These are the only places to find supplementary material, such as publishers' notes, editorials, or letter columns, all of which are of interest to the analyst of comic books as cultural artifacts. Many of the stories, however, are becoming available through inexpensive reprint volumes such as the Marvel Essentials or DC Showcase series. Finally, the comic book is a corporate product involving many different producers. During the 1960s it became common for the publisher to list all who contributed to the product, while prior to that time a writer and artist were generally the only creators listed. Appropriate citation of comic books, attributing proper credit to their creators, has thus been inconsistent and not formally established. I have followed the citation format preferred by the Comic Art and Comics area of the Popular Culture Association in referencing source material.[43]

The Organization of This Book

This study is organized into relevant periods in the unraveling and reconstruction of American national identity throughout the Cold War as defined by both the narrative consistency of comic books and changes in the comic book industry. For instance, 1968 saw both editorial and distributional changes at Marvel Comics that affected how the company related to its market; 1976 appears as a cutoff year not only because of the changing cultural narrative but also because of the beginning of a profound decline in sales that led to a new form of marketing comic books. Table 1.1 offers the relevant periods and the significant reasons for their definition.

What follows is an analysis of the transformation in American national identity during the later Cold War and post-Cold War periods. The subject of this study is the relatively continuous narrative of the two Marvel comic books (*Captain America* and *Iron Man*), other books of relevance (those of the Avengers, the Hulk, and Nick Fury), and their relation to the national identity crisis of Cold War America. To demonstrate changes in the definition of the American self I analyze general trends in this continuity over the periods, with in-depth analysis of representative and seminal texts to explore specific transformational moments.

TABLE 1.1:   Narrative and Industry Changes Used to Define Relevant Periods

Period	Continuity	Industry
1961–1968	Support for Cold War consensus and Cold War policy Comic Code remains strong Emergence of Marvel method and new style superhero	Marvel displaces National as industry leader End of Marvel's distribution deal with National Marvel sold to Cadence Industries (1968) Kirby and Ditko leave Marvel
1969–1976	Identity issues come to the Fore Social Relevance Movement in Comics	Expansion of titles, but declining sales. Loss of editorial direction at Marvel (five editors in chief b/w 1972 and 1977)
1977–1985	*Captain America and Falcon* reverts to *Captain America* (July 1977) Domestic and personal issues dominate stories	Jim Shooter becomes editor at Marvel (1978–86) Rise of the direct market
1986–1996	Vigilantes and violence become the norm—darker superheroes. Major books end their numbering in 1996 and are restarted under "Heroes Reborn"	New World Entertainment buys Marvel (1986). Jim Shooter leaves as editor Ron Perelman buys Marvel (1989) and takes it public; reader rebellion launched by Bob Kunz (April 1996); bankruptcy declared (December)
1997–2007	"Heroes Return" gives a reboot to continuity. "Neo-classical" treatment of heroes as reaction to violence of preceding period. Emphasis on ill-defined enemies and relation between villain and politics. War on Terror brings politics back to comics in a big way. Civil War and Death of Captain America (2007)	Bob Harras becomes editor (1998–2002). Toy Biz buys Marvel out of bankruptcy (1998). 2002—Marvel opts out of Comics Code and develops its own ratings system

Chapter 1 analyzes the emergence of the liberal consensus within the context of the Cold War and identifies certain tensions inherent within it. This consensus is constructed out of rhetorical elements that have served as the basis of the definition of the American self since the seventeenth century. Readers more interested in the readings of the comic book continuity might wish to start with chapter 2 and return to chapter 1 later. Those more interested in the trajectory of American national identity might wish to start with chapter 1.

Using the discussion in the first chapter as a baseline, subsequent chapters analyze the changing portrayal of identity in the various superhero comics, following the periodization described above. Chapter 2 begins in the early 1960s with an America characterized by the ferment of growing disillusion with the national security state spawned by the Cold War and a desire to maintain a notion of national consensus and normalcy in the face of continued threats from communists. This desperate attempt to create a consensus had been one of the sources behind the U.S. Congressional investigation into comic books in the 1950s. The Comics Code was still strong in the 1960s and limited the ability of comics to challenge the mainstream consensus directly. Thus the attempt to maintain a pro Cold War consensus had infiltrated comic books and would be reflected in the story lines of the 1960s. Unsurprisingly, the stories of this period tend to reflect the American consensus, asserting that the major threats came from outside the United States, generally in the form of communist plans for world domination. The only threat from within was from those who were too willing to shirk their public duties to stand up to the communists. The government played a benign role, protecting the security of citizens from this outside threat. Still, the ferment of the 1950s, which created an audience receptive to the troubled antiheroes who populated the Marvel universe, appeared within the comics of this period. While comic books still endorsed the Cold War consensus, by 1968 there were emerging challenges.

Chapter 3 examines the late 1960s and early 1970s. By the end of the 1960s, the clear Cold War consensus had blurred into a greater ambiguity concerning American national identity and its role in the world. Identity became the central theme of comic books early in this period, with mistaken identities and multiple maskings of heroes and villains a common element of stories. This represents both a crisis of identity and a collapse of the ideology of the Cold War consensus, and the ambiguity surrounding that ideology was represented in both the story lines and the artwork of the comics. This signifies a growing disillusion with the idea of consensus and increasing confusion about the American identity. While still politically conservative, a growing number of story lines now identified the problems faced by America as less the product of communism and more the product of American society. As the Comics Code was weakened in the early 1970s, direct challenges to American government and policy emerged. Stories increasingly treated civil rights, the antiwar movement, Vietnam War policy, and other critical issues with a sympathetic portrayal of those who challenged the government and its policies. Significantly, communists become increasingly scarce in these story lines, while American corporate and government actors appear more frequently as villains or dupes of villains. Challenge to these policies were portrayed as right and just, but the idea that there is an absolute right or wrong faded. The moral certainty of the consensus of the 1960s became the existential ambiguity of the 1970s.

As the 1970s came to an end, the age of affluence that had reigned during the 1950s and 1960s became the age of limits to growth. The economic crisis, oil crisis, and confidence crisis all replaced the national security crises that defined the earlier Cold War era. Americans became less concerned with public affairs and more concerned with personal issues, rejecting the demands of public duty and retreating into privacy. This is reflected in the comic books of the late 1970s and early 1980s, as stories became increasingly concerned with the private histories of characters— both heroes and villains. Pop psychology reigned in several books, as witnessed in expansive retellings of characters' origins and stories about their childhoods, love lives, and private battles. This was due in part to changes in the comic book industry (due partially to the retreat from public affairs that was represented by the resurgence of film and new forms of leisure-time entertainment), but reflected the disillusion with the public realm that characterized the morally ambiguous 1970s. This is the subject of chapter 4.

Chapter 5 examines the polarizing politics of the administration of President Ronald Reagan and the rebirth of the Cold War after a decade of détente, thus bringing politics back to comic books in the mid-1980s. This politics was not, however, one of the supportive stance of the 1950s, nor of the challenging stance of the 1960s, but an angry and disillusioned politics of distrust and betrayal. Heroes became disturbingly vicious and angry, and it became harder to tell the difference between heroes and villains, who increasingly became equated. There was also a growing self-awareness to the comic books of the 1980s; after thirty years of continuity and fifty years of existence, the comic book industry now became a venue that had its own culture, its own clichés, and its own tropes that could be worked and reworked for significant commentary. The voice is one of self-conscious irony portraying the politics of the Cold War as a politics of betrayal. Betrayal, in fact, is the key motif of this period, signifying a final fatalistic disillusion with Cold War America.

The economic boom of the 1990s, apparently a return of the era of abundance that characterized Marvel's first decade, saw a return to earlier ideas of moral certainty and heroic identity. As discussed in chapter 6, the story lines in the 1990s were less connected to real-world events than in the 1960s heyday but now represented an almost nostalgic recall of the Cold War, when some form of common identity was held, even if it was a fleeting and illusory one. Much of this fell apart with the terrorist attacks of September 11, 2001. The real world now intruded again, and comics became more consciously political than at any time since the early 1970s. As the so-called War on Terror unfolded the superhero comics failed to support this national mission as they had earlier missions. The rhetorical elements used to define the American self lost cohesion, and while the tropes of the 1960s continued to be utilized the content became more obscure, making it increasingly difficult to identify the enemy and the hero in clear moral terms. The complexity of the post–Cold War world, including growing globalization and the War on Terror, were thus represented by increasing ambiguity about the American self.

The 2007 death of Captain America serves as an epilogue to this tale of identity crisis. The Cold War had come to be defined in these books as an era when America betrayed its own ideals, weakening the very rhetoric of American identity. This generated a conflict about the very possibility of heroism that plays out in Marvel's "Civil War," culminating in the death of the ideological center of the Marvel universe. The aftermath of these events, in which the heroes try to come to terms with their changed reality, mirrors the contemporary quest to define the American self in the postmythic, postconsensus moment. The absence of the mythic definition of what it means to be American renders difficult a collective action, but it may create opportunities to proceed toward a future free of the blinders of myth. No longer capable of defining America as free, progressive, and virtuous without irony, Americans may more realistically aspire to achieve an ideal they had previously defined as reality.

1

The Cold War and the Forging of the Liberal Consensus

T THE END OF THE SECOND WORLD WAR the United States emerged as a military and economic power of global proportions, with both the resources and the will to assume a role in world affairs that was unprecedented in its history. This would require a transformation in the American political economy that empowered the federal government—especially the executive branch— to intervene in both domestic and international affairs in ways never before imagined. It was fueled by the vast expansion of the American economy that would grow at an almost unbroken— and even quickening—pace for two decades, generating an affluence never before known. In so doing, however, this increasingly globalized, centralized, and bureaucratized reality of postwar America conflicted with the reigning vision of national identity: a new-world nation of virtuous individuals, blessed by God to follow a mission of progressive reform, free of entanglements with the immoralities of petty tyrannies of the old world. The changes in the material reality of America—particularly the assumption of a global role and a political economy that had become nationally integrated—required a reformed vision of the American self. By the end of the 1950s, such a reformation had not only been achieved but had become the hegemonic discourse of American national identity to such an extent that many refer to the decade as a period of national consensus and conformity. Drawing on the major elements that have always defined the American identity, the Cold War American was viewed as an individual who lived in the most virtuous political system in the world, as evidenced by American prosperity, and whose divine mission was to extend the benefits of that prosperity to all American citizens and promote the virtue of its governmental system around the world by defending against the evil forces of totalitarianism. But this American identity was marred both by internal contradictions and by its very hegemony, which would be difficult to maintain in any period of American history given the extent of divisions—regional, ethnic, class, racial—in American society. As this consensual identity increasingly came under challenge during the later years of the Cold War, it would shatter. Rather than a momentary collapse, however, this time it would undermine the very rhetorical elements that had been used to define what it meant to be American, rendering problematic any reconstruction of the American self.

The Cold War Transformation

The postwar period during which the Cold War emerged was an epoch of startling transformation in the American political economy. The United States assumed, for the first time, a leading role in international affairs, devising a global policy to contain communism and export its own political economic system. Scientific and technological breakthroughs created a variety of new consumer products, medical treatments, and military applications, of which the atomic bomb was the most significant. Large capitalist organizations—both business and labor—combined with government intervention to create conditions for the economic enfranchisement of the majority of Americans who would benefit from expansive economic growth in an age of abundance.

The origins of these transformations lay in the late nineteenth and early twentieth centuries, as the United States developed a nationalized economy and began systematically to reach out to the world. The architects of early Cold War policy all came of age between the Spanish-American War and World War I. Having participated in the first wave of American internationalism and empire, they would see, as had no generation before them, the importance of international relations for both political and economic well-being. Two world wars and the Great Depression demonstrated to them that neglecting international affairs threatened both national security and prosperity. They would thus link national security and economic welfare in the construction of a new global political economy.[1]

The United States became the richest, most productive country in the world in the early twentieth century. By the 1940s it had achieved an unrivaled international competitive position. With more than 50 percent of the world's productive capacity and gold reserves, the United States was in a position to play the role of international hegemon. In the late 1940s, the nation was the major actor (along with Great Britain) in constructing the global political and economic institutions that defined the noncommunist international playing field of the Cold War. This entailed establishing the dollar as the linchpin of global finance to assure exchange-rate stability for international transactions. It also meant capitalizing global financial institutions such as the International Monetary Fund and the International Bank for Reconstruction and Development (later known as the World Bank) to provide enough capital to the global economy to avoid major slowdowns of global economic activity. The United States also provided loans under less formal auspices, most famously the Marshall Plan, sending thirteen billion dollars to help rebuild Europe. The nation opened its markets to most countries of the world under the General Agreement on Tariffs and Trade, and it would serve as a buyer of last resort for other countries' exports.[2] While all of this seems costly for the United States, as noted by political economists, playing the hegemon was not a disinterested role. By assuring an open, stable, liberal capitalist global economy, the nation would benefit. Rich, liberal capitalist foreign countries provided markets for U.S. exports and safe havens for U.S. investment. The economic well-being of the United States necessitated an open global economy; a prosperous Europe made for a prosperous America.

The new global economic order also served the U.S. security goals of containing communism. While the North Atlantic Treaty Organization guaranteed Western European security from a Soviet invasion, the Marshall Plan, the International Monetary Fund, and the World Bank were all designed to achieve the open global economy the United States wanted, and to secure sufficient prosperity for Europe to prevent popular support for Soviet-sponsored communist movements. A prosperous Europe thus also guaranteed greater security for the United States.

As World War II came to a close, the antagonism between the United States and the Soviet Union became increasingly intense. While who started the Cold War and why are questions that continue to be debated even today, there is no doubt that the USSR was the nearest rival in economic and military power to the United States and seemed to be following a series of policies designed to enhance its power at the expense of the United States. National security soon became defined monolithically as security from the USSR and its allies. Since a bipolar conflict necessarily becomes a zero-sum game—where a gain for one is a loss for the other—security came to be defined as keeping the USSR and its allies from expanding their sphere of influence, of containing communism. The battle between the two powers would not be a hot war, but a cold one, fought not directly with troops so much as with economics, technology, politics, and ideology.[3]

These global commitments—to maintain an open international economy and contain communism—created the conditions for a massive growth in U.S. government, particularly of the executive branch. The federal government had been expanding for sixty years, from the early Progressive Era through the New Deal and World War II, but now a massive reorganization in government was undertaken to provide national security and economic prosperity. The National Security Act of 1947 created twelve new agencies, including the National Security Council and the Central Intelligence Agency.[4] A year earlier Congress had passed the Full Employment Act, which, while falling short of guaranteeing full employment, did make the government responsible for the state of the domestic economy and created the Council of Economic Advisors.[5] These two acts greatly expanded the size of government and recognized the increased scope of its interventions; following the Executive Reform Act of 1938, they more specifically enhanced the role of the executive within the U.S. government.[6] The historical moment was right for Americans to accept, and even advocate, an increasingly interventionist and powerful national government centered on its executive branch.

During the Great Depression Americans had turned to the federal government for help and hope as never before. The New Deal programs of President Franklin Delano Roosevelt had responded with massive government outlays and new legislation in areas previously seen as illegitimate for government intervention. Banking, labor, public works, farm prices, housing, and poor relief now fell under the purview of the federal government. The national mission to defeat the forces of fascism in World War II only extended the government's reach. After passage of the 1946 Full Employment Act the government formally assumed the major role in insuring the performance of the U.S. economy. This, too, would become linked to national security as the government subsidized industry through defense procurement and rebuilding efforts in Europe. The knowledge industry would also be brought into the service of security and prosperity as the government subsidized new university enrollments through the GI Bill and made available federal grant moneys for research and education in natural and social sciences to develop new technologies for defense and methods for intelligence gathering to understand the enemy.[7]

Centering power in the executive branch implied that proper administration (rather than politics) could resolve social and economic problems. Faith in government experts mirrored the growing influence of knowledge in many other aspects of American society, and experts from both business and academia came to have greater influence than ever before. While the role of the expert had been exalted from the Progressive Era through the New Deal, science took on a newly popular role during the Cold War. Having developed the atomic bomb and other technologies to defeat the Nazis, scientists and engineers now created new consumer marvels available to middle-class Americans. Economists, led by John Maynard Keynes, had apparently solved the problem of the business cycle and were now heeded as oracular visionaries. A sociologist appeared on the cover of *Time* magazine, and the report of sex researcher Alfred Kinsey would become one of the best-sellers of the 1950s; a 1957 study would reveal that

14 percent of the population reported having consulted a professional for expert advice.[8]

Extending national commitments overseas, government intervention into new areas of domestic affairs, and expanding government administration was made possible by the rapid growth
of the U.S. economy over the two decades that followed the end
of World War II. Fueled by pent-up demand during the war, new
government initiatives, and the expansion of productivity and
technology during World War II, the U.S. economy grew through
the 1950s, with economic growth accelerating in the 1960s. The
new science of management that had developed in the 1920s and
1930s saw American industry dominated by large-scale, horizon-
tally integrated Fordist firms, employing thousands of workers in
both production and management.[9] By the 1950s most working
Americans were employed in white-collar jobs for the first time,
as organized capitalism replaced the individual entrepreneur and
yeoman small-holder of American myth. The growing wealth of
the nation would fund the expanding national security apparatus
and other federal programs, while making available to American
consumers a new standard of living. Americans would accept
such expanded government power if it continued to extend the
benefits of abundance; thus a key feature of the postwar era was
the economic enfranchisement of the majority of Americans.
By the decade's end, more Americans than ever owned their
own homes, equipped with a variety of new labor-saving devices,
automobiles, and television sets. Newly constructed suburbs such
as Levittown, New York, would provide an affordable suburban
existence to middle-class America, whose ranks were swelling
daily. It seemed, as Warren Sussman notes, that the United States
had achieved its goals—widespread economic well-being, self-
sustaining growth, and liberal democracy.[10]

This new abundance was made possible by the transformation of the political economic system that was celebrated in
American culture. From Thomas Jefferson and Andrew Jackson
to Free-Soilers and Progressives, the story of American success
was a story of individuals, sometimes banded together as a popular coalition against the corrupt influence of big, moneyed interests, but always for the goal of expanding the scope of individual
opportunity. Whether Southern plantation owners, monopolistic

trusts, the New England banking establishment, or the House of Morgan, the enemies of the popular American yeomanry were always defeated by the virtue of the small-holding, individual entrepreneur. But the new reality of the postwar political economy was an organized capitalism in which the individual was in fact a part of the great capitalist organizations. Big business, big labor, and big government were the reality. The new suburban homeowner was not the yeoman farmer of free-soil myth, but an other-directed, team-playing organization man. In this new world, political conflicts were of little consequence, as historians, politicians, and social scientists all confirmed. Ideology had come to an end, and future progress was guaranteed by linking natural and social scientific experts to business and government. The issue—as late–Cold War presidential candidate Michael Dukakis would claim—was not ideology but competence.[11]

While this age of affluence gave more people the opportunity to own their own homes and fill them with the latest labor-saving technology, the newfound abundance it produced also served the other goal of postwar America: containing communism. With its great wealth, the United States would be able to export its political economic system around the world, and the inevitable success of that system would keep communism from expanding. To do this, the nation made economic and military commitments throughout the world, asserting itself as a global power as never before.

Many of these transformations predate the Cold War or are not directly related to the East-West conflict, but they all are tied to it and influenced by it. While the American corporation had been transforming independent of U.S. foreign policy, the Cold War brought government and business elites into close cooperation on defense contracting and other policies. While the university had been changing on its own, the influence of government Cold War expenditures on research and analysis had a determining effect. While the abundance that reigned through most of these two decades was not a direct product of the Cold War, it was enhanced by government defense spending and became a central weapon in the American ideological arsenal, used to demonstrate the superiority of the capitalist system to that of communism. In 1948, rather than respond militarily to a Soviet blockade of West Berlin, the United States and its allies began a massive airlift of goods into the beleaguered city, supplying it completely by air. In 1959, Vice President Richard Nixon engaged in the "kitchen debate" with Soviet Premier Nikita Krushchev at an American exhibition in Moscow. In a mock-up of a ranch-style home replete with all the consumer products available for sale in the United States, Nixon used American economic abundance to challenge Krushchev's claims that the USSR would soon overtake the United States. So pervasive was the use of abundance as a weapon that it would come to be lampooned in David Reisman's famous essay "The Nylon War."[12]

By the end of the 1950s the American political economy had been transformed. The federal government, now centered on the presidency as never before, was seen as responsible for both national security and economic prosperity. This entailed permanent foreign involvement that had been eschewed for 150 years since George Washington warned against entangling alliances and an expansion of the scope and power of government interventions within the United States. American workers found themselves in a postindustrial economy that provided them with a standard of living they had never imagined, but which saw them working as members of large organizations in which they were merely one player among thousands. While they might own their own homes and enjoy the benefits of abundance, this was not the free-soil dream most of them had aspired to from birth. Others, most notably African Americans, were still struggling for access to this abundance; many others—particularly women— were wondering why this abundance did not make them happier. Over the heads of them all hung the apocalyptic possibility of atomic warfare amid the constant crises of the Cold War.

The Cold War Cultural Consensus

Defining national identity became an obsession in twentieth-century America. The nationalization of the economy and the massive influx of immigrants through the nineteenth century combined with America's first sustained forays at empire building to lead Americans to try to define who they were. Debates about the ability of immigrants to assimilate—the melting pot versus cultural pluralism—began in the second decade of the twentieth century. Allan Carlson sees the attacks on "hyphenated Americans," the Red Scare and Palmer raids, and the restrictive immigration laws of the 1920s as reflecting "a national search, however crude, for a common identity."[13] It was during these decades that the American Studies movement was born, with its major project being to define the meaning of America in the nation's literature, symbols, and myths. Warren Sussman has demonstrated that a new concern with national culture and the search for an American way of life characterized the 1930s.[14]

By the end of World War II, that American way had been found. Historians began to reinterpret American history as based on a cultural consensus. Richard Hofstadter, the most famous of the consensus historians, argued that American history was best understood as a consistent pattern of pragmatic, liberal capitalism, with ideological extremism as a major threat.[15] Similarly, Eric Hoffer warned of the threat posed to society by ideological "true believers."[16] Political scientists saw a basic value consensus and the presence of a large middle class as preconditions for a stable democracy.[17] In the mid-1950s, theorists of political and economic development argued that modernization required the development of a large middle class and a consensual consumer culture.[18] By the end of the 1950s, Daniel Bell would argue that ideological conflict was at an end; technology, linked to industry and politics, rendered a pragmatic solution to all social and economic problems possible.[19]

Taken together these arguments suggested an America characterized by minimal conflict among its citizens. What conflict existed would be over the means to achieve the ends of expanding liberty, democracy, and opportunity, but not over the ends themselves. This conception of the American nation envisioned consensus rather than conflict as the norm, and thus justified characterizing any dissent from the consensus as un-American. Asserting the anti-ideological nature of American identity, ironically, masked a strongly ideological position that used the rhetoric of American national identity to achieve cultural hegemony.

This cultural consensus is often seen as a unique moment in American cultural history. Lary May argues that it represents a new phase in American history characterized by a "remarkable reorientation of national values and artistic norms." It was an era of boundless faith in American politics and economics in which "politicians and businessmen spoke with one voice in praise of the modern corporation and an affluent society where conflicts over scarce resources were a thing of the past."[20] This differed, May and others suggest, from the previous view of American cultural history, which had been seen as a story of conflict rather than consensus. Whether it was Americans versus the English, New England versus the Mid-Atlantic, North versus South, populists versus moneyed interests, or Jeffersonians versus Hamiltonians, the story of American culture had been one of conflicting conceptions of the American self.[21] While the degree of cultural consensus achieved by the end of the 1950s might have been unprecedented, the definition of the American self developed during the Cold War did not emerge sui generis out of the new, increasingly global American experience. Instead it drew heavily on the rhetorical elements that had been used to construct the American identities through which cultural conflicts had been conducted. Thus the consensus was made possible, in part, by the existence of a shared language and rhetoric of American national identity that can be seen in various diverse formulations of the American self from the seventeenth century on.

The Rhetoric of America: Freedom, Progress, and Providence

[I]t is by a mutual consent through a special over-ruling providence, and a more than an ordinary approbation of the Churches of Christ to seek out a place of Cohabitation and Consortship under a due form of government both civil and ecclesiastical. In such cases as this the care of the public must over-sway all private respects, by which not only conscience, but mere Civil policy doth bind us; for it is true that particular estates cannot subsist in the ruin of the public. . . .

The end is to improve our lives to do more service to the Lord the comfort and increase of the body of Christ whereof we are members that ourselves and our posterity may be better preserved from the Common corruptions of this evil world. . . .

. . . for the means whereby this must be effected they are two fold, a conformity with the work and end we aim at, these we see are extraordinary, therefore we must not content

> ourselves with usual ordinary means whatsoever we did or
> ought to have done when we lived in England, the same must
> we do and more also where we go. . . .[22]

Thus did John Winthrop both admonish and encourage his fellow Puritans aboard the *Arabella* before they disembarked on their errand into the wilderness of Massachussetts Bay in 1630. In this brief description of their mission, Winthrop wields a rhetoric of community to bind the individual saints of the Puritan settlement into a single entity. He acknowledges that they are free individuals, noting that they have each given their "mutual consent" and that each has a private interest. These free individuals, however, have come together under the dispensation of providence to build a world free of corruption's influence. They are on a progressive mission to build a better world, one more moral and virtuous than that which they left in England. To complete this mission of moral regeneration, they must take extraordinary measures, placing the public before the private and acting as a community to assure their individual salvation.

These rhetorical elements—freedom, progress, and providence—would become the common language of American community, one that the Puritans would bequeath to the generations that followed them. While Winthrop's sermon sees them as individual saints, each with an individual relationship to God, they are at the same time charged by that God to create a virtuous community that is morally superior to all other communities. In this they "must be knit together in this work as one man . . . to entertain each other in brotherly affection." This is an extraordinary situation, blessed by God. "Thus stands the cause between God and us, we are entered into Covenant with him for this work." Their virtue has providential dispensation, rendering them superior to the corruption they have fled. Their mission is of dire historical import, "for we must consider that we shall be as a City upon a hill, the eyes of all people are upon us."[23] Their mission is one of world historical significance, not merely for themselves and their posterity; the eyes of the world are upon them, and they must succeed.

Such rhetorical elements would be reconfigured in various periods to construct different visions of the American community.[24] At the core of these visions is the free individual, the

Puritan saint, the citizen, or the freeholder who serves as the constituent element of society. The free individual thus predates the liberal revolution of the eighteenth century, and is encoded in the cultural DNA of the United States, dedicated even before its birth, to "life, liberty and the pursuit of happiness." The persistent rhetorical power of the individual in American culture is represented in the American vision of heroism, ranging from Daniel Boone and Natty Bummpo through the cowboy on the frontier and the private detective in urban America to the super-hero in comic books. Politically, celebrating the individual leads to arguments that advocate individual liberties rather than corporate rights and free markets rather than public intervention.

The peculiarly liberal notion of equality—all having equal access to the same individual liberties—renders it a by-product of freedom rather than an independent rhetorical element in its own right. While occasionally portrayed as an autonomous value (most notably prior to the Cold War in arguments concerning abolition), the American notion of equality nevertheless continued to emphasize extending legal rights to all equally—perhaps most obviously with the equal protections clause of the Fourteenth Amendment—rather than extending into notions of group rights or equality of condition. In the Cold War and after, political claims based on group identification (race, gender, ethnicity, or sexual orientation) would be accepted only to the extent that they were limited to members of the group gaining individual access to the full rights of citizenship. Hence, arguments about equality rested on equal *individual* access to the political sphere.

A second rhetorical element was the belief in unending progress. From the Puritan vision of making the world ready for the return of Christ, to Benjamin Franklin's story of upward mobility and the postrevolutionary pragmatic reformers,[25] to Ralph Waldo Emerson's vision of "Young America,"[26] to the emphasis on economic growth and innovation in the twentieth century, Americans have accepted a vision of progressive improvement as a basic constituent of their cultural discourse. The most important formulation of progress coming into the twentieth century was the free-soil thought of nineteenth-century Republicanism. Linking individual freedom to prosperity, it was the dominant discourse of progress prior to the Great Depression.

Free-soil thinkers constructed a definition of American identity that stressed economics more than government as the basis of American virtue. Abraham Lincoln, for instance, draws a connection between virtue, liberty, and economic progress, noting that a community of free individuals, owners of land or self-employed artisans, is a necessary basis for progress:

> The prudent, penniless beginner in the world, labors for wages awhile, saves a surplus with which to buy tools or land, for himself; then labors on his own account another while, and at length hires another new beginner to help him. This, say its advocates, is free labor—the just and generous, and prosperous system, which opens the way for all—gives hope to all, and energy, and progress, and improvement of condition to all. If any continue through life in the condition of the hired laborer, it is not the fault of the system, but because of either a dependent nature which prefers it, or improvidence, folly, or singular misfortune.[27]

Free labor *is* progress. A society of autonomous producers is just and generous and gives hope. Continuing as a wage laborer, for Lincoln, is to be immoral because of the failure to achieve the autonomy of the free individual. The object of American society is to create the virtuous community of freeholders, and progress is measured by the extent to which all citizens are autonomous freeholders.

Southern slaveholders, ironically, saw industrialization and constant labor as demeaning to humankind, and thus saw themselves as the civilizing force of progress in America. Relegating menial labor to slaves (who were defined as inhuman) released the slaveholder from the need for toil. He was capable of pursuing the civilized arts and creating a progressive, virtuous society. Thus slaveholders would argue that they were the progressive force in American society, creating a civilization of virtuous individuals freed from the need for demeaning menial labor.[28]

The third rhetorical element was, and continues to be, the belief in American moral superiority and exceptionalism. From the blessings of providence bestowed on the Puritan errand to the manifest destiny to fill the continent to moral crusades to end all wars or make the world safe for democracy, Americans have conceived of themselves as the bearers of a virtuous mission, frequently referring to providence as the source of their virtue. It was, for instance, in 1954 during the Cold War that "one nation, indivisible" celebrated in the Pledge of Allegiance became, in fact, "one nation, under God."[29] American virtue was manifest in the superiority of American political and economic institutions.

While these three rhetorical elements do not themselves constitute a national identity, the intermingling of them, their arrangements and relations, constitutes the basic building blocks of all competing visions of American national identity. The Cold War, emerging after the national mobilizations of the Great Depression and World War II, created a space in which a particular vision of cultural history could be used to serve the political economic ends of major actors in the United States. Seeking a return to normalcy after two decades of crisis, Americans were complicit in this development, permitting themselves to subordinate public debates over American identity and its implications for policy making to private concerns of work, consumption, and family. In a country that still celebrated a Jeffersonian yeomanry and bathed in a Washingtonian isolationist moral superiority, the global commitments of the emerging Cold War and the large-scale organization of American life created material conditions that did not conform to the rhetoric of American identity.

The Necessity of Consensus

Justifying and gaining acceptance for these political economic changes was clearly on the minds of American policy makers. George Kennan's famous call to contain Soviet power acknowledged the long-term nature of the conflict (it might last as long as seventeen years, he prophesied) and the difficulty in maintaining public support over that time.[30] More directly, National Security Council Memorandum 68 of 1950, the major document defining Cold War policy, stated the most significant problem in fighting the Cold War was getting U.S. citizens to accept the costs and the new role they were being asked to play, and it noted the government would need to educate the citizens into a crisis mentality to maintain the course. The document warns that "A free society is vulnerable" because it is easy for citizens to lose sight of "evil design." It is thus important to evoke the full power of the American people by ensuring "that sufficient information regarding the . . . present situation be made publicly available so that an intelligent popular opinion may be formed. Having achieved a comprehension of the issues now facing the Republic, it will then be possible for the American people and the American Government to arrive at a consensus." This is vital, because the major threat to achieving America's "fundamental purpose" is identified as the "lack of will to maintain it."[31]

Thus, three streams converge to create the Cold War consensus. First, the national mobilizations of the Great Depression and World War II brought a sense of national community that had never before held such sway with mainstream America or among its intellectual elites. Second was the need for the government to channel this sense of community into a mobilization in support of the newly expansive and internationalist American government. Third was the persistent rhetoric of American culture, emphasizing freedom, progress, and providence. The rhetoric would be adapted to serve the needs of Cold War America, in the form of a consensus on national identity.

The Rhetoric of Consensus

During the 1950s the virtue of the American political system and the unending economic progress of its free-market economy became inextricably linked to the Cold War. Science, free markets, and individual rights had defeated the Nazis and created the conditions for affluence. The forces of totalitarian communism posed a threat similar to that of the Nazis and would be defeated by these same—peculiarly American—strengths. What emerged has been often characterized as a new cultural consensus. Promulgated by government, professional, and academic elites and enforced by loyalty oaths, Congressional hearings, and public censure, this consensus was constructed throughout the 1940s and 1950s and became nearly hegemonic by the start of the 1960s. While dominant, this consensus did not, in fact, represent a unitary national identity for Americans. Intimidating dissent into silence is not the same as eradicating it. Jackson Lears sees the consensus as an imposed vision, from a Gramscian hegemonic "new class of salaried managers, administrators, academics, technicians and journalists."[32] Similarly, Leerom Medovoi suggests the consensus was merely imaginary, imposed by "a dominant bloc within the nation-state that valorized a shared system of political signs—the various tropes and rhetorics of American democracy as they were relationally defined against the communist enemy."[33] To claim it is the hegemonic discourse of a dominant new class or that it is a language used by a dominant bloc within the nation-state negates neither its existence nor its impact. It does imply—more directly than a strict notion of consensus—that, while dominant, this set of beliefs was not the sole definition of national identity, national culture, or ideology. But while this consensus might be challenged by competing visions, it remains nonetheless that there was developing throughout the 1950s an argument of an American consensual identity. By the end of the decade, this was the dominant vision, the one that would carry into the 1960s.

There were four main components to the Cold War consensus that characterized American identity as it entered the 1960s. The first of these was that affluence was produced by free individuals. While there was some challenge to this notion from sociologists who suggested that the bureaucratized organization man was increasingly the norm, the individualism that had been a key element of American national identity since the eighteenth century continued to characterize mainstream discourse.[34] While most European countries had adopted some form of social democracy, and economic critics of the affluent society such as John Kenneth Galbraith advocated similar developments in America,[35] free-market liberalism dominated American thinking. Critical claims on the American social product from civil rights advocates or women's groups would be acceptable only if they were couched in the terms of individual rights and liberties. America's economic wealth was seen as the product of the free market and the individual entrepreneurship it made possible.

The second element was the belief that individualist America produced virtuous leadership. The American system of democracy was heralded as the best system in the world, still blessed by divine providence to be a beacon of light to suffering peoples around the globe. Rather than maintain its moral virtue by shunning the immoralities of petty kingdoms, as Washington had suggested, America now was called to lead actively, to defend free people wherever they may be in their struggle to follow the American example. Thus, America's global role and the expansive, interventionist national security state created to play it were justified by continued reference to the moral superiority of the United States that had been a hallmark of American identity since John Winthrop spoke aboard the *Arabella*.

The opposite of the virtue of free-market individualism was the controlling force of totalitarianism that the United States must oppose. This presented the third element of American ideology. The greatest threat to the United States and the world was the inhibition of free individuals by the forces of "ruthless, godless tyranny."[36] The USSR was portrayed not merely as a rival for power, nor as a political economic alternative, but as a force for immorality and corruption. The Cold War was neither a power struggle only nor an ideological conflict but instead the latest stage in the age-old battle between good and evil. Since free market individualism produced both affluence and virtue, the inhibitions on freedom must necessarily produce squalor and evil. The virtuous United States could not help but oppose such evil wherever it manifested itself, at home or abroad.

The fourth element was the growing emphasis on inclusion. Inclusion was not necessarily a product of the Cold War, but its role in the construct was enhanced by it. It was produced in part by the experiences of the Great Depression and World War II. The Depression had demonstrated to a generation that contrary to both later Puritan and free-soil formulations, poverty might not necessarily be produced by immorality. As God-fearing middle-class Americans found themselves without work, without homes, and without prospects in the 1930s they realized that economic catastrophe could befall anyone, irrespective of individual work ethic. They thus came to accept that there was a need for American society to provide for all its members, as was done through the series of programs constructed during the Roosevelt administration. Facing the Axis powers in a collective effort in World War II, and sharing in the collective guilt of the "final solution," Americans saw that the virtue of their system would only persist to the extent that all were able to benefit from the age of affluence. The immorality of the communist system during the Cold War could not be permitted any leverage to challenge American virtue, and thus inclusion of all citizens, irrespective of race, gender, or ethnicity, would become more important throughout the period.[37]

The interweaving of the rhetorical elements of American identity into the Cold War consensus is easily seen in President Dwight D. Eisenhower's first inaugural address. After humbly asking permission to open with a prayer, Eisenhower proceeded to invoke the deity six times in the first third of the speech as he defined American faith. At the center of this faith was the freedom of the individual—particularly, the right to elect leaders and the "right to choose our own work and to the reward of our own toil."[38] Economic freedom was the source of the vast productivity of America that was the "wonder of the world." Freedom became almost synonymous with equality, as all who contributed to the power of the country must be accorded freedoms. Equality was thus defined as inclusion within the system of freedoms and was essentially a by-product of freedom, a common liberal move. The major threat defined within this faith was the "mockery of the tyrant." Eisenhower never once mentioned the USSR in the speech, referring instead to tyranny and evil. Melding freedom and providence, Eisenhower defined tyranny as evil, the opposite of the divinely inspired freedom. Three times in the speech Eisenhower evoked a Manichean vision of the United States–USSR conflict, as good versus evil; "[f]reedom is pitted against slavery; lightness against the dark." This conflict was defined as global, in which America was the torchbearer of freedom to the world, the hope and defender of free people. The economic and military power of the United States was not solely for national defense, but "a trust upon which rests the hope of free men everywhere." America must exert itself globally because of the economic necessity of markets and materials, but also because it must defend and inspire all those people who shared the "noble idea" of freedom. As Eisenhower asserted, "This faith we hold belongs not to us alone but to the free of all the world. This common bond binds the grower of rice in Burma and the planter of wheat in Iowa, the shepherd in Southern Italy and the mountaineer in the Andes. It confers a common dignity upon the French soldier who dies in Indo-China, the British soldier killed in Malaya, the American life given in Korea."[39] Having linked American moral virtue with the export and defense of freedom and defined totalitarianism as the evil that threatens the security and expansion of freedom, Eisenhower outlined nine principles that were to implement this faith. These advocated maintaining military strength and will while remaining open to arms control, supporting "proven friends of freedom" with military and economic aid while honoring each country's special heritage, maintaining economic growth to support the military, and respecting the negotiating framework of the United Nations. These principles, Eisenhower's translation of the American faith into action, would require strong support from the American people and would reach into all areas of life: "Moral stamina means more energy and more productivity, on farm and in factory. Love of liberty means the guarding of every resource that makes freedom possible—from the sanctity of our families and the wealth of our soil to the genius of our scientists." Such an extensive definition of security interests and such an expansive vision of America's global interests would require total commitment on the part of American citizens: "So we are persuaded by necessity and by belief that the strength of all free peoples lies in unity; their danger, in discord."[40]

For Eisenhower, individual freedom was the bedrock value to be preserved because it was God-given. He saw the United States as the moral force for good in promoting the global progress of freedom against tyranny. Defending against tyranny required that the government reach into every aspect of domestic life, because all Americans must be dedicated to the defense against tyranny included in the progressive mission, and must also support an expansive foreign policy, to serve as a beacon of light to those who seek freedom from the oppressor's yoke. The American self was thus a free individual, charged by providence to serve the progress of freedom at home and around the world, defending against the evil forces of tyranny.

By the end of the 1950s, most Americans accepted that they existed in a virtuous society of free individuals, with the best form of government and the greatest possible economic system in the free market. The most compelling evidence of this was the rising standard of living and growing equality that was made possible by this virtuous system. If this was to continue, Americans needed to be vigilant against the tide of totalitarian control that flowed outside their borders and lapped at their shores. Soviet advances in rocketry that permitted the USSR to launch the first satellite into orbit, and the establishment of a potential Soviet satellite state off the coast of Florida, demonstrated that the threat posed by the Soviets to the American virtuous society was clear and present. The major domestic issue confronting Americans was to assure that all were included in the abundance that their land produced, as long as they were willing to accept the premises of the liberal consensus; for this, as for national security, the government played the deciding role. While accepted by most Americans, this consensus was not without tension. The tensions arising around it, though, while emergent in the 1950s, would not be fully apparent until the mid- to late 1960s.

Anxious Contradictions

One set of tensions arose between the belief that Americans were endowed with individual liberties and the government's desire to root out communist influences within the United States. The anticommunist Red Scare of the 1940s and '50s contributed to the strengthening of the federal government and promoted the Cold War consensus but challenged Americans' belief that they had freedom of thought and association. Hearings held by the House Committee on Un-American Activities (HUAC) contributed to the idea that there was some set of beliefs and behaviors that was peculiarly American while also using the power of the federal government to stifle opposition. The loyalty oaths required during the administration of President Harry S. Truman beginning in 1948 squelched dissent from within the ranks of government. Government propaganda films on discerning the communists among the population, or offering tragic visions of the failure to maintain vigilance against potential communist infiltrators, sought to delegitimize communist ideologies and create fear that communists were lurking around every corner. John Kenneth White sees this anticommunist battle as a partisan conflict between Republican anticommunists and Democratic liberals in the State Department, comparing it to a Stalinist purge.[41] While this is perhaps an extreme interpretation, there is no doubt that the anticommunist crusade did foster ideological conformity within the United States. Victor Navasky argues that the HUAC hearings were instrumental in developing the U.S. Cold War consensus: "A major contributor to this . . . was the ex-Communist whose testimony helped create, confirm, and fix the image of the Soviet Union as subverter of American capitalism, to link Soviet imperialism abroad to the 'red menace' at home, to persuade Americans that 'the Russian fifth column in the United States is greater than Hitler's ever was.'"[42] The histrionics of Senator Joesph McCarthy in seeking out communists in the State Department and the military were another form. While the backlash against the senator's tactics quashed the major phase of the anticommunist crusade, it did not end it altogether. HUAC continued to function into the 1970s.

The popular fear of communists infiltrating the United States and undermining it from inside was manifest in the wide array of popular entertainments. The success of Matt Cvetic's book *I Was a Communist for the FBI*, spawning both feature films and a television series, suggests that this fear was extensive. Films such as *Big Jim McClain* (1952), *My Son John* (1952), *Pick-Up on South Street* (1953), and *Invasion of the Body Snatchers* (1956) all played on it.[43] In most of these works, as well in such government propaganda films as *Red Nightmare* (1962), the major threat posed by the communists was toward the family. Children were frequently turned against the American father by the communist-sympathizing mother. The rhetoric of the government and anticommunist experts—that the family was the bulwark of American values and thus the greatest weapon against the communists—linked the popular fear of communists to fears about the breakdown of the family.[44] The Senate hearings into juvenile delinquency and comic books can only be understood in the context of the anticommunist crusade that preceded it.[45]

There was strong opposition to both HUAC and McCarthy from various groups such as the Hollywood Ten, or in popular entertainments such as the 1952 film *High Noon* (whose writer, Carl Foreman, intended it as an allegory for Hollywood's capitulation to HUAC). Some voices were raised against McCarthy early in his attacks—most famously that of Maine Senator Margaret Chase Smith—and he was ultimately censured by the Senate. Still, when the CBS television network finally challenged McCarthy two years into his crusade on an episode of *See It Now* in 1954, its sponsor, Alcoa, received hate mail and was publicly criticized by conservative columnists. A poll showed that more people trusted McCarthy than the show's host, respected reporter Edward R. Murrow, and that one-third believed that Murrow was a communist sympathizer.[46] As more details of the government's domestic anticommunist activity became apparent over the next several decades—from FBI domestic surveillance to infiltration of the American Communist Party, as well as covert foreign activities—the controversy over the Red Scare would become but a moment in the tension between a belief in individual rights and virtuous government and the reality of the Cold War.

That the government would go to such ends to stop the communists would continue to be a source of tension. In an unintentionally ironic statement, NSC Memorandum 68 pointed to the heart of the problem in defining the extent to which America should go to defeat the communists, noting, "The integrity of our system will not be jeopardized by any measures, covert or overt, violent or non-violent, which serve the purposes of frustrating the Kremlin design, nor does the necessity for conducting ourselves so as to affirm our values in actions as well as words forbid such measures, provided only they are appropriately calculated to that end and are not so excessive or misdirected as to make us enemies of the people instead of the evil men who have enslaved them."[47] Were the ends of defeating the enemy sufficient to justify the virtue of the means? Could America retain its virtue if it engaged in unvirtuous acts, even to defeat communist totalitarianism? Might not America become its own enemy? Increasingly throughout the next three decades, Americans would seek to define themselves and the enemy. While the communists were clearly defined in the 1950s, the enemy became increasingly ambiguous as the 1960s unfolded. Tom Engelhardt sees the plethora of conspiracy theories surrounding President John F. Kennedy's assassination as evidence of a growing ambiguity concerning the enemy's identity, noting that "the public was increasingly ready to entertain the thought that some kind of enemy-ness, some kind of organized evil, had managed to creep close to the president with deadly intent. As a result, the most unbelievable, un-American, and horrifying act since Pearl Harbor . . . was open to any interpretation except the most obvious anti-communist one."[48] Ultimately, their quest for an enemy would lead Americans to turn back upon themselves. Walt Kelly's comic strip *Pogo*, while referring to pollution in the mid-1960s, gave a new sense of identity to Cold War America: "We have met the enemy, and he is us."

From the other side of the ideological consensus would come criticism from those who accepted the severity of the communist threat but believed that the government was insufficiently dedicated to confronting the moral threat it posed. The peaceful coexistence of the Eisenhower administration and the internationalism represented by the United Nations was seen as part of a grand conspiracy to undermine America. Having accepted the claims of a communist conspiracy at the end of World War II, many saw the government abdicating its mission of stopping communism by the end of the 1950s. Organizations such as the Christian Anti-Communist Crusade and, most famously, the John Birch Society led the way. The rhetoric of the Birch Society would be used by Ronald Reagan and Barry Goldwater in the early 1960s; by 1965, at its height, the Birch Society numbered between 80,000 and 100,000 members. Birch members supported the radically conservative presidential campaign of Barry Goldwater, and society membership was a stepping stone in the early ideological formation of many conservatives.[49] Defending the virtue of American freedom (particularly of property) these countersubversives saw politics in "value" terms. American values were threatened by the expansion of communist influence, evidenced by the launching of Sputnik, the Cuban Revolution, and the growing conflict in Southeast Asia. Increasing conflict over civil rights and the centralization of federal power over states' rights suggested to them that the American government was not meeting its burden of defending values. While fringe thinkers at the start of the 1960s, they would be able to capture the Republican presidential nomination (but lose in a landslide) in 1964, but would gain governorships, most notably in California. By the 1970s, they would emerge as a major force in American politics.

The tensions surrounding American public virtue would be coupled with anxieties about individual identity. While the liberal consensus was an expression of faith in politics and economics—arenas of public life—the major goal of most Americans was the development of their private lives. As Lary May notes, the public identity of anticommunist, liberal America was meant to create the opportunities for personal fulfillment and consumption.[50] Public and private became linked in ever new ways during the high Cold War. Elaine Tyler May has shown how women were encouraged to return to the home as mothers and wives through the advice of experts who saw the nuclear family as essential to maintain social stability in the face of the communist threat.[51] James Gilbert has linked theories of child rearing, delinquency, and Cold War national security in the 1950s.[52] Allan Carlson demonstrates that U.S. foreign policy and a vision of national character based on strong families were specifically connected.[53] But the contradiction between public and private became increasingly difficult to solve. As the expansive national security state pervaded American society to protect the public, it frequently did so by invading the private, or attempting to call the private to its service. Could it be possible to have such an expansive public realm while maintaining, if not strengthening, the rhetoric of individualism and celebration of the private in American life?

Whither the individual in the age of organized capitalism? With the arenas of politics and economics populated by big organizations driven by competence rather than ideology, the American citizenry was cast out of the two areas that had been heralded as the main arenas for self-fulfillment. Thus, while economic problems seemed a thing of the past, and the abundance produced by the economy would permit a social transformation that ended political conflict, people became increasingly uneasy. The age of abundance was also the age of anxiety.

These anxieties were profound. The science and technologies that were creating the conditions for abundance were also producing atomic bombs, heralding an apocalyptic rather than a rosy future. The vast diversity of goods for sale, ranging from televisions and automobiles to houses, was creating a mass consumer culture that homogenized consumption, leaving little room for individual expression, and many have posited that it undermined the development of high culture in the United States. The development of new forms of mass media—television, comic books, phonograph records—gave youth access to new forms of cultural education that could be seen as promoting immorality and heralding a breakdown in social norms, as seen in the rise of juvenile delinquency. The virulence of these fears led to mass protest. Public burnings of comic books occurred during the first anticomic crusade in the late 1940s, and again in the mid-1950s.[54]

The impact of these anxieties was readily apparent. Engelhardt notes that the threat of atomic annihilation was the "big fear" that characterized American society. To it were added myriad "little fears" centering on the breakdown of the family under the onslaught of communist infiltration. The new magazine for men, *Playboy*, with its philosophy of male consumption, tried to give men an identity indoors, whereas the traditional locale of masculinity had always been outside.[55] This had to be married with laments throughout the decade of the 1950s concerning the crisis of masculinity; for much of the 1950s, writers from Arthur Schlesinger to Philip Wylie lamented the decline of manliness and how the lack of virility was undermining the American ability to stand up to the communists.[56] Senate hearings into juvenile delinquency, focusing particularly on comic books, were held after the successful publication of Fredric Wertham's *Seduction of the Innocent*. The culture of mass consumption was indicted in everything from *Invasion of the Body Snatchers* to John Kenneth Galbraith's *Affluent Society*. Anxieties about the atomic bomb were easily seen, from the building of fallout shelters to best selling novels and films about nuclear apocalypse.

Further anxieties were felt by those not sharing in the promised abundance. Women, who had returned to the home as mothers and wives after the war, felt increasingly empty. "The problem with no name," Betty Friedan called it, the unease at having achieved everything that women were supposed to want but still feeling unfulfilled.[57] The rise in the use of prescription tranquilizers by suburban housewives attests to this anxiety. Miltown was launched in 1955, and by 1956 one in twenty Americans was taking Miltown or some other tranquilizer.[58] Less subdued, African Americans fought for access throughout the decade. After the NAACP's legal successes in 1948 and 1954, the civil rights movement escalated, although it would not be until the early 1960s that it caught the attention of the American mainstream.[59]

The rhetoric of American identity celebrated the individual in political, economic, and social terms. Free thinking, rights-bearing, individual producer in free markets for both economic and political competition was the role of the American citizen. In an age of organized late capitalism, with a newly expanded central state creating an organized nation, the place of the individual seemed decreasingly real. How could one live the meaning of America in an America where that meaning no longer seemed relevant? The contradictions inherent in the Cold War identity would become increasingly pertinent in the 1960s and '70s, and the Cold War consensus would unravel. This would have deeper ramifications than the fading of the myth of consensus. The very rhetorical elements that had constituted the language of American national identity for two centuries would become increasingly impotent.

The economic abundance and apparent social cohesion of the early 1960s generated a social exuberance that aspired to eliminate the problems of American society. In the context of the liberal consensus, the chief problem was to include those who were not reaping the benefits of the age of affluence: the poor, minorities, and women. The hopes of transforming American society while still contesting the Cold War were shattered against the rocks of the Vietnam War, the stalling of the civil rights movement, the imperial presidencies of Lyndon Johnson and Richard Nixon, and the exhaustion of the postwar economic boom. The enhanced power of the presidency to prosecute the Cold War encouraged imperial excesses, the consequences of which led Johnson to decline running for a second term and forced Nixon to resign. Perception of Cold War policy as perverse arose with the Vietnam War. As details of U.S.-sponsored covert operations became public in the 1970s, in the wake of Watergate and Vietnam, faith in the virtue of American institutions began to wane. While the role of the media in showing the clay feet of politicians is important, the media would not do so had Americans not been willing to see their politicians as lacking virtue. Faith in progress was diminished by the great inflation of the 1970s and the collapse of the Fordist economy that had seemed the epitome of the American dream. Only the celebration of the individual and the free-market economy in which she existed would retain its rhetorical power, but without the supports of progress and providence, that individualism could not provide a rhetoric of national identity, a coherent meaning. Thus the end of the Cold War, the collapse of the Soviet Union, and the return of economic prosperity in the early 1990s did not bring a renewed sense of national purpose, nor did it generate the kind of exuberance evident in the early 1960s. Instead, profound anxiety and social dissatisfaction prevailed. Americans felt betrayed and looked to themselves as their betrayers.

But this was all to come later. As the 1960s dawned the threat still came from outside, from the totalitarian communism that threatened the American way of life. That way of life was composed of individuals whose virtue was rewarded by a growing standard of living, who knew that their system of government was the best and most virtuous in the history of the world, and who sought to remake the world in their own image.

2

The Enemy Without: 1961–1968

A S THE 1960S DAWNED, the Cold War was heating up. The era of "peaceful coexistence" that had been the hallmark of the first six years of the presidency of Dwight D. Eisenhower had ended, and increased tension between the United States and the USSR lent greater credence to the notion that America was a bastion of freedom and virtue amid an increasingly threatening world. Moscow was seen as the sole source of threat, having seemed to expand its sphere of influence to Southeast Asia, into the Middle East, and even into space with the launch of Sputnik in 1957. That influence had even reached the Western Hemisphere with the Cuban Revolution in 1959.

In this context of a reinvigorated conflict with the communist other, Americans continued to share a vision of themselves as virtuous, free individuals on a progressive global mission to defend the world from the evils of totalitarian communism. Buoyed by the affluence of the long postwar economic boom, Americans continued to see their prosperity as evidence of their virtue. Affluence might offer evidence of American virtue, but anticommunism was the ideological heart of the consensus. Godfrey Hodgson refers to the "liberal conservatism" that "blanketed the scene and muffled debate."[1] He sees support by both presidential candidates John F. Kennedy and Richard M. Nixon for anti-Castro rebels as evidence of this ideological coherence. Todd Gitlin argues that "anti-communism was the very crucible of . . . identity" for liberals.[2] Similarly, anticommunism was the basis for the conservative revival of the late 1950s.[3] American identity continued to be defined largely by what Americans were not; the external enemy—ideological, totalitarian communism— was the opposite of the pragmatic, free democracy that was the virtue of the United States.

Within this context of consensus, however, the tensions of the 1950s were ever more apparent. Those excluded from American affluence were becoming more active in making themselves heard. On February 1, 1960, four black students from North Carolina A & T University staged a sit-in at the whites-only counter of a Woolworth's department store. While there had been such sit-ins before, this action spawned a movement throughout the Southern states.[4] Clearly the tensions of the 1950s were beginning to erupt into full-blown social conflict.

Howard Brick defines the 1960s as an age of contradiction, most fundamentally a conflict between the glacial pace of social and political transformations and "the deceptive ease with which reformers thought great change could be achieved: that kind of confidence fostered dramatic aspirations for a new society but failed to recognize or nurture the social and political means that could bring change about."[5] Brick focuses on the unsatisfying consensual identity that pervaded the early 1960s and the quest for meaning—both social and personal—that was a product of it. The dominant language might be one of consensus—in economics, academia, and politics—but there were several enclaves of dissent. The growing conservative movement, centered around the *National Review,* the Young Americans for Freedom, and even the more extremist positions of the John Birch Society, represented one such form of dissent. The breadth of this movement would be revealed with the 1964 nomination of Barry Goldwater for president and the subsequent election of conservative candidates to various state offices—most notably, governor of California.[6] From the left, voices of dissent against the consensus were also rising, particularly among youth. While the Beat movement was never very large it garnered much attention and attracted scores of weekend tourists.[7] On college campuses, for both the

Left and the Right, the philosophical rage was existentialism with its quest for authentic identity.[8]

It was two years before the Port Huron Statement, three years before Betty Friedan's *Feminine Mystique* was published and Martin Luther King Jr. described his dream at the March on Washington, four years before the Berkeley Free Speech Movement and the Goldwater crusade, and five years before the first major antiwar protest. In 1960, these potential dissents lay beneath the surface of consensus and were overshadowed by a presidential election in which the two candidates focused on foreign policy and tried to outduel each other for the laurel of most rabid anticommunist. In a speech at Brigham Young University in September, candidate Kennedy defined the enemy not as the USSR but as "the Communist system itself—implacable, insatiable, increasing in its drive for world domination. . . ." The Cold War was thus not merely a military conflict, but "a struggle for supremacy between two conflicting ideologies: freedom under God versus ruthless, godless tyranny."[9]

In 1961, the year the new president took office, the constant crises of the Cold War seemed to be the only political reality. The disastrous U.S.-sponsored invasion of Cuba at the Bay of Pigs in April was followed in July by President Kennedy's request for a 25 percent increase in defense spending. In August, the East Germans closed the border to Berlin and began to construct the wall that would divide that city and, metaphorically, the East and West for the next three decades. The Cold War extended its reach beyond Earth on April 12 when Soviet Cosmonaut Yuri Gagarin became the first human to orbit the earth; the United States could only muster suborbital missions with Alan Shepard in May and Gus Grissom in July. It was nearly a year before President Kennedy would deliver his famous speech at Rice University, committing the United States to a manned mission to the moon when, in November 1961, four intrepid Americans bent on beating "the commies" into space launched their own private rocket. Encountering dangerous cosmic radiation they aborted the mission and returned to Earth, finding themselves endowed with superhuman powers. Thus was born the Fantastic Four out of the Cold War.

Constructed between 1962 and 1965, consciously set in the context of Cold War America, and required to conform to the strictures of the Comics Code, the political economy of the Marvel universe could not but reflect the liberal consensus that was the core of the American Cold War identity. Constantly under threat from the USSR, these superpowered Cold Warriors both articulated and represented the anti-ideological, free-market individualism that was its core. The strength of the consensus is apparent in the moral certainty with which Marvel's heroes battle communists and their stand-ins, physically, verbally, and visually. Celebrating free markets, independent scientists, and individual rights, Marvel's Cold Warriors continually faced and triumphed over secret societies, communist agents, and their superpowered Soviet counterparts, frequently leading Soviet agents to defect once freed from totalitarian controls. If this was insufficient to convince the reader of the rightness of the American position, the communists were frequently equated with (and often directly linked to) the Nazis of World War II, an objective evil against which to define an objective virtue. The fault lines in the consensus of the 1950s, however, would open into rifts by the middle 1960s. As the dissents of the 1960s became more vocal and more overt, the moral certainty of Marvel's Cold War would gray into increasing ambiguity; even while continuing to assert the orthodoxy of the American consensual identity, the characters, stories, and art would begin to render that orthodoxy problematic.

Moral Certainty and Marvel's Cold War

The Marvel superhero is born into the Cold War and has Cold War rhetoric and ideals ingrained in his four-color DNA. Marvel comic books of the 1960s take the consensual national identity for granted, depicting a valiant and virtuous America defending itself from immoral and corrupt communists bent on world domination. While not all books deal with the Cold War directly, all of the major characters who populate the Marvel universe were created between 1961 and 1964 (the major exceptions being the Submariner and Captain America, who were created in 1941 and revived in the early 1960s), and most were created as Cold War products or in Cold War circumstances. Table 2.1 offers the dates and venues for the first appearances of the major Marvel heroes of the 1960s.

TABLE 2.1: The Origin of the Marvel Universe

Date	Character	Magazine
November 1961	Fantastic Four	Fantastic Four 1
May 1962	Hulk	Incredible Hulk 1
	Submariner	Fantastic Four 4
August 1962	Spider-Man	Amazing Fantasy 15
	Thor	Journey into Mystery 84
September 1962	Antman	Tales to Astonish 30
March 1963	Iron Man	Tales of Suspense 39
September 1963	X-Men	X-Men 1
	Avengers	Avengers 1
December 1963	Doctor Strange	Strange Tales 111
March 1964	Captain America	Avengers 4
April 1964	Daredevil	Daredevil 1
August 1964	Nick Fury and SHIELD	Strange Tales 135

Of the ten new characters created in these years (excluding Captain America, the Submariner, and the Avengers, who were a group assembled from already existing characters), eight either gained their powers through radiation or within specific Cold War contexts. Only Thor, who was an immortal (and hence had no discernible origin), and Doctor Strange, who becomes a student of the "mystic arts" after an auto accident ends his career as a surgeon, were thus born from something other than the Cold War.

Anticommunism and Marvel Comics

Even Thor, however, was not exempt from the Cold War, as the East-West conflict pervaded the earliest Marvel stories. The Mighty Thor battled communists when he became a "Prisoner of the Reds."[10] Iron Man was the most ardent of Marvel's Cold Warriors, and over one-third of the stories between 1963 and 1966 pitted him against communist adversaries. Tony Stark, playboy millionaire munitions industrialist, was field testing a new weapons system in Vietnam when he was caught in a communist trap and forced to create the body armor that would turn him into Iron Man. His earliest tales had Iron Man face the communists indirectly, as several stories involved thieves trying to steal Tony Stark's military inventions for sale to the highest bidder (generally, the Soviets). He also directly combatted various Soviet agents, including the Black Widow, the Crimson Dynamo, and the Titanium Man. His major nemesis, however, was the Mandarin, a Chinese anticapitalist who in the early stories worked for the communist government although he was not himself a communist. Similarly, the Hulk would alternate between battling Soviet agents bent on stealing American nuclear technology (one-quarter of the stories between 1962 and 1966) and powerful aliens, all while trying to avoid capture by the U.S. military.

The stories represented the moral certainties of the Cold War, with plotlines that defined the conflict in stark contrasts between good and evil. With the exception of the deeper character development of the heroes, the books mirrored the comics of World War II in their unquestioning portrayal of American virtue. The visual representation of the communist enemies reinforced the assertion of the moral superiority of America, which was also very similar to the racial stereotyping common to World War II comic books. Where the Japanese had been portrayed as subhuman—with large foreheads, buck teeth, and sinister, elongated fingers—the Soviets would now bear that stigma. An early story, for instance, pits Iron Man against the Red Barbarian.[11] The villain, clearly intended as a Soviet, is named the Barbarian and is depicted with an overhanging brow, bad teeth, and a constant sneer. He engages in numerous acts of brutality before Iron Man defeats his agent. Notably, the Red Barbarian himself is not defeated, suggesting the ongoing nature of the struggle.

This stereotyping, in which the Soviets, Chinese, and Vietnamese appeared inhumanly sinister, was rendered even more obvious when contrasted with the clear attractiveness of most of the Marvel heroes, all of whom are tall, strong, and clean-cut.

Figure 2.1. The Subhuman Communist

"Iron Man: Trapped by the Red Barbarian,"
Tales of Suspense 42 (June 1963), 7.

From the blond, blue-eyed Steve Rogers (Captain America) to the urbane and sophisticated Tony Stark (Iron Man), Marvel's heroes are all handsome and, by association, virtuous. The exceptions, of course, are the Hulk and the Thing, whose ugliness is part of the price they pay for their strength. They may be monstrous, but they are not depicted as less than human. Stan Lee, editor and chief writer for Marvel Comics in the 1960s, in fact, recalls asking artist Jack Kirby to create a "good looking monster" for the Hulk.[12]

The physical deformity of the communist villains in these stories implies that the political economic system they represent is not only ideologically repulsive but morally bankrupt. The representatives of this system must thus exhibit a physical appearance that marks their lack of virtue. In this way, the attractiveness of the Americans necessarily lends them an aura of virtue. In his first appearance the Hulk battles a hideously deformed Soviet superscientist, the Gargoyle.[13] During the tale it is revealed that the deformity that gives the villain his name is also responsible for his genius. American scientist Bruce Banner (the Hulk's alter ego) can cure the Gargoyle of his deformity, but he will lose his supermind. This is an exchange the Gargoyle is willing to make, coming to understand that his communist masters have kept him ugly so that he could produce superpowered weapons for them. Once cured of his deformity he becomes only normally intelligent, but remains smart enough to recognize the virtue of his American rescuer. He turns on his Soviet bosses, destroying them, his weapons, and himself in a virtuous sacrifice.

The virtue Banner displays in helping his foe implies the moral superiority of America to the Soviet Union. This virtue rests on America's willingness to reward the individual (Banner) as opposed to the Soviet's attempt to control the Gargoyle. Offered the opportunity to become an attractive individual rather than an ugly slave of communism, the villain chooses the beauty of freedom and individualism, even though it costs him his life. The pervasive anticommunism of these books thus reflects not only the ubiquity of the Cold War conflict in American culture but also a core element of the American national identity: the individualism that opposes communist control.

Celebrating the Individual

An ardent individualism underlies the superhero in general. A private citizen who becomes a vigilante to seek justice, the superhero almost by definition champions the private over the public. Like the frontiersman, cowboy, or private detective heroes who preceded him, the superhero has a more certain sense of justice than legal authorities who are limited by bureaucratic procedures, legalities, or politics. This can lead to conflict, although this is rarely the case in these books of the 1960s because of the continued influence of the Cold War consensus and its manifestation in the comics industry, the Comics Code Authority.[14] Taking the superhero—one in the line of individualist American heroes—and placing him in opposition to those seeking total control celebrates the American virtue of individualism.

One key Marvel character type that reflects the dominance of individualism is the scientist-hero. Of the many geniuses who populate the Marvel universe, none are academics. All are independent scientists whose autonomy makes their scientific breakthroughs possible. Reed Richards (Mr. Fantastic), Henry Pym (Antman), and Tony Stark (Iron Man) are all private actors; only Bruce Banner works for the military directly, and he suffers the most violent of transformations. While Stark builds weapons and has many military contracts, he is still a private entrepreneur, the head of his own company who works in his private laboratory. In an age when the links among the government, academia, and business are at their greatest, not one of the scientists in Marvel participates in organized science. This celebration of the maverick scientist brings the cowboy into the atomic age, riding his microscope or computer to the frontiers of knowledge in ways organizational scientists cannot.

The rhetoric of the heroes also celebrates the free individual, defining him as the element that gives America its moral power. This rhetoric is clearest in the mouth of the ideological center of the Marvel universe—Captain America. After defeating the Red Skull's latest plan to resurrect the Third Reich and conquer America, Captain America is called a hero, to which he responds, "So long as we cherish liberty—so long as the bitter weed of tyranny can never take root upon our shores—then all of us are heroes—and the dream which is America will long endure."[15] Battling alongside his superheroic allies in the Avengers, Captain America must also face bigotry. Having defeated a clandestine organization—the Sons of the Serpent, a racist group resembling the Klu Klux Klan (although they wear cobra masks rather than white sheets)—the Avengers wonder how such intolerance could be possible. The superarcher Hawkeye complains, "He almost got away with it! Why were we so blind, so gullible?" to which Captain America responds, "That's the courage of a free country—any man has a chance to sway us—any man may be heard. And it is also our strength—it's the creed by which we live . . . for whenever the deadly poison of bigotry touches us, the flame of freedom will burn a little dimmer."[16] The free individual with the right to speak his mind is offered as a creed, signaling the centrality of individualism to the American self. Bigotry and intolerance are defined as "deadly poisons," indicating that the corollary to a nation of free individuals is the inclusion of all citizens in this creed. This instance, however, is not a product of internal contradictions but another moment of conflict with communism. The source of intolerance, the Sons of the Serpent, turns out to be led by a Chinese communist spy, General Chen, who seeks to fuel race conflict in order to weaken the United States and thus make it ripe for conquest.

The veneration of individualism in the Marvel Cold War story generates a logic to the ideology of the books. Because the core value is defined as liberty, the central evil of the communist system is its trampling of individual freedom. The books suggest there is an inherent desire among all humans for such freedom, even among communist agents. A distinction will thus be drawn between the communist government and its subjects. Because humans inherently desire freedom, the communist government must necessarily be vulnerable to opposition from inside whenever its ability to control its subjects weakens. This is demonstrated in several stories throughout the period. The Gargoyle's rebellion in *Hulk* 1 is followed by the defection of the Crimson Dynamo, another Soviet scientist-foe of Iron Man, who ends up working for Tony Stark's American munitions company after Iron Man convinces him that the communists will kill him, fearing his power.[17] The Black Widow, an undercover Soviet agent who frequently plagues Iron Man, breaks with the Soviet government and becomes a covert operative for the Supreme Headquarters International Espionage, Law Enforcement Division (SHIELD) operative after living in the United States and falling in love with the superhero archer Hawkeye.[18] A Vietnamese scientist, Half-Face, rebuilds the Soviet supervillain the Titanium Man to fight Iron Man, but repents his alliance and becomes an anticommunist when he finds that his family, whom he believed to be dead, is in fact alive.[19] In each of these instances, the inherent desire for freedom is articulated and comes to the fore when the ability of the communists to control their subjects is weakened. The American identity, centered on the freedom of the individual, is more authentically human than the total control exerted by the communists, and thus more virtuous.

Not only does the narrative of the stories offer a vision of moral certainty but the art of the books reflects this as well. Dominated by the style of Jack Kirby, Marvel's major artist of the period, the artwork is characterized by very clear lines, stark contrasts, and a formal, contained look. Text boxes remain tied to the top edge of the frame and the artwork does not extend into the gutters. All action is contained clearly within the six to nine panels per page. Such tight containment, clear lines, and limited contrasts suggest a perspective of certainty in the narrative, reinforcing the moral certainty of the texts. This is very different from the style Kirby used in the Captain America books of the 1940s. In those tales he would frequently violate the boundaries of the panels, having his characters reach across the gutters. He would also vary panel shape and location, at times separating panels by a jagged gutter resembling a lightening bolt. These techniques gave his art of the 1940s an exuberance, suggesting unbounded opportunities and the "grand expectations" that James Patterson suggests characterize that period. When contrasted with his 1960s artwork in the Captain America series, one can only see the tightly contained frames in the latter as representing something mundane yet certain. There is little exuberance in this art, although there is stronger sense of clarity.

Nazis and Communists

The identification of Cold War communists with World War II fascists is the major trope used in comic books to assert the moral certainty of American Cold War activity. As World War II was seen as a "good war," with a clear vision of the allied "good" versus the axis "evil," such an equation translates the Cold War conflict into a Manichean clarity. This was a common move not only in comic books but also among politicians and scholars seeking to support Cold War policy. The identification of a governmental form, totalitarianism, common to both Nazi Germany and the

Stalinist USSR, has been offered by Ron Robin as evidence of the service political science offered to Cold War policy.[20] If the Soviets are the same as the Nazis, then the kind of commitment necessary to defeat the Nazis is justified against the Soviets, even though there is no Pearl Harbor to mobilize Americans to action. Politicians would find World War II analogies useful in justifying Cold War policies. In justifying aid against communist insurgents in Turkey and Greece while articulating his famous doctrine of global anticommunism, President Harry S. Truman equated aid to these beleaguered governments with U.S. expenditures in World War II, defined as an "investment in world peace and freedom."[21] The domino theory for Southeast Asia and the whole structure of containment would be justified in part by the need to avoid the failure of Munich. Military preparedness in peacetime was justified by the need to avert a future Pearl Harbor. The Kennedy administration's rhetoric constantly referenced Pearl Harbor in justifying increased military expenditures. This rhetoric came to be used against them when Curtis LeMay equated the Cuban Missile Crisis with the Munich crisis to advocate stronger military action than the president was willing to take. Demonstrating resolve in the face of enemy encroachment would avert the possibility of future war.

By the time Stan Lee and Marvel began to redefine the comic book superhero this language had become pervasive throughout American culture. It is unsurprising that the same narrative structure that was used to justify Cold War policy would emerge in the comics of the period. Under the watchful eye of the Comics Code Authority, which prohibited comics from portraying politicians or government as anything but benign and knowledgeable, Lee would take the same trope used by politicians to justify their actions to render a fantastic representation of them.

The continuity between the Second World War and the Cold War is clearest in the characters of Captain America and Nick Fury, both of whom are tied directly to World War II. Trying to stop a V-2 rocket launched by Nazi scientist Baron Zemo at the end of the war, Captain America is lost in the Arctic and presumed dead, although he is frozen in an ice floe. Found floating by the supergroup the Avengers, he is revived in 1964 and joins them. His young sidekick, Bucky, however, is not so lucky, being killed in the explosion.[22] Captain America gains his own title (sharing *Tales of Suspense* with Iron Man) in November 1964. After a handful of contemporary adventures (including a trip to "battle-torn" Vietnam to rescue a captured helicopter pilot[23]) the stories treat events occurring in World War II, in which Captain America and Bucky battle the Nazis, most notably his World War II nemesis, the Red Skull. It is not until issue 72 (November 1965) that Captain America stories become current, and even then he is fighting robots left behind by the Red Skull to re-create the Nazi regime. The Avengers are not immune to the impact of Captain America's tie to World War II; for several issues they battle the Masters of Evil, led by the same Baron Zemo who caused the death of young Bucky and who will himself die while battling Captain America.[24]

Similarly, the government spy organization of the Marvel universe, SHIELD, is headed by Nick Fury, the leader of a commando unit in World War II (he also stars in *Sgt. Fury and His Howling Commandoes*). Now a colonel, he has been transformed from noncommissioned officer grunt to blue-collar officer and superspy. In accord with the need for Marvel heroes to pay for their powers in some way, Fury's promotion comes with the loss of an eye, and Colonel Fury sports an eye patch that Sgt. Fury did not need. During the first four years of its run, Nick Fury and SHIELD battle two different evil organizations: Hydra and Advanced Idea Mechanics (AIM). Hydra is a terrorist organization bent on world domination, while AIM is an organization of evil scientists who engage in terrorist activities with the goal of world domination. Both of these secret organizations bear striking resemblances to the Bundist espionage groups that Captain America fought in World War II and to the covert Soviet spy rings of Cold War paranoia. Their goals of total world control link closely to the totalitarian goals attributed to the Soviet Union. In keeping with the identification of Nazis and Communists, Hydra is run by Baron von Strucker, Nick Fury's nemesis from World War II, and AIM is secretly headed by the Red Skull. The covert organizations that serve as stand-ins for the communists in the 1960s are offered as continuities from Nazi Germany, and thus pose the same obvious moral threat. Given the clarity of the evil posed by these Nazi holdovers, it stands to reason that those who oppose them (Nick Fury, SHIELD, and Captain America) possess the same obvious virtue of those who opposed the Nazis. The connection between World War II and the Cold War is maintained, making the Soviet threat of the Cold War synonymous with the Nazi threat of World War II, and thus rendering the U.S. Cold War position morally superior.

In the first Captain America story not dominated by World War II (*Tales of Suspense* 75), Captain America directly states that the virtues of the World War II era still apply in the 1960s. A product of World War II revived in 1964, he is a man out of time, trying to apply his moral certainties to an age of increasing ambiguity. While musing over his situation he will think, "Today it's all behind me! This is a new world—a new age! An age of atomic power, space exploration, social upheaval—yet, an age over which the threat of war hangs heavy once again. And so long as danger beckons, there is still a need for an old relic like Captain America. A need that must be met!"[25] The assertion that even under the new conditions of 1960s America—where the Cold War, nuclear weapons, and postindustrialism have transformed life—the values of the 1940s are still relevant harks back to the consensus history argument concerning the essential continuity of American identity. More specifically, it links the conditions of the 1960s with those of the 1940s, reinforcing the equation of Nazis with communists.

The stories of this period describe a pervasive conflict between the United States and the communists, defined as an ideological battle of freedom versus totalitarian control, the same conflict America faced when it fought the evil of Hitler and the Nazis. In this conflict the individualism of America creates a space in which scientist heroes can develop the tools and abilities to defeat communists wherever and whenever they pose a direct threat. The very freedom that permits this individual achievement, however, renders America vulnerable to subversion from military or industrial spies, or from the forces of intolerance. As the consensual national identity emphasized pragmatic individuals, the only potential threat from within is from ideological action. This is seen in a telling sequence from *Amazing Spider-Man* 38 (July 1965). A year after the Berkeley Free Speech Movement, and in the midst of growing campus protests over the Vietnam War, college student

Peter Parker finds himself walking across the campus of fictional Empire State University and into the midst of student protesters. "What are they after *this* time?" he asks a fellow student. "They're protesting tonight's protest meeting," he is told. The protesters ask him to join them: "C'mon Parker, if you join our protest meeting we'll join one of yours sometime!" "Sure!" another adds, "And if you've got nothing to protest, don't worry about it, that won't stop us."[26] The protesters are portrayed as seeking excuses to cut classes or gain attention rather than as actually committed to a cause. A true hero, Spider-Man will not join them, because he seeks neither notoriety nor strict ideological goals. By 1965, while there may be growing public dissent, Marvel still adheres to the consensus identity.

Fault Lines

While still strong, the liberal consensus began to lose its clarity by the mid-1960s as the tensions inherent within it became increasingly apparent. The growing agitation for civil rights and the white backlash in the South challenged the belief in the growing equality of American society. Betty Friedan's *Feminine Mystique* (1963) exposed deep anxieties felt by American women. These trends indicated the growing politicization of identity within the Cold War context. This was also apparent in cultural experimentation in new forms of expression in literature by the likes of John Barth and Thomas Pynchon, in film under the influence of foreign (particularly French new wave) cinema, and, in music, jazz by Thelonious Monk, Ornette Coleman, Miles Davis, and others. The increasing influence of existentialism on college campuses also embodied this search for individual meaning unmet by the liberal identity of the Cold War consensus. This quest for authentic experience also fueled the passion of the conservative crusaders who pushed Goldwater to the Republican nomination in 1964, supported Ronald Reagan for governor in California, and formed the nucleus of what would become the New Right in the 1980s. From both the Left and the Right, the assumptions that underlay the liberal consensus and the policies it produced would come under increasing question as the decade progressed. Films such as *The Manchurian Candidate* (1963) would parody the paranoia of earlier Cold War films; *Failsafe* (1964) expressed anxieties linking nuclear war, uncontrollable technology, and dehumanizing bureaucratization. Most famously, *Dr. Strangelove* (1964) would lampoon Cold War nuclear strategy, unsubtly linking it to the crisis of masculinity articulated during the 1950s. *Catch-22*, an absurdist novel of a bombardier squad in World War II—which was, in fact, more about the mass-consumption, Cold War society of the 1950s—would become a best-selling novel of the decade. By the mid-1960s, the Cold War consensus was coming apart along the fault line of identity.

While the comic books of this period revel in the moral certainties of the high Cold War, there are ever-present areas of anxiety and ambiguity that expand and create a space within the form for challenges to both the liberal consensus and Cold War policy. Anxiety concerning the bomb is one clear area. The previously unchallenged virtue of American government—both its institutions and its leaders—begins to be questioned. More important, national identity and self-identity become increasingly contested terrains. The character-driven subplots of the stories render problematic the authenticity of the identity of the heroes in their civilian and public personae. This is manifest in the tensions between personal desire and public duty that start to emerge and in the decreasingly clear identification of heroes and villains. By the end of the period cracks would appear in the Cold War consensus around these fault lines of technology, virtuous government, authentic identities, and an increasingly ill-defined enemy.

Technology

The portrayal of the effects of radioactivity, creating unpredictable and perverse transformations of human beings, represents continued anxiety over the role of atomic weapons and nuclear energy. This was a change from the comics of the early 1950s, where the bomb had been portrayed as a benign tool for national security, albeit a highly destructive one,[27] and it presages a major change that is to come. Still, while the effects of radiation may cause some anxiety, the effects in the early Marvel universe are largely benign, imbuing the irradiated actor with special powers. None of this is without a price; for Stan Lee, with great power comes not only great responsibility but a great personal cost.

Peter Parker may gain the powers of a human spider, but he is partially responsible for the murder of his uncle. The Fantastic Four may gain superpowers, but Ben Grimm is turned into an inhuman pile of rock, and Reed Richards must live with the guilt of having caused it. The X-Men may have special abilities, but they are feared and shunned by humanity. Tony Stark becomes the powerful Iron Man but must wear his armored chest plate or else die from the shrapnel moving inexorably toward his heart. Daredevil is blinded. Bruce Banner suffers the worst fate, gaining immeasurable strength and invulnerability, but becomes a rampaging green beast. From the origin of the Marvel universe, then, there is some ambiguity about the ethical value of the bomb, technology, power, and responsibility.

These ambiguities become more pronounced as the decade neared its end. In a telling departure from Cold War orthodoxy, technology becomes the villain in an Iron Man story. Tony Starks's best friend and chauffeur, Happy Hogan, injured in a battle between Iron Man and the villainous Black Knight, is transformed into the powerful but mindless Freak through the use of an experimental medical technology (the "enervator") designed by Tony Stark. Stark muses, "Can this be Happy? Have my worst fears thus been realized? There's no trace of intelligence in his eyes! Nothing but hatred—bestiality!! Is this what my enervator did to him?"[28] Where Tony Stark and the other Marvel heroes had been unstinting believers in the use of technology (at least nonatomic technology) now even Iron Man sees it as potentially undermining humanity. Technology run amok has changed a pleasant, helpful, and generous man into a mindless, hating beast. That the technology in question is helpful—offering medical miracles in hopeless cases—creates a particularly troubling issue. If benign technology can generate such disastrous results, what might be the potential effects from technology that is more destructive in its use?

Virtuous Government

The virtue of the government also becomes more ambiguous by the late 1960s. An unquestioning Cold Warrior, supplying weapons to the U.S. government, Tony Stark finds himself at odds with that government beginning in December 1965.[29] Stark and Iron Man are investigated by the Senate Armed Services Committee, which wants to know the identity of Iron Man. This is not a major transformation of Cold War ideology, however, as the subplot revolves around the activities of Senator Harrington Byrd, a stereotypical Southern politician with graying longish hair, three-piece suit, and smoking cigar. Byrd is not playing politics, but is, in accordance with the Comics Code, a dedicated public servant seeking to protect Americans. His desire to gain access to the Iron Man technology is motivated by his strong goals of public service. He subpoenas Tony Stark to testify before his committee, but when Stark fails to attend—because, as Iron Man, he is fighting supercriminals—Senator Byrd cites him for contempt of Congress and cancels all of his military contracts, shutting down Stark Enterprises. The return of the communist armored superfighter Titanium Man, who challenges Iron Man to an epic, televised battle, gives Tony Stark and Iron Man more credibility as staunch anticommunists, particularly with the government.

Having reestablished his credentials as an impeccable anti-communist, Tony Stark and Iron Man can face Senator Byrd's committee. When Stark testifies, however, he has a heart attack, and the world discovers how ill he is. At this point, Senator Byrd becomes a Stark supporter, telling a reporter, "Hang the inquiry. I want to go and pray for the life of a brave man."[30] To demonstrate that this has been no mere politically motivated investigation, we are given a final scene of Senator Byrd and his political adviser. The adviser wants him to drop his investigation of Iron Man because he and Stark are so popular and it is an election year, to which Senator Byrd responds, "I have a duty to the American public! I've got to do that duty whether the cause is popular or not. I'd rather lose an election than betray my ideals or my Senatorial oath."[31] The hearings do not resume, however, and the Senator Byrd subplot ends at this point.

While ultimately affirming the virtuous intentions of politicians, the story still places the government and the superhero in confrontation. To the extent that the hero is assumed to be virtuous this weakens the moral standing of the government, even with a resolution that demonstrates the senator's dedication to public service. This is reinforced by a scene of Lyndon Johnson and Robert McNamara watching the Titanium Man battle Iron Man on television. LBJ comments, "If only the day would come when force is no longer necessary—when men would reason together instead. But until such a time we should be thankful that power such as Iron Man's exists and can be used in behalf of freedom."[32] While this was no doubt a device to reinforce for the reader the notion that the government still supported Iron Man even in the face of the Senate investigation (presidential support trumps a senatorial investigation), the message of this panel is problematic. The need for Iron Man to fight on the side of freedom suggests that the government is unable to secure that freedom by itself. That the president makes such a claim implies that the government recognizes that it is incapable of securing the interests of the nation and requires some external help in the form of a superpowered hero. While overtly offering support for the hero, and linking the virtue of the hero with the virtue of the government, the statement also seems to raise the hero above the government and, in so doing, generates doubts about the government's material and moral value.

Authentic Identity

In the early years, the stronger focus on character was intended merely to offer more compelling stories. By developing more realistic characters, Marvel opened the door to story lines more engaged with the real world, and thus more easily affected by the cultural shifts that would be ongoing through the next several decades as the Cold War played itself out. It also created greater scope with which the books could treat the private lives of the heroes, and this would become very significant in subsequent years as the personal began to compete with the political as an avenue of social protest.

Howard Brick notes the growing interest in existentialism in the late 1950s and early 1960s, and Todd Gitlin recalls how influential Albert Camus was in his own intellectual and political development as a freshman math major at Harvard University in 1960.[33] Likewise, Sharon Jeffrey, a leading figure in the Students for a Democratic Society, notes her passion for organizing and politics was driven by her desire to find "a meaning of life that [was] personally authentic."[34] The particular translation of existential thought into the United States, primarily through Walter Kaufman and Richard Barnett, leant the philosophy a liberating tone centering on the theme of authenticity.[35] While Stan Lee may simply have been trying to tell a good story, the new depth he gave to his characters and the angst many of them experienced over the cost of their new powers found a receptive audience in search of authentic characters. The very success of his innovation reveals a concern with authentic characters, real individuals seeking an identity that gives to them meaning. This aspect of Marvel comics will come to dominate the 1970s and 1980s, but it began to emerge in the later 1960s.

The concern with authenticity can be seen in mistaken-identity stories. These had always been one stock Marvel story line. Iron Man's conflict with the Red Barbarian hinges on an actor impersonating Tony Stark, and before receiving his own book in 1964 Captain America had twice fought Marvel heroes (*Strange Tales* 115; *Tales of Suspense* 58); in both instances it was someone posing as Captain America. The mistaken identity rarely extended beyond the hero/villain conflict, and it was never more than a plot device. In the second half of the 1960s, however, this plot device took on a new complexity. At the end of 1966, both Iron Man and Captain America have stories that focus on mistaken identities. The Avengers are infiltrated by an AIM robot (the "adaptoid") that can mimic any human shape. It uses that power to drug Captain America and then assume his form, fooling even the hero's friends.[36] After Tony Stark has a heart attack, doctors find his Iron Man chest plate under his clothing, and reporters begin to question whether he is Iron Man. To protect the superhero's secret identity, Happy Hogan (who had already figured it out) dons the Iron Man armor to protect his boss. Mistaken for the real Iron Man, he is captured by the Mandarin, requiring Tony Stark to leave his hospital bed to save him.[37] In both stories, the scope of the mistaken identity has now widened to include allies and nemeses, raising questions about the character's authenticity. How authentic can the identity be if those who know the hero best are easily deceived? While not particularly interesting stories, these are some of the first examples of Marvel playing with the dual identity of its heroes. Creating ambiguities concerning identity, seeing identity as a problematic element within the story rather than a convention of the genre, would become increasingly important to Marvel story lines in the 1970s.

Private identities also started to become more important as the decade progressed. In *Tales of Suspense* 95 (November 1967), Captain America falls in love with a female agent of SHIELD known only as Agent 13 (her real name is Sharon Carter).[38] When she refuses to marry him because of their shared commitments, he decides to quit being Captain America so that his alter ego, Steve Rogers, can have the life that has been denied him. Unlike most Marvel superheroes, Captain America's alter ego is less defined than his costumed identity. Where the turmoil in Spider-Man's life comes from his Peter Parker persona and Iron Man's from his Tony Stark persona, prior to this point Steve Rogers played almost no part in the story of Captain America. The emergence of a meaningful Steve Rogers identity now signaled his incorporation into the fold of the new Marvel heroes, but it also demonstrated the increasing politicization of the personal within the Cold War culture. This hiatus from his costumed identity would be brief, and in the next issue he would decide to become Captain America yet again. Asserting the authenticity of his costumed identity, Captain America justifies his return: "A man can't ever stop being . . . something that he was born to be."[39] This portends a growing debate within the book over which identity is the authentic one, Captain America or Steve Rogers, and will become a dominant aspect of the character over the next several years.

The Ill-Defined Enemy

Increasingly during this period, the moral certainty surrounding Cold War images and actions begins to fade into ambiguity. As the enemy against which the consensus identity had been defined becomes less clear, the moral certainty of the American Cold War position also becomes more tenuous. While there is still a verbal commitment to American supremacy and Soviet inferiority, the clear distinctions become blurred, and the books begin to present these ideas in a cloudier context.

Iron Man's battle against the Freak—his friend turned into a mindless brute—offers a case in which the villain is not truly evil but is merely incapable of controlling his actions. Is the villain the brutish Freak, or is it the technology that created him out of a kind and gentle man? Perhaps the villain is the inventor of the technology (Tony Stark) who blindly trusted his invention, using it on his friend without proper testing. This amorphous problematizing of the villain becomes much more specific in the Nick Fury, Agent of SHIELD stories. When Jim Steranko took over the artwork from Jack Kirby in 1966 (and ultimately the writing of the tales as well), the Nick Fury stories became one of the most innovative series of the period. Influenced early by the neat lines and contained frames of Kirby, Steranko slowly developed his own style in which frames bleed into one another, characters frequently overreach the gutter, and increasingly psychedelic effects become prominent, blurring the clear contrasts of the Kirbyesque art that characterized Marvel. Less prominent but similar effects can be seen in Gene Colan's cinematographic and impressionistic artwork for *Iron Man* (beginning in 1966) and John Buscema's gutter-crossing work in the *Avengers* (beginning with issue 57, October 1968). The boundaries between events in comics began to break down, and while this did not signal a revolution underway, it did point to an increasing unease with the certainties of the early 1960s.

The story lines in the Nick Fury stories represent a break with the moral certainty of public duty expressed in the earlier comics. While Hydra had been linked to the Nazis through Baron von Strucker, and AIM through the Red Skull, the menace that emerges during the Steranko run is linked only to the Cold War. The most significant is the extended battle between SHIELD and the Yellow Claw (*Strange Tales* 161–67, October 1967–April 1968).[40] Bent on world domination, the Claw, a Chinese villain who had a brief run in an eponymous comic in the late 1950s, was resurrected—along with his nemesis from the 1950s, FBI agent Jimmy Woo—by Steranko. The political motives of the characters are intertwined with personal motives, as Jimmy Woo seeks to defeat the Yellow Claw not because he is evil but because Woo loves the Claw's niece, Suwan. Nick Fury's actions are heavily influenced by his growing relationship with SHIELD agent Valentina Contessa di Allegra. Additionally, to draw distinctions between the new kind of antihero and traditional, caricatured good guys,

Steranko adds agent Clay Quartermain to SHIELD; noble and handsome, he is a contrast to the gruff Nick Fury. Quartermain, whose name conjures images of the fictional nineteenth-century British adventurer, is drawn in that mold. He has a timeless quality, being a classic adventurer from a wealthy background who joins SHIELD to pursue his innate sense of justice, and who will become an important ideological symbol in future stories.

The Yellow Claw story (which ran into 1968) signals another interesting twist. Near its end (*Strange Tales* 167, April 1968), as Nick Fury defeats the Yellow Claw while Jimmy Woo mourns the dead Suwan who has been killed by her uncle's weaponry, it is revealed that the Yellow Claw is a robot, manipulated by Dr. Doom, the nemesis of the Fantastic Four. In the issue's final panel, a full two-page spread, Dr. Doom is shown playing chess with a robot, and the chess pieces are modeled after the agents of SHIELD and the minions of the Yellow Claw. The image of the major U.S. spy agency and FBI agents manipulated by an outside force for Dr. Doom's own amusement suggests the futility of U.S. Cold War policies, the growing credibility gap between the U.S. government and its citizenry, and the increasing belief that Americans were being manipulated and thus out of control of their own lives. This would appear again in the next issue, Steranko's most daring in terms of his art effects, in which Nick Fury faces an alien superbeing and fails to stop it from destroying the world, only to wake and find it was a nightmare. The penultimate page, a full-page spread with pop-art effects, offers an oversized full moon shining over a crumbling New York skyline. In the lower right-hand corner is a sign declaring "dead end."[41]

While there is by the end of this period a growing ambiguity and anxiety in some facets of these books, a core sense of certainty at the moral virtue of the United States in the Cold War remains. Returning to Vietnam to test new ammunition designed by Tony Stark, Iron Man is drawn into conflict with the communist Titanium Man, now working for the North Vietnamese scientist Half-Face. Titanium Man initially defeats Iron Man and is sent by Half-Face to wreak destruction on peasant villages in the north, which will be blamed on U.S. bombing and thus secure the communists a propaganda victory. Regaining his power, Iron Man races north to stop Titanium Man and Half-Face. While the

Figure 2.2. Pop Art Meets Comic Books
From "Today Earth Dies!" *Strange Tales* 168 (May 1968) 10.

metal-clad warriors battle over a peasant village, the peasants sit in fear, believing all is lost. One peasant notes, "If the American should fall—there will be no safety for us anywhere! We can only wait . . . and place our faith in him who is known as Iron Man."[42] Standing on the outskirts of the village, Half Face recognizes his wife and child, whom he believed dead. Reunited with his family, he realizes that he has been wrong to support the communists and drains the power from Titanium Man, giving Iron Man the victory and declaring, "No longer do I serve those who are the oppressors! From this moment on . . . I fight for freedom . . . as do those whom I love."[43]

Similarly, after his brief retirement to develop a private life, Captain America returns to fight lingering Nazis and communists for most of 1968. Between issues 97 and 100 he again faces Baron Zemo,[44] and he will spend the next four issues battling the Red Skull. These tales are followed by one in which the Chinese communists (obviously Mao Zedong) have hired a Hollywood producer to use a robot replica of Captain America to make films showing him brutalizing and executing prisoners in order to discredit him in the public's eyes.[45]

Iron Man, meanwhile, fights the secret societies that no longer plague SHIELD, although here the stories begin to delink Nazis and communists. AIM returns to be defeated by Iron Man, although the group is no longer connected to the Red Skull. An organized crime syndicate, the Maggia, is also important. As in the Captain America stories, issues of identity and the personal begin to outweigh the public. This is seen in *Iron Man* 10, the conclusion of a Maggia story line, in which the head of the syndicate, Big M, is masquerading as Whitney Frost, a beautiful socialite. In this guise she becomes the recipient of the affections of Jasper Sitwell, a SHIELD agent assigned to Tony Stark's munitions factory. In the final scene, as Big M escapes toward a waiting helicopter, Sitwell points his gun to stop her, but fails to do so, exclaiming, "I can't! Shortly after she began seeing me, her over-interest in my security work made me suspicious. After that it wasn't difficult to figure who she was . . . I've known what she was doing all this time! But now why couldn't I stop her? Why?"[46] Not only does the story contain the masquerade of a mistaken identity, it also offers the private interest getting in the way of public duty, even though that duty is clear. Sitwell, portrayed as a rigid, by-the-book agent, is not the character one would expect to forsake his obligations, but even his personal life begins to outweigh his public duty.

Offering a Marvel Philosophy

In 1967, Marvel comics began including a box on the "Bullpen Bulletins" page titled "Stan's Soapbox" in which Stan Lee would push new products or, more significantly, seek to define the Marvel philosophy, much as Hugh Hefner defined *Playboy*'s philosophy.

In his first installment (June 1967) Lee offers a portrayal that emphasizes profit and entertainment with some side-elements: "We think we've found the best formula of all—we merely create the type of fanciful yarns that we ourselves enjoy—and, if we like 'em, 'you oughta' like 'em too; after all, you're our kinda people. Now then, in the process of providing off-beat entertainment, if we can also do our bit to advance the cause of intellectualism, humanitarianism, and mutual understanding . . . and to toss in a little swingin' satire at you in the process . . . that won't break our collective heart one tiny bit!"[17]

There is nothing particularly interesting here save for the attempt to appear hip and to create a sense of camaraderie between the writers and the readers. Over the next year, however, the Soapbox would be used to discuss the relevance of comic books to contemporary social issues and to offer Lee's opinions on them. By the end of this period, the Soapbox defined the "Marvel philosophy" in terms similar to those portrayed above, but with a very different emphasis that represents the breakdown of the Cold War consensus.

The year 1968 was a key one for Marvel. Publisher Martin Goodman sold Marvel to Cadence Publications, and Marvel's distribution deal with National Periodicals expired. This deal had limited Marvel to eight titles per month, creating the need to limit stories to twelve pages so that magazines could have two different heroes in them. A new distribution deal permitted Marvel to expand its output and to give solo magazines to each of its heroes. Thus, Iron Man got his own magazine starting at issue 1, while *Tales of Suspense* became *Captain America*, beginning at issue 100. Nick Fury and the Hulk also got their own magazines (as would the Submariner, Dr. Strange, and Thor). Marvel was also able to create new titles, and it would do so extensively over the next decade.

1968 was also the last year that the original group who created Marvel stayed together. Lee had been relinquishing writing duties piecemeal and was scripting only one or two books a month by the end of the year. Several of the artists who had created characters—most notably Jack Kirby and Steve Ditko—left Marvel, angry over the lack of acknowledgment for their contributions to the success of Marvel and its stable of characters. A new group of writers and artists—notably, Roy Thomas on scripts, and Gene Colan, John Romita, John and Sal Buscema, and Herb Trimpe on art—would lead Marvel into the new decade. Some characters would not survive either; after Jim Steranko stopped working on the Nick Fury series it struggled through 1969, began reprints in 1970, and was dead by 1971.

As this new group took over, still under the editorship of Lee (until 1972, when Roy Thomas would take the reins), it reflected the changing context of comic books. As the high Cold War tensions and certainties of the Cuban Missile Crisis were replaced by the ambiguities of the Vietnam War and Watergate, the world of the Marvel universe would become increasingly ambiguous, critical, and uncertain.

3

The Enemy Within: 1969–1976

T HE TUMULTUOUS EVENTS OF 1968 suggested to many people that the Cold War consensus was dead. The year began with the launching of the Tet Offensive in Vietnam, demonstrating that the North Vietnamese and their Southern allies were far from beaten, irrespective of the reports from the military and from Washington, D.C. The assassinations of Martin Luther King Jr. (April) and Robert Kennedy (June) seemed to indicate the death of the aspirations for democratic expansion and authentic existence that had characterized the start of the decade. Distrust of authority and growing disillusion with politics as normal would generate the chaos of the Democratic Party's national convention in Chicago and the antiwar march on Washington in August. Continued conflicts between the highly publicized counterculture of the New Left and the less well known but equally influential emerging New Right of the Young Americans for Freedom (YAF) revealed a growing ideological divide. All of these events and conflicts indicated a growing generation gap, racial gap, gender gap, and credibility gap between government and citizens. With these growing chasms in American politics all vision of consensus seemed to have disappeared. Most Americans continued to support the government and did not take part in demonstrations or experience the counterculture except through television news or *Life* magazine. In fact, among youth, support for the Vietnam War, for the reactionary policies of George Wallace and the American Independent Party, and for Richard Nixon ran higher than in the population at large. The costs of the Vietnam War and the War on Poverty waged by the administration of President Lyndon Johnson were beginning to be felt as inflation rose to post–World War II highs, threatening the affluence that permitted the consensus to persist for so long. Richard Nixon's conciliatory campaign rhetoric of 1968, in which he offered a secret plan to end the Vietnam conflict and a willingness to listen to the divergent voices in American society (albeit if they would speak quietly), attracted many voters who feared the increasing conflicts in society. This conciliatory stance would prove as chimeric as the secret plan to end the war, and the gulf between government and citizen would widen over the next several years. The centrist, pragmatic, consensual American self that had been the basic unit of the postwar era had developed a spiderweb of cracks by 1968; it was shattered in the 1970s. Bruce Schulman sees 1968 as the transition year when the postwar consensus finally came undone, and the fragmentation of the 1970s began.[1]

The era of limits had begun. No more would faith in the unending progress toward an affluent, equalitarian society be the core of an American consensual identity. These would be replaced by fears of creeping inflation, the exhaustion of cheap fuel supplies, and the fear of too rapid population growth outstripping the planet's carrying capacity. While fear of a nuclear war seemed to diminish with détente, apocalyptic fears were commonplace, from Hal Lindsey's *The Late, Great Planet Earth* (the best-selling book of the 1970s) to the popularity of disaster films.[2]

Perhaps no statement better captures the fragmentation of American identity in the 1970s than Jimmy Carter's introduction of himself to America in 1975. "I am a Southerner and an American," he writes. "I am a farmer, an engineer, a father and a husband, a Christian, a politician and a former governor, a planner, a businessman, a nuclear physicist, a naval officer, a canoeist, and, among other things, a lover of Bob Dylan's songs and Dylan Thomas's poetry."[3] Carter, the hope of a return to innocence and virtue after the conflict and cynicism surrounding Vietnam and Watergate, defines himself in terms of class, occupation, family and social roles, education, training, and taste. Nowhere does he say he is a Democrat, and he precedes his Americanness with his Southernness. In his psychobiography of Carter, Kenneth Morris suggests that Carter never developed a "unified self that grows naturally from a community that sustains it. Instead, his selves were many and fragmented. . . ."[4] Lacking a core identity, Carter may well have been the exemplary American leader of the mid-1970s.

The erosion of the national identity consensus generated several redirections of the American political economy. Without a consensus the most extreme versions of containment were difficult to maintain. One result was that the slow and oft-interrupted U.S. withdrawal from Vietnam began in 1968. As support for containment waned, the Cold War appeared less threatening, and the two superpowers entered a period of détente. This period of greater cooperation between the capitalist and communist worlds witnessed two summits between Soviet and U.S. leaders, numerous cultural exchanges, and the opening to China, isolated since 1949. *Cooperation* rather than *containment* was the watchword of the period. Arms control, begun with the test ban treaties of the John F. Kennedy and Lyndon Johnson administrations, topped the agenda of superpower issues. China would be rehabilitated in the eyes of the United States and begun to be brought back into the comity of nations. As tensions appeared to ease, popular support for U.S. Cold War policies declined, further lessening the tensions between the superpowers and removing one of the key factors generating the liberal consensus. If the USSR was not as threatening as it had seemed in 1962, then the "us versus them" attitude that generated consensus was no longer pertinent; the weakening of consensus became a factor in further weakening the consensus. But if the USSR was not the enemy against which Americans defined themselves, who was?

One legacy of the liberal consensus and the popular mobilizations of the 1960s was a continued engagement by citizens with public life. The American identity remained a public identity, although as the scope of government action increased, what constituted public and private became less clear. Now, however, the counter to the public action of Americans was no longer an external threat, but the continued problems that beset American society, the very gaps that had become apparent in the 1960s. The enemy was no longer an external entity threatening American security, but the internal problems besetting the richest society in the world. These threats involved continued racial tension, gender inequality, poverty, and, most important for the political economy, a government that was viewed as secretive, hubristic, and controlling.

This view of government as the enemy was common to both the Right and the Left. While the Left focused on foreign policy, internal surveillance, and the excesses of the Nixon administration, the right looked to government more generally. The expansion of federal power into labor relations, poor relief, business and consumer regulation, and health care was seen by conservatives as illegitimate national action subverting the prerogatives of the states and the individual citizens. This had been the case since the mid-1950s, fueling the conservatism of Barry Goldwater, Orange County, California (epicenter of California's conservative renewal), Ronald Reagan, and the YAF. This language would be deployed by Nixon in the guise of the "new federalism," which sought to return some autonomy to states through the use of block grants. It was a language that was useful to Southern segregationists and would become a cornerstone of the rhetoric of the postsegregation, postdemocratic South. Individual freedom and liberty from improper federal action would be the rhetoric of western and Southern conservatism and the basis on which the New Right would build its electoral future.[5]

Trust in government declined well into the 1970s, hitting all-time lows in polls by mid-decade (29 percent in 1974 according to the American National Election Survey). The slow pullout from Vietnam punctuated by increased bombing, the revelations in 1969 of the massacre at My Lai, and the 1971 invasion of Cambodia offered a mixed message and suggested that the government had hidden agendas. Such agendas would only seem more real when rumors of dirty tricks turned into revelations of links between the Nixon White House and the men who burglarized the office of the Democratic National Headquarters at the Watergate Hotel in June 1972. As those links became clearer, new revelations— about the "Plumbers" breaking into Daniel Ellsberg's office, of Nixon's enemies list—confirmed the fears that government was not serving the people but controlling them. As both inflation and unemployment rose, the government seemed incapable of governing effectively or morally. Rather than the virtuous exception, the American government was just another petty tyranny.

The outside enemy that had defined American identity for the first two decades of the Cold War had been replaced by an enemy within. That enemy, though, was not perceived as monolithic as had been global communism. It was defined differently by the various groups who now found a space to assert their own visions of identity. Identity politics thus became the defining feature of postconsensus America.

Todd Gitlin notes that by 1968 his major concern was with the issue of identity. "Who were we?" he wanted to know of the New Left. The politics of identity had also become central to the civil rights struggle, as the integrationist impulse of the Southern Christian Leadership Council was challenged by the growing militancy of Student Nonviolent Coordinating Committee, the Black Panthers, and the violence in northern black enclaves. For most of the 1970s, racial politics would emphasize issues of identity rather than integration and would spread beyond African Americans to include Native Americans and Latinos.[6] The working class would also be resurgent in its attempt to fight against economic downturn and retain its own identity in the wake of 1960s countercultural influences.[7] The women's movement, always closely tied to concerns of self-awareness, was torn by identity issues, particularly over the question of biological differences versus socioeconomic equality.[8] In a series of actions designed to enhance civil rights, promote economic opportunity, and protect the privacy of citizens, government had brought politics into direct confrontations with the personal and the private lives of citizens. Revelations of domestic surveillance and "dirty tricks" would show the government invading personal lives in obviously illegitimate ways. As the decade of the 1970s began, the personal had been politicized as never before, and the lines had blurred between public and private, self and society. The collapse of the liberal consensus and the politicization of the personal meant that the politics of the 1970s could not help but emphasize identity. This quest for a public identity is the key theme to understanding comics of the late 1960s and 1970s.

Comic Books at the End of the 1960s

By 1969 Marvel Comics had displaced National Comics as the industry leader, selling close to a quarter million copies of each title per month.[9] This success had been a product of the new style of storytelling, emphasizing character and antiheroes, combining action and soap opera, and creating a sense of narrative continuity, as well as through the salesmanship and hucksterism of Stan Lee. As Lee relinquished writing and, later, editorial duties largely to Roy Thomas, Marvel continued its success. Following Lee's lead, Thomas continued the trends that had begun in the mid-1960s.[10] As the Cold War consensus eroded, the moral certainty of the comics also became a thing of the past. Increasingly, the story lines would see the U.S. government as a threat, question the values of the American Cold War generation, and become ever more challenging in tone. Unlike the previous period, where the Cold War consensus dominated the comic books both in theme and perspective, growing anxiety and a fear of American institutions and leaders characterize this period.

The political tumults that marked the late 1960s found their way only obliquely into superhero comics. Still constrained by the Comics Code, comic books did not become specifically critical of Cold War policy, nor did they reflect the political upheavals that were raging in the world around them. This does not mean that social changes of the late 1960s and early 1970s were not influential in the comic book world, but it does indicate that the degree to which the comic books were reflecting the "youth rebellion" was never as high as Marvel suggested at the time or after. Readers, however, were finding in the stories various elements that led them to confront social issues, particularly identity issues. The letters pages in *Captain America* from 1969 to 1971 reveal much of this. Extended debates occurred between readers discussing the meaning of patriotism and antiwar protests, the morality of political apathy, the role of violence in conflict resolution, nationalism versus global community, and the Vietnam War. Letters asserted a vision of the meaning of (Captain) America, and then defined actions for the hero based on that meaning. Several argued that he needed to be fighting in Vietnam.[11] Others argued that he was an agent of the establishment and needed to be shown rethinking his position.[12]

Frequently when Marvel writers tried to treat social issues, it was done in a patronizing and often counterproductive manner. In an industry dominated by middle-aged white men, story lines with a feminist bent often turned into revelations about the creators rather than reflections of women's struggles. For instance, *Avengers* 83 (December 1970) and *Incredible Hulk* 142 (August 1971) feature a well-endowed feminist Asgardian warrior called the Valkyrie who leads a group of women heroes against the male heroes, all the while denouncing the "male chauvinist pigs."[13] More ridiculous (in retrospect) is the creation of an all-female Supreme Headquarters International Espionage, Law-Enforcement Division (SHIELD) unit called the Femme Force,[14] in which the buxom female agents are beset by catfights over who is flirting with Captain America. Similarly, as discussed below, treatments of race often reflected a patronizing attitude.

The counterculture and youth cultures did have some direct representation. Several issues of various books noted campus conflicts as backdrops to superhero conflict. The representation of student protest, of extrasystemic action, still had to be treated within the context of the Comics Code, affirming the anti-ideological basis of the liberal consensus; while the students often might have legitimate concerns, the more extreme forms of protest were generally attributed to some outside, villainous influence. For instance, in *Captain America* 120 (December 1969) student demonstrations turn violent even after the administration has agreed to the students' unspecified demands. The students' minds, it is revealed, are being controlled by the evil organization Advanced Idea Mechanics. Drugs would occasionally appear, although always as a dangerous and illegal activity.[15] The famous three-issue story in *Amazing Spider-Man* (96–98, May–July 1971) in which Peter Parker's friend Harry Osbourne becomes addicted to some kind of pill was published without approval of the Comics Code Authority (CCA), even though the story came at the behest of the U.S. Department of Heath, Education, and Welfare. The Comics Code's inability to adapt to changed circumstances and the pedagogical uses of comic books weakened its power and altered the terms of its activity.[16] Dennis O'Neil and Neal Adams ran an antidrug story in *Green Lantern/Green Arrow* 85–86 (August–December 1971) in which Green Arrow's sidekick, Speedy, was using drugs (heroin this time), and the book was approved by the CCA.[17]

Two events that demonstrate the erosion of support for Cold War policies are the cancellation of the Nick Fury, Agent of SHIELD series after only eighteen issues and the transformation of the character of the Hulk. In both instances, the decreasing concern with the East-West military conflict plays a part. If the major enemy facing the United States was not the communists but instead the divisions internal to American society, then support for spy agencies was not going to be as high. The romance of the spy was also diminished as the Vietnam War ground on and revelations of covert actions began to darken the beacon of American virtue. Readership of *Nick Fury, Agent of SHIELD* thus began to decline, and the stories became increasingly fantastical, with Nick Fury battling ghosts and space aliens, before the book was canceled.

The Incredible Hulk was able to adapt to the weakening of Cold War tensions, and thus did not fall under the editor's axe as had Nick Fury. The Hulk, previously characterized as a malevolent and uncontrollable force kept in check by the military, began to be portrayed more as a victim than a threat. He is driven largely by his anomie, his separation from all social connections; throughout this period his major quest is to end his loneliness and find a friend. He will develop several friends who serve as supporting cast for a time, but they always become victims of the conflict between the Hulk and the military. They either try to help the army for the Hulk's own good (which the Hulk perceives as betrayal) or they are physically hurt in a conflict between the Hulk and General Thunderbolt Ross's "Hulkbuster" brigade. The frequent refrain "Why won't men with guns leave Hulk alone?" reflects a sense of persecution that resonated with readers. Declining purchasing power, the draft, COINTELPRO, images of body bags, riots, and police brutality could only give to people a sense that the authorities were out to get them. While the Hulk faced increasingly fantastical supervillains, it was still the military, now seen as obsessively hounding this poor, misunderstood creature that was the constant backdrop to the stories. Declining support for political and military authority made readers respond to a victimized Hulk who faced the same barrage of ambiguity that they did, leaving them tired and desirous of just being left alone.

An antiwar impulse was also very pronounced within the Hulk. A frequently used plot of the early 1970s has the Hulk locating a haven of peace in which he can be free from the hounding of the military.[18] Some force brings violence into this oasis, requiring the Hulk to battle, defeat, and expel it, but at the cost of being driven from this peaceful paradise himself. In this tale, the Hulk represents both humanity's desire for peace and its innate violence. That he is violent only in response to some external threat suggests that humanity can suppress its violence and achieve peace if it truly desires; if even a rampaging, irrational beast such as the Hulk can do it, surely humans can turn their swords into ploughshares. If only the state, represented by the coercive power of the army, would leave private individuals alone, there would be no more war.

More commonly, the overt message of the comics was continued support for the liberal consensus: anti-ideological, proindividual, proequality, and progovernment. While continuing to articulate such support for this consensus, the comics now exhibited a profound crisis of identity. Rather than offering convincing visions of heroes who knew who they were and what they were doing, the stories were populated by heroes who were continually mistaken for villains, villains who were mistaken for heroes, secret identities that multiplied, unexpected faces that appeared under masks, and—when the masks come off—ambiguous identities. This identity crisis undercut much of the support the story lines offered for the liberal consensus, creating instead a deep ambiguity around its meaning, its purpose, and ultimately its components. Three moments in particular are representative of the collapsing center in the Marvel universe. The first is the increased salience of identity in the Nick Fury, Iron Man, and Captain America books from the late 1960s onward. The second is the transformed relation to governmental power and policy, represented by Iron Man's return to Vietnam and Captain America's encounter with Watergate. The third involves the changing portrayal of race in the treatment of Captain America's partner the Falcon, the first African America superhero in the Marvel universe.[19] These three moments are particularly important because they target the major elements of the liberal consensus directly—an accepted American national identity; belief in the virtue of American leaders, government, and the policy they produce; and the growing equality of American society. In each of these areas the liberal consensus would fail to meet the challenge posed by events and require reconstruction.

Ambiguous Identities

The issue of identity—often mistaken, generally confused and ambiguous—is a central feature of comic books of this period, reflecting the loss of faith in a consensus identity. The first issue of the Nick Fury, Agent of SHIELD series (June 1968) opens with a two-page sequence of narrow panels without words in which Nick and a masked opponent stalk each other, ending with the masked opponent shooting Nick. The narrowness of the panels gives a claustrophic feel to the sequence, heightening its tension. The third page reveals that the masked entity was Nick Fury testing the abilities of an android version of himself (a Life Model Decoy, or LMD, in Marvel speak). "Kinda funny feelin' shooting yourself," Fury comments.[20] Eight of the fifteen original issues of this book would involve mistaken identities.[21]

Between 1969 and 1970, one-third of the Captain America stories hinged on mistaken or switched identities, the same number that have the superhero fighting ex-Nazis, although only one of the ex-Nazis espouses a fascist agenda (Baron von Strucker).[22] For Iron Man, ten of the twenty-four issues focused on identity. Only one issue of either book has a battle with communists,[23] and even then they are not really communists but Caribbean revolutionaries who are controlled by an alien machine known as the Overseer. This is a major change from the previous period, when communists and Nazis abounded. The linkage between the Cold War and World War II has become much more tenuous, demonstrating the weakening of the liberal consensus and of the American self it defined. The multiple maskings in both the Iron Man and Captain America books indicate the increasing complexity of identity issues within the comic stories and suggest a growing unease with the moral certainty of the American Cold War identity.

Jim Steranko (w/i) and Joe Sinnott (i). © 2018 Marvel Characters, Inc. Used with permission.

Figure 3.1. Nick Fury Stalks Himself
From "Who Is Scorpio?" *Nick Fury, Agent of SHIELD* 1
(June 1968), 3.

The Captain America stories of this period begin with
a retelling of his origin that brings him more in line with the
Cold War Marvel comic books. The 1941 origin, and most subsequent retellings, offer the story of Steve Rogers, rejected as
4-F because of his physical frailty when he tried to enlist in the
army, who becomes a guinea pig in a government experiment to
create supersoldiers to fight in World War II. Drinking a serum
developed by Dr. Erskine, puny Steve Rogers is transformed
into the most perfect physical specimen of humanity—his body
is transformed such that he operates always at peak human

performance. A Nazi spy who has infiltrated the experiment kills Dr. Erskine and is accidentally killed by Rogers, who tries to stop him but does not realize his new strength. Since Erskine has kept no notes his formula dies with him, and Rogers becomes the only supersoldier.[24] Given a costume and a shield he becomes Captain America. To this story is added a new element in the retelling in *Captain America* 109 (January 1969). Rather than simply drinking the formula, Rogers is then bombarded by "vita-rays."[25] The introduction of radioactivity into the Captain America origin brings him into the modern Marvel continuity, under the shadow of the bomb, and will prove an important feature of the story lines during this period.

Captain America's origin is revised just as even he was moving into a period of greater moral ambiguity. Jack Kirby would draw only one more issue of the book during this period, replaced first by the pop-art comic artist Jim Steranko and then the more impressionistic and atmospheric Gene Colan. While Lee would continue to write the stories, they became increasingly focused on the moral dilemmas posed by the divergence between Captain America's 1940s upbringing and the social upheavals of the late 1960s, and by the conflict between the public identity of Captain America and the private identity of Steve Rogers. In both cases, the growing identity crisis that results from the breakdown of the liberal consensus is reflected in the stories.

Immediately after the retelling of his origin, Captain America has to face a renewed assault by Hydra, now led by Madame Hydra, who has no ties to World War II whatsoever (*Captain America* 111–14). The four-issue sequence is fraught with the disturbing imagery of gas attacks, mass murder, and a final battle in a cemetery. The theme of identity is a central element of the story. Because Captain America revealed his secret identity as Steve Rogers when he briefly retired (*Tales of Suspense* 95) Hydra is able to find him and target him for assassination. He is thus driven to re-create the secret of his identity. A subplot involves teenager Rick Jones, a supporting character in several Marvel books. It is Rick Jones whom Bruce Banner saves from an atomic test when Banner himself is caught in the explosion that turns him into the Hulk. Jones also is a member of a ham radio operators club, the Teen Brigade, who help the Avengers, and is an honorary

Jim Steranko (w/) and om Palmer (i). © 2008 Marvel Characters, Inc Used w th pe mission.

Figure 3.2. The New Look 1969
From "The Strange Death of Captain America,"
Captain America 111 (March 1969), 10.

member of that group. Now Jones attempts to become Captain America's sidekick, donning the uniform of Bucky Barnes, the dead sidekick from World War II.

In the process of fighting Hydra, Captain America is apparently killed, falling into New York harbor. Dredging the harbor fails to produce a body, but it does retrieve his uniform and a mask of Steve Rogers's face, leading people to believe that the Steve Rogers identity was a fake. When Captain America reemerges to rescue Rick Jones and defeat Hydra, he claims that he faked his death and planted the mask so that he would again have a secret identity.[26] After this he will wander alone, questioning his own identity. "So it's farewell to the man known as Steve Rogers," he muses. "And yet, how can you say farewell to a man who never lived? Can I truthfully say Steve Rogers was ever more than just a name? Did he really have a life, a meaningful identity to call his own? No! Ever since adulthood I've lived under the all-pervasive shadow of Captain America. My costume has become as much a part of me as my skin. It's only when I dress in civvies, as I'm doing now, that I feel like a pretender."[27] Given the publicness of the American identity developed in the Cold War consensus, Captain America's questioning of his private identity signals a major shift in concern. The public identity of Captain America dominates the private identity of Steve Rogers and leaves Captain America feeling alienated. Absent a private self to support his public self, the hero is left alone, dislodged, and without meaning. As the avatar of an American creed, Captain America's dilemma implies that emphasizing the public side of the creed undermines the private, or, to draw the line further, focusing on external affairs leads to the neglect of the internal affairs that are necessary to sustain national identity.

At the end of this adventure he will search for a hotel room, only to be rejected for lacking a driver's license, address, or luggage—any evidence of his identity. He finally finds lodging at a single-room-occupancy fleabag for ten dollars a night. Again ruminating on his anonymity and lack of meaningful identity provided by his public persona, he asks, "Must I live out the rest of my days as a human symbol, as an emotionless, masked fighting machine?" At this point the Red Skull returns, telling Rogers, "Did you think a mere disguise could hide you from the Red Skull?"[28] Rogers may have no identity and be lost, but the ultimate villain can always identify him and will always find him.

The theme of identity will continue into the next story arc (issues 115–19) in which the Red Skull returns armed once more with the Cosmic Cube that translates the holder's thought into reality. The Skull will exchange bodies with Captain America, send him to an island filled with the Skull's former allies who now wish to kill him, and try to take over the superhero's life. In the process, Captain America meets a young black man, Sam Wilson, who has a pet falcon. He trains him to be a crime fighter like himself and makes him a costume. Sam Wilson will become the Falcon, and he will eventually become Captain America's partner for most of this period (issues 134–212, January 1971 to September 1977).

The Skull's use of the Cosmic Cube further hints at the transformations underway in American national identity. In the previous period, the Skull had used the cube to create beings to defeat Captain America and fulfill his own goals of global conquest. Now he uses the cube to take over Captain America's identity. The villain's ultimate goal, resurrecting the Third Reich with himself as führer, has been replaced by defeating Captain America by changing places with him. Rather than achieve his political economic goals, the Red Skull now sees victory in furthering the American identity confusion that is already present, transforming hero into villain.

While this identity crisis suggests a deep-seated anxiety over the meaning of America, it is insufficient to change the overt support for Cold War policies or for authority in general. In an oft-referenced story,[29] Captain America wanders through Manhattan contemplating his anachronistic role as a defender of American values. "I'm like a dinosaur—in the cromagnon age," he thinks. "In a world rife with injustice, greed, and endless war who's to say the rebels are wrong? . . . Perhaps I should have battled less and questioned more." But as his ruminations come to an end, he decides, "So I belong to the establishment, I'm not gonna knock it. It was the same establishment that gave them a Martin Luther King, a Tolkien, a McCluhan, and a couple of brothers named Kennedy. We don't claim to be perfect, no generation is. All we can do is learn to live with each other, learn to love one another." While the questioning of his role represents a concern with American identity, the sequence serves to confirm the timeless justice of the values of the 1940s, a reiteration of the ideological position of the character since 1964.

In *Captain America* 125 (May 1970) the personal identity crisis is transferred directly to the Cold War. In this story Captain America goes to Vietnam to rescue a doctor who has been helping the wounded on both sides but has been captured. Both North and South Vietnam have claimed the other side had captured him and engage in vicious firefights. The doctor was in fact captured by the Mandarin, the nemesis of Iron Man, to keep East and West fighting one another. Captain America rescues the doctor and returns to the United States. While the story ultimately offers support for the Cold War, it is fraught with mixed messages that render that support ambiguous. Only North Vietnam is described as using propaganda, although both sides are described as fighting with fanaticism. Thus the conflict is implied to be a product of ideology run amok (rather than the pragmatism that is a central element of the American consensus), and the communist enemy lies with propaganda, but the American allies do not. More significant is the inability of the hero (or the reader) to identify the villain in the story clearly. Until the last few pages there is no inkling that the captors were neither the North or the South. That the captor was a third party who saw the conflict as a means of getting his two ideological opponents to defeat each other renders the politicomilitary context of the story morally problematic. It remains unclear at the end of the story exactly who is the enemy. Indeed, the book seems to indict those who stay at home and do nothing more than it indicts ideological extremists; the splash page that opens the issue shows Steve Rogers violently flinging his Captain America costume away from himself and declaring, "I've got to get involved!" The crisis of identity that plagues these stories makes it difficult for a public actor such as Captain America to become involved since he is unclear in his own beliefs and in the identity of the enemy. The ambiguity surrounding the hero thus renders the book incapable of offering convincing support for Cold War policies.[30]

Iron Man stories early in the period also emphasize the issues of identity that face Tony Stark, aka Iron Man. An electronics genius, industrialist, and millionaire but also a playboy who is frequently considered frivolous and coldhearted by those around him, Tony Stark encases himself in an iron armor that lends him superpowers but also represents increasingly his isolation from other people. While he acquired a cast of supporting players in the earlier period—secretary Pepper Potts, chauffeur Happy Hogan, and several potential love interests—it is not until the late 1960s that these elements of the story become central. The introduction of Janice Cord drives these issues to the fore. She is the daughter of a rival industrialist who is killed despite

Figure 3.3. Indicting the Reader.
"Captured in Vietnam!" *Captain America* 125
(May 1970), 1.

Iron Man's intervention and after what appears to be his deser-
tion by Tony Stark. Janice will appear for over a year as a love
interest for Tony Stark, at one point thinking of suing Stark for
the death of her father while at another considering selling her
father's business interests to Stark. Because she does not know
that Tony Stark and Iron Man are the same person and believes
one of them to be responsible for her father's death, at each
appearance she creates a greater ambiguity for the reader and
other characters about where the identity of Tony Stark ends and
where Iron Man begins. Janice's lack of knowledge is highlighted
in issue 9 (January 1969), which also begins a three-issue series
in which Iron Man fights the Mandarin, who has deduced that

Iron Man is Tony Stark. Yet when he unmasks Iron Man, he finds a blond-haired human inside, who tells him that Stark is not Iron Man; at the same time, he sees Stark on a live television broadcast. As it develops, the image on television is an LMD and the man in the armor is Tony Stark, wearing a mask.[31]

The maskings become increasingly complex, until the LMD Stark used to confuse the Mandarin becomes self-aware and tries to take over Tony Stark's life. Driven out of his firm and unrecognized by his closest associates, Stark is captured by the crime boss Midas. Meanwhile, the robot has assumed the armor of Iron Man and is accepted by both SHIELD and the Avengers as the real thing. The only person who recognizes the true Tony Stark is his foe, former Maggia leader Whitney Frost (also known as Big M), whose face was hideously disfigured in a helicopter crash while escaping Iron Man. She now hides her disfigurement behind a golden mask and is known as Madame Masque. The only person who sees through the multiple masks and role confusions of Tony Stark is someone who is equally masked even though she is a foe. After defeating the LMD, and back in the clutches of Midas, Madame Masque reveals herself to Tony Stark as the former Whitney Frost. His startled response leads her to cover her face, crying, "You're no different than the others." Taking her in his arms, he kisses her and says, "Maybe I am just pasteboard playboy. Maybe I come with a manufactured line. But I know a real woman when I hold one, and I know there's a kind of beauty that can't be destroyed because it's on the inside."[32] Both hiding behind masks, both offering a false front to the world, Tony Stark and Madame Masque share a mutual understanding that is not available to the unmasked; only those whose identity is unknown or ambiguous have the insights necessary to understand. The multiple identities suggest the collapse of the hegemonic myth of consensus. Being freed of the myth and recognizing the ambiguity of the world allows the actor to discern reality. Ironically, in this tale, being masked renders the hero capable of seeing the true faces behind the masks of others. It is only the awareness of ambiguous identity that gives this special insight. It does not matter on which side of the law they reside, nor on which side of the Iron Curtain.

In a later tale, Janice Cord's director of research turns out to be the son of the former Soviet superpowered agent Crimson

Dynamo, who returns to defeat Iron Man for leading his father to defect, and because he is also in love with Janice. For several issues, the identity of the scientist and the Crimson Dynamo remain unknown, increasing the role confusion. That this Soviet hero is attacking Iron Man for a personal rather than political goal adds to the ambiguity. The other Soviet hero, the Titanium Man, arrives to return the escaped scientist to the USSR, but he, too, is defeated by Iron Man, although in their battle Janice is killed.[33] The battle between Cold War enemies, fought for private reasons, results in the death of a woman Tony Stark loves; the private desire is sacrificed to the public necessity, although the motives behind the public identity are ambiguous. All of these maskings, all of this confusion between public and private identities, symbolically suggests the hero lacks an authentic self and portrays the moral certainty of the Cold War as unaware, limited, and myopic.

Cold War Reflections

By 1972, support for the Cold War had become much less staunch in comic books. Within the Iron Man series this took the form of criticism of the military industrial complex, as Tony Stark transformed his firm from a munitions industry to one focusing on "peace industries" (although this would not be specifically articulated until 1975)—notably, the environment and space exploration—and through the emergence of new villains who specifically target corporate industry, replacing the Cold War enemy spies who had characterized the 1960s. The Captain America books became the prime venue through which political commentary on the Cold War was offered. Aside from the specific focus on American values that have always been a major piece of the Captain America story line, two elements of the continuity in the stories make this possible. The first is the link between Captain America and World War II. As demonstrated in the previous chapter, this linkage was at the core of the moral certainty pervading Cold War policies offered in the text. By breaking that link, by having Captain America through word and action specifically deny the isomorphic relation of World War II and the Cold War, the moral certainty of U.S. Cold War policies lost one of its principle underpinnings.

The second element of the continuity is the twenty-year period that Captain America is supposedly frozen in ice. Moving directly from 1945 to 1964, Captain America does not experience the fall of Nationalist China, the anticommunist crusade of the 1950s, the Korean War, the rise of an arms race, and nuclear blackmail—none of the events that are seen as shaping the high Cold War culture into which he will reemerge. He is thus unaffected by these events and remains ideologically pure (or naive). He is thus able to bring a moral vision untainted by the early Cold War to the Cold War of the 1970s.

Both of these elements are used by Steve Engelhart and Sal Buscema in one of the most compelling Captain America stories of the early 1970s (*Captain America and the Falcon*, 153–56, September–December 1972). Having spent his time since his resurrection working with either the Avengers or SHIELD, Captain America rejects Nick Fury's most recent offer to join the organization formally, arguing that he needs to remain loyal to his partner, the Falcon. Nick Fury, angry over the rejection and his fear that his girlfriend, Val, is in love with Captain America, bars Captain America from SHIELD and forbids Agent 13, Sharon Carter (Captain America's girlfriend), from seeing him.[34] After a series of adventures in which Sharon violates this command, they return to Captain America's apartment to find Nick Fury waiting to fight with Captain America. The battle between the two Marvel heroes connected with both World War II and the Cold War is portrayed largely as a personal conflict over the rejection of SHIELD and jealousy. But the underlying reason is finally given as Fury tells Captain America, "Pal, do you know I used to be your age before you got yourself frozen solid for twenty-years? I kept on livin', fightin' for my country. Through World War II, the Korean War, the Cold War, I lived those 20 years, gettin' gray for America. And then you pop up, all blond, blue-eyed and young. When people think of American heroes, they don't see old, unsung types quietly bustin' our backs for 'em. No, they see you, glory-boy!"[35] Fury sees Captain America's purity as an affront. While the battles of the Cold War that undermined the moral certainty that Americans had felt in World War II rendered the hero Fury unheroic, Captain America has not been so sullied. Fury sees this youthful innocence and purity as the attraction for his girlfriend, and it is only after Val appears to tell Fury that she loves him, even with all of his failings, that he can forgive Captain America and end the fight.

Breaking the link between World War II and the late Cold War, between Fury and Captain America, is only a prologue to the story that will run for the next three issues. Having resolved his battle with Fury, and having no immediate enemies to fight, Captain America changes into civilian Steve Rogers and leaves for a Caribbean vacation with Sharon Carter, leaving the Falcon to watch over New York. In the Falcon's civilian identity as Sam Wilson, Harlem social worker, he seeks out his sometime girlfriend, Leila, who tells him that Captain America is beating up African Americans in Harlem. Having put Steve Rogers on a plane, the Falcon knows this cannot be true, but as he scours Harlem, he witnesses Captain America beating up a black man. When he confronts him, he hears Steve Rogers's voice. Ripping off the mask, he sees Steve Rogers's face. As he stares in disbelief he is hit from behind. The last panel shows him facing Captain America and Bucky Barnes.

As the battle resumes in issue 154, the dialogue of Captain America is changed. After stunning the Falcon with a blow, he tells Bucky, "He's harder to put away than I figured, Bucky. When we decided to lure him to us by roughing up some coloreds, I should have taken that into account."[36] After Captain America defeats the Falcon, the black community comes to his aid, bursting into the warehouse where Captain America and Bucky are torturing the Falcon in hopes of getting him to reveal the location of his partner. Captain America tells him, "I am Captain America. Your friend's some pinko who's duped the American public, who's trying to sell out this great nation to the reds! I am the true force of our democracy."[37] The Falcon is rescued at this point by the Harlem residents, while Captain America and Bucky flee. They go to the Avengers and take a jet, having learned the whereabouts of Steve Rogers. Issue 155 reveals these two to be the Captain America and Bucky of the 1950s. For three issues of *Young Men Comics*, there were Captain America stories, and three issues of *Captain America Comics* were also published in 1954 (titled *Captain America, Commie Smasher*). Within the current continuity, however, these could be rationalized only by arguing that the star of these stories was not the true Captain America, who had been frozen in ice during this period. So a new origin is told for this character.[38]

A young man so idolizes Captain America in the 1940s that he gets a history degree with a thesis based on Captain America. In his research he rediscovers the supersoldier serum and convinces the U.S. government to let him be the new Captain America for the Korean War, and he has his face surgically altered to look like Steve Rogers. His dream is shattered, however, when the war ends, and the era of peaceful coexistence leads the U.S. government not to antagonize the USSR by creating a new Sentinel of Liberty. Taking a job teaching at a prep school, he meets a young boy who resembles Bucky and also adores Captain America. When the Red Skull reemerges to threaten the UN, Steve and Bucky take the serum and become their heroes, now fighting communists, for whom the Red Skull works (it turned out not to be the same Red Skull). Having failed to be bombarded by the vita-rays introduced into the origin story in *Captain America* 109, however, the serum has a deleterious affect on their minds, so that they "began finding reds where others saw nothing, like in Harlem and Watts. In fact we found that most people who weren't pure-blooded Americans were commies." Viewing their bigotry as "schizophrenic paranoia" the government places them in cryogenic suspension, from which they are released in 1972 by a government official who sees Nixon's opening to China as appeasement of the communists.[39]

The final battle between the two Captain Americas presents a variety of ideological conflicts. The battle between Fury and Captain America has broken the equation of the morality of World War II with the morality of the Cold War. This becomes more evident when the brain-damaged Captain America of the 1950s is released from captivity by someone who specifically references that isomorphism, further weakening the trope that had given containment its moral legitimacy in the 1950s and '60s. The anticommunism of the 1950s is equated with racism, undermining the moral certainty of the Cold War consensus. While the unthinking, bigoted chauvinism of the 1950s Captain America is contrasted with the more liberal tolerance of the 1970s Captain America, there is also a clear connection between the two. As he heads for the battle, the real Captain America thinks, "I've never fought the evil side of my own nature. And that's what he is after all, a man who began with the same dreams I did and ended an insane, bigoted superpatriot. He is what he is because he admired me, wanted to copy me. . . . In a very real way I'm responsible for all the evil he's done."[40] At the end of the battle, his potential culpability is transformed into identity, as he tells the Falcon and Sharon that "he could have been me." Patriotism is portrayed as having a high potential to degenerate into chauvinism and bigotry. That which makes Captain America an interesting character, gives him his unique position, his defense of American values, is a slippery stance, easily becoming a defense of all aspects of the American position. In accord with the liberal consensus, the extremism of the superpatriot is contrasted unfavorably with the more tolerant ideological position of Captain America. Still, the potential for fascism inherent in the superhero, particularly the superpatriot, is made very clear.

The narrative offers a direct commentary on the effects of Cold War policies. Because the story begins with the battle between Nick Fury and Captain America, highlighting the effects of Captain America's not experiencing the high Cold War, the emergence of a Captain America from that period gives a strong argument that the loss of moral clarity is a product of the Cold War itself. The two Captain Americas represent different relations to the period—one slept through the high Cold War of the 1950s, the other was directly produced by those same events. Facing a specifically Cold War reflection of himself Captain America is no longer morally or empirically able to deny the effects of the Cold War. Facing this reality, the real Captain America tells his double, "America's in danger from within as well as without."[41]

This is a far cry from the battles of the 1960s, either against the Nazis or against their communist avatars in the Cold War. Captain America identifies the threats from within as organized crime, racism, and fascism, which his double takes to be an accusation. Communists are not identified as threats, nor are totalitarian governments. The threats from within are seen as greater than the threats from without, and they are here portrayed as having been spawned or given greater prominence by the Cold War events through which Captain America slept.[42]

Making the Connection: Captain America and the Secret Empire

Beginning in issue 163 (July 1973),[43] an extended story pits Captain America against the Secret Empire. Released just as the U.S. Senate began holding televised hearings into the Watergate scandal, the tale begins when the Viper, former ad executive turned supervillain, launches an advertising campaign to unsell Captain America. This campaign is operated by Quentin Hardeman, director of the Committee to Re-establish America's Principles (CRAP). With innuendo and lies, the campaign uses television to destroy Captain America's reputation. Over the course of a year it is revealed that Hardeman and his committee are a front for the Secret Empire, a group bent on conquering the United States. They are led by Number One. Using their civilian identities to infiltrate the Secret Empire, Captain America and the Falcon discover their plot to use mutant energy to fuel their plans and to establish their own superhero, Moonstone, in Captain America's place. The final battle between Moonstone and Captain America (cover-dated the month before Nixon resigned) takes place on the lawn of the White House, where Moonstone is defeated. Number One runs into the building. Captain America captures him in the Oval Office and unmasks him (although readers never see his face). Number One is a high-ranking government official seeking total power. His plans in shambles, he takes out a gun and kills himself.[44]

The Watergate parallel is unmistakable, from the similarity between Quentin Hardeman and H. R. Haldeman, the Nixon administration's Committee to Re-Elect the President (CREEP) and CRAP to the final denouement in the Oval Office, suggesting that Number One is the president.[45] Had the story stopped here it would be an interesting allegory that might merit a footnote, but the story would extend for another eight months as Captain America faced a crisis of identity because of the failings of American leadership.

Having defeated the Secret Empire in issue 175, Captain America spends issue 176 reflecting on the events of his life and the implications of the failings of the American government. In a medium known for spandex-clad beefcakes beating each other continually, this issue is an exception—there are no physical battles, no villains, only an internal moral conflict. As a parade of associates tries to give him reasons to continue, Captain America contemplates giving up his superhero identity. The final and most potent argument is given by Peggy Carter, his girlfriend from World War II who had been in a coma until recently (she is also the sister of his current girlfriend, Sharon). A woman out of time, much as Captain America, she argues, "Sure we've had scandals, but we've exposed them publicly and gotten back on the right track. There's nothing wrong with us, at least no more than at any other point in history. I know it sounds corny, Cap, but you're more than just an example. You're a symbol, a symbol of the country that's given everything it has to light the torch of liberty throughout the world. . . . Lots of people fight crime or

Figure 3.4. Answering Peggy Carter
From "Captain America Must Die!" *Captain America and the Falcon* 176 (August 1974), 27.

provide inspiration, but only you do it for the United States of America."[46] To this Captain America responds, "There's just one problem with that argument, Peggy. America is not the single entity you're talking about. It's changed since I took my name. There was a time, yes, when the country faced a clearly hideous aggressor, and her people stood united against it. But now nothing's that simple. Americans have many goals, some of them quite contrary to others."[47]

Representing a nostalgic vision that does not understand the modern world, Peggy Carter's argument fails to account for the changes America has experienced during her coma. Having a decade of experience under his belt since his own resurrection, Captain America can recognize these changes and realize that the world in which he lives is different from the world in which he came of age and adopted his costume. Sal Buscema's art highlights the multicultural aspect of the changes the superhero is describing and their effects on the equivalence of World War II and the Cold War. The unity of the consensus is clearly imagined in the flag on the rifle piercing the swastika. The centrality of the flag imagery is maintained in the next panel, which centers on Captain America's flag-draped costume as he explains that there are "many different versions of America." The final panel, wider than the other two, offers a series of faces, multihued and ethnically diverse, surrounding a determined (and larger) face of Captain America. The unity of purpose identified in World War II is thus shattered by the multicultural reality of 1970s America. While there is no reference to the Soviets, there is both visual and narrative reference to the Second World War and the clear menace of Nazi Germany, and an assertion that the modern world does not parallel World War II. In the course of this issue, Captain America will note three times that the world has changed since he was given the supersoldier serum on the eve of World War II. The first is after he recounts his origin, the second is his response to Peggy. The final time is a soliloquy at the end of the issue in which he will indict Cold War America as a period during which government virtue has vanished. He muses, "The government created me in 1941—created me to act as their agent in protecting our country, and over the years I've done my best. I wasn't perfect. I did things I'm not proud of, but I always tried to serve my country well. And now I find that the government was serving itself . . . I'm the one who's seen everything Captain America fought for become a cynical sham."[48] He has tried to do his best, but finds that the government he serves has lost its virtue. (Captain) America has lost the sense of self.

Since he no longer has a clear definition of his own identity ("Which America am I supposed to symbolize?") and has no faith in the virtue of those he should serve he decides to stop being Captain America. For the next eight issues, he will not be Captain America. He will become a new hero, called Nomad. Others will try to be Captain America, most successfully a young Brooklynite named Roscoe who works at the gym Steve Rogers frequents. In issue 183, Nomad will find Roscoe crucifed upside down on a chimney in New York. The Falcon tells him that it was the Red Skull who killed Roscoe as a pretender. Nomad spends two pages soliloquizing over the decision he has made, noting that the reason he quit being Captain America was "Because the others who acted in America's name were every bit as bad as the Red Skull." He continues,

> And yet, I didn't want to know about those people. The Skull was Okay to oppose, and still is, but Number One wasn't, because he was supposed to be on our side. Oh Lord! If I wasn't prepared for any and all threats to the American dream, then what was I doing as Captain America. I'm not the poor, abused hero I've been telling myself I was. I'm not even a fool. I'm a failure. I thought I knew who the good guys and the bad guys were. I thought, as usual, that things weren't as complex as they are, and I couldn't understand how the good guys could put their faith in a man so bad. But my naivete is my problem, not America's. The country didn't let me down, I let her down by not being all that I could be. If I'd paid more attention to the way the American reality differed from the American dream, if I hadn't gone around thinking the things I believe in were thirty years out of date, then I might have uncovered Number One and stopped him before it was too late.[49]

Captain America's crisis of faith is not merely political but personal as well. He defines the problem not as one of good government, but of authentic identity. In resolving this crisis he regains his faith, loses the costume of Nomad, and redons the flag-colored garb of Captain America. In the final splash page (drawn by Frank Robbins) a determined Captain America stands at the center with the discarded Nomad costume laid out behind him as if under that costume had always been the Captain America uniform. The suggestion is that beneath the cynicism of Nomad there always remained an American romantic who wanted to believe. An editorial note announces that this is thirty-fourth anniversary of Captain America's first appearance.

Steve Engelhart (w), Frank Robbins (p), and Frank Giacoia (i). © 2008 Marvel Characters, Inc. Used with permission.

Figure 3.5. Captain America Reborn

From "Nomad: No More!" *Captain American and the Falcon* 183 (March 1975), 32.

The artwork of Sal Buscema in these stories offers a strong contrast with the Steranko and Colan runs of the early 1970s. Where the complexity of their art rendered a more conventional message unsettling, Buscema's seems more of a throwback to the Kirby style of visual storytelling. His clear lines and square, contained panels offer an easily accessible visual form. As the story becomes more complicated, the morality of the tale more ambiguous, the art suggests greater certainty to the message. Where the image dominated the story for Steranko, for Buscema the image supports the arguments of the narrators. Thus Captain America's moral dilemma is given strong support by the artwork and becomes the moral dilemma of the reader. The art leads readers to conclude that his embrace of uncertainties is a valid response to the growing ambiguity of moral action.

Readers engaged with the politics of both the Watergate and the Nomad story line parallel intensely. While the earlier story of the two Captain Americas seems to have been read largely as a patch on the narrative continuity, these stories were read as political statements. Several writers voiced their distrust of the government. Some readers suggested that Captain America's questioning of "American values" was unpatriotic. A common argument was that government had become so untrustworthy because American citizens failed to exercise their votes. Future Marvel editor Ralph Macchio opined, "If these scandals occurring almost daily are making citizens of this country shake their heads in despair, I hope they don't forget that they shoulder part of the responsibility for the mess."[50] Another letter writer commented that "Steve [Engelhart] portrayed validly the susceptibility of the American people to demagoguery and mass media saturation."[51] Many letter writers debated the various reasons friends offered Captain America for retaining his heroic identity. During this run, few of the letters emphasize story or art so much as the interpretation and meaning of the story for understanding the world around them. One writer concluded, "Hate, wars, and government corruption had destroyed Steve Rogers' faith in America (as it has also done to us)."[52] The letters also accepted the reconciliation of Captain America as he redonned his costumes. Ralph Macchio wrote again, claiming, "Because of a mag like CAPTAIN AMERICA the youngsters of today are being offered an opportunity to open their minds and see what's at the core of liberty,"[53] Another writer commented, "Let's face it, we all do love America, even though we realize she's not perfect. . . . We are all like Steve Rogers . . . disillusionment and frustration make us divorce ourselves from America, but after weighing the alternatives, they just don't stack up."[54] "So much cynicism, so much lethargy lately in America. Where has the dream gone?" asked another writer. "Marvel has provided the answer: it never left. . . . The questions laid down during Cap's monologue seemed nothing if not a challenge to the common man—a challenge to believe in yourself and your ideals."[55]

The Secret Empire–Nomad stories represent the apogee of the crisis of identity that had been ongoing in the books for nearly five years (and which would continue, albeit in a less prominent way). The reemergence of Captain America at the end of the sequence has redefined him in several ways and has thus redefined the vision of American culture he represents. No longer does the symbol of the American dream see himself as a creation and agent of the American government. That government is no longer perceived as virtuous, but is populated by villains "every bit as bad as the Red Skull." When Captain America identified the enemies from within in issue 156, he referred to organized crime and fascism. That definition now includes corrupt politicians and a variety of potential threats that are not defined in American popular culture as evil. When Captain America refers to America, he has defined it as contested terrain and no longer a monolithic cultural ecology. The Cold War consensus of national identity is a thing of the past, no longer descriptive of America, if it ever was. In fact, that consensus seems to be defined as a mask behind which a government grew increasingly corrupt and the problems of a plural society were ignored. These transformations have been clearly identified as effects of the Cold War, the period between Captain America's creation and the scandal that so shocked him. While still holding faith in the basic rhetorical elements of progress and liberty, he no longer takes these as defined for him by a government that is peopled by potential culprits but seeks a redefinition based on a conception of American pluralism. His reeducation in the politics of identity has been profound.

The Education of Tony Stark

As late as 1972, Iron Man continues to justify his anticommunist stance and Tony Stark's manufacture of munitions, albeit a defense that is convincing neither to the reader nor, apparently, to Tony Stark. A funeral for a friend lost helping Iron Man, at which a man named Gilbert accuses Tony Stark of causing the death, is the impetus for a retelling of the Iron Man origin that is virtually identical to the first telling. The story ends with the modern Iron Man looking at his original armor in a glass case and questioning his role:

> Maybe . . . I was wrong to think a golden galahad made any sense in 1972. How about it, Stark? How about it? No! You've been fooling yourself, Tony, trying to take the simple way out. It'd be too easy to give in to the Gilberts of the world, because for every person killed because he encountered Iron Man, a hundred more have lived. You've been looking at it all wrong, Stark. You're not a civilian, you're a soldier, albeit a reluctant one, a soldier in the battle for human rights, human dignity. There's a war being fought every place, every day, a war that's going to be won someday, somehow, and one man who's going to help win it is Iron Man.[56]

While the anticommunist Iron Man of the 1960s is not specifically identified, the origin story—in which the Vietnamese communists ensnare Tony Stark and force him to build the armor—and the presence of that armor during the soliloquy as if it were an interlocutor clearly call it to mind. The redefinition of the battle against the communists as a battle for human rights is a revision of history rather than an encounter with it. The scene's portrayal, with one suit of armor talking to another but referring to it by the human name, implies a lack of control on the part of Tony Stark. The most jarring image is of the current Iron Man's image, reflected in the glass casing of the older armor. The human eyes of Tony Stark behind the gold and red face mask seem mournful and then determined in the next panel. In the final panels, the perspective has shifted farther out, and as Iron Man declares himself a soldier, no human elements are visible.

Figure 3.6. Self-Reflection

From "Why Must There Be an Iron Man?" *Invincible Iron Man* 47 (June 1972), 20.

By 1975 there are no more justifications offered, and the past is confronted rather than redefined. *Invincible Iron Man* 78 (September) tells a story set in 1969 (the same year investigative journalist Seymour Hersh broke the story of the My Lai massacre) of Iron Man going to Vietnam to field test a new laser-guided cannon developed by Stark Industries. The test is to destroy a peaceful village that had been targeted by the U.S. Army, even though there is no official order and the action violates international law. During a firefight with the North Vietnamese, Iron Man becomes enraged and begins to attack a guerrilla who keeps shooting at him, saying, "Fire away, Red, 'cause it's the last thing you'll ever do." He finds that his assailant is a young boy blinded by the destruction of his village. Finding the village destroyed and everyone dead, Iron Man uses his power to build a mass grave, over which he writes the word WHY as an epitaph. He returns to the United States and transforms Stark Industries from a munitions manufacturer into Stark International, with an emphasis on "peace industries"—space exploration and the environment.[57]

The story is told in flashback and is bracketed by a reference to Iron Man's origins and past in the front and by a declaration of Iron Man and Tony Stark's principles at the end. The Iron Man of the 1960s is defined as ignorant and naive, locked within Cold War blinders that gave him a sense of moral certainty that was unrealistic. Transforming the visual trope from issue 47, Tony Stark gazes into a mirror in which the reflected face of Iron Man in an older version of his costume peers back at him and comments, "And what about you, Tony Stark? Once you were do or die for America and Mom's Apple Pie. You didn't do much soul searching back then, did you? As Iron Man you beat the commies for democracy without ever questioning just whose democracy you were serving, or just what those you served intended to do with the world once you'd saved it for them. Vietnam raised all those questions didn't it, Tony? Didn't it? Like, what right had we to be there in the first place?"[58] Having seen his weapon destroy innocent civilians, and himself assume that the use of that weapon, untested, was justified because of the communist threat, Stark/Iron Man develops guilt and a sense of responsibility for those whom he formerly sought to destroy. After his recollection, he dons his armor and offers a rededication of his life, noting,

> that was one of the things that forced you to re-evaluate your image of yourself as a manufacturer of weapons of war and your dual role as an avenger, whose prime purpose for existing is to avenge the wrongs of the world! Wrongs such as hate, intolerance, and war, Avenger. War is the culmination of all those evils. War is the condition that devalues any of mankind's gains, and I swear as the man Tony Stark, as the Avenger fate chose to cast in the role of Iron Man, that I will live to avenge those whose lives have been lost through the ignorance of men like the man I once was, or I will die trying![59]

An editorial note at the bottom of the final page declares, "Dedicated to Peace."

In addition to increasingly questioning the morality of Cold War policy directly, the Iron Man comics also come to challenge the ability of capitalist enterprise to promote equality or justice in American society. This is perhaps best represented by the emergence of the villain Firebrand. As his name suggests, Firebrand is a militant, antiestablishment, anti-industry activist, one

Figure 3.7. Redefining the Enemy
From "Long Time Gone" *Invincible Iron Man* 78
(September 1975), 30.

who uses violence and destruction. He first appears in *Iron Man* 27 (July 1970), rousing a black community to violence against an unscrupulous developer. Iron Man thinks he is a mercenary, but Firebrand replies, "I'm just an all-American boy, Iron Man, one of those wide-eyed innocents who started out to make this nation a better place. I sat in for civil rights, marched for peace, demonstrated on campus, and got chased by vicious dogs, spat on by bigots, beat on by 'patriots,' choked by tear gas, and blinded by mace until I finally caught on. This country doesn't want to be changed! The only way to build anything decent is to tear down what's here and start over."[60] After defeating Firebrand and achieving some form of reconciliation, Iron Man explains to a police officer, "It's not Firebrand's escaping that bothers me. It's wondering where the rest of us went wrong that someone like him should have to come into being at all."[61]

The Iron Man comics thus directly question Cold War policy, particularly in Vietnam, and the faith that the liberal consensus placed in the ability of the American economy to provide a just distribution of social product. The "grand expectations" that James Patterson suggests guided America through the 1960s were not realized, creating more militant action on the part of those who had not gained access to the age of abundance.[62] While Iron Man opposes Firebrand's methods, he understands the frustration that produces them and the part he has played in creating that frustration.

This version of direct questioning of public affairs in comic books will not last long in the Iron Man series. When Firebrand returns (*Invincible Iron Man* 48, July 1972) he will still espouse his anticapitalist rhetoric, but he is revealed to be the son of Simon Gilbert, an abusive father and unscrupulous member of the board of directors of Stark Industries who has recently been fired by Tony Stark. Simon Gilbert allies with Firebrand (not knowing his identity) and dies while trying to blow up a Stark production plant. Firebrand's revolutionary militancy is thus transformed from a product of a failed society to that of a failed family. His subsequent appearances have him avenging his father's death, for which he blames Iron Man (issue 59), or in the mold of a power hungry supervillain (issues 80–81).

The Sidekick's Struggle: The Falcon and Civil Rights

Having rejected Rick Jones as a boy sidekick for Captain America, Stan Lee gave him an African American sidekick, the Falcon. Trained by Captain America during the period when the Red Skull had switched their bodies, Sam Wilson becomes the Falcon in *Captain America* 117 (September 1969). They became partners in *Captain America and the Falcon* 133 (January 1971). Now in New York, Sam Wilson is a social worker in Harlem who is also the crime-fighting Falcon. In his civilian role he frequently confronts the radical black power activist Rafe Michel, with whom he also vies for the affection of the beautiful Leila. Meanwhile, he is constantly plagued by the inferiority he feels toward Captain America and the lack of respect he thinks is accorded him as Captain America's sidekick, although the term that Captain America and the editors/writers always use is "partner."

Jeffrey A. Brown argues that the introduction of black heroes into comics was driven largely by the commercial success of blaxploitation films and the desire of comics executives to capitalize on this market.[63] While the blaxpoitation portrayal of race seems to have had some influence on the development of the Marvel characters—particularly Luke Cage—the treatment of the characters, and in particular the Falcon, seems to be an attempt to deal with racial issues in a more serious manner. The creation of the Falcon in the Captain America books coincides with an Iron Man story in which Tony Stark selects a black boxer, Eddie March, to take his place in the hero's armor for a short-lived retirement (*Iron Man* 21, January 1970).[64]

While race may have become an increasingly salient issue for the comic book industry, the industry was still dominated by white men who often adopted a patronizing tone, particularly when treating issues of black identity. A prominent story is *Captain America and the Falcon* 143 (November 1971), in which Sam Wilson is beaten by a group of radical black power activists, including both Rafe Michel and Leila. The group is inspired by men in blue masks and yellow tunics with a red fist on their chests. These men have mobilized a mob of African Americans to beat up Wilson and Reverend Garcia, the voices of moderation in the community. The conflict is offered between two different trajectories for racial relations. Sam Wilson and Reverend Garcia represent the integrationist impulse, moderate in tone, inclusive of all people of color. The black nationalist vision is represented by Rafe Michel and Leila. Frequently referring to Sam Wilson as an Uncle Tom and telling him that black is beautiful, they see integration as crumbs offered from the table of white America. Given that the inclusive, integrationist impulse is represented by the hero, this voice is clearly the privileged one in the book. Less ideological and more pragmatic, the integrationist voice fits the vision of the consensus identity better than the extremism and violence of Rafe Michel's black nationalism. While both Sam Wilson and Michel vie for the affection of Leila, she will ultimately become the Falcon's girlfriend, further delegitimizing the black nationalist voice.

After being rescued by Captain America, Sam Wilson and his partner try to stop the radicals from burning Harlem to the ground. Fighting the mob and the masked leaders, they discover that under the blue hood is the face of the Red Skull, who escapes, although the racial warfare is now over. Black nationalism—like communism, portrayed as a militant ideology—is thus equated with Nazism and further undermined as a relevant voice in racial debate. That Leila becomes Wilson's girlfriend suggests that the rift between the older civil rights movement and the new identitarian black nationalism can be bridged.

Torn between his partnership with Captain America and the needs of the black community, the Falcon sees his relationship with Captain America become increasingly tense. Having focused on the Red Skull, Captain America admits that he had forgotten the "racial crises" that still need to be resolved. The Falcon replies, "Think nothing of it. White men have been forgetting us darkies for centuries! That's why there is a crisis." Seeing that the current crisis has been averted, Captain America tells the Falcon, "Well, all's quiet for now, but who knows what little something it will take to make them explode again," to which the Falcon replies, "I don't think I like the way you put that, partner. They . . . *we* got reason to blow up. I got some reassessing to do! I'll get in touch when I know where I stand." Coming later to mend fences, Captain America sees Sam kissing Leila and thinks, "Sam . . . kissing that militant girl! I can see this is no time to try and square things with him."[65] That is not to happen right away, as the Falcon breaks his partnership with Captain America to serve his own people better and to become proud of his black heritage (notably, he does this by making a new, white costume).[66] This independence will be short-lived, as he will soon reunite with Captain America and remain his partner for the next several years, until the magazine reverts to being *Captain America* at issue 223 (July 1978).

Throughout their partnership, there will be tension between the blond-haired, blue-eyed Captain America and the African American Falcon. Frequently feeling inferior and patronized, the Falcon will seek his own identity apart from the man who trained him. He will get the Black Panther, Marvel's first black superhero, the king of the African nation of Wakanda and a scientist of note, to modify his costume with glider wings to give him more power. For his part, Captain America will try to understand, but the presence of the Falcon in the book gives his attempts at understanding a patronizing tone. There is an element of condescension to him, suggesting that the degree of understanding possible between white and black America is not as great as the Captain and other liberals might want it to be. It reveals a one-sidedness to the race debate in the 1970s, in which the liberal whites seem to be accommodating but desire accommodation on their terms alone, failing to appreciate that there might be another voice to be heard.

Just as these tensions seem to be resolved after the Nomad interregnum, it is revealed that Sam Wilson is an identity constructed by the Red Skull. Seeking to create a weapon to use against Captain America when he possessed the Cosmic Cube, the Skull had created the identity of Sam Wilson in Snap Wilson, a street-savvy gang member and drug dealer. The Skull activates him in *Captain America and the Falcon* 185 (May 1975),[67] and his story is told in the next few issues. No longer is there tension between Captain America, the naive but patronizing white liberal, and the African American Falcon. The crisis of identity has become twofold. Captain America has been misled and has never understood the true face of his black partner, whose very identity has been constructed to defeat him. This implies a basic lack of understanding between the white and black communities, such that the moderate liberal integration impulse that motivates Captain America is presented as having failed to see clearly across the racial boundary. Second, the Falcon's identity is now obscured, rendering him incapable of representing an ideological position within the civil rights discourse. Instead, the tension is within the Falcon, reconciling the urban street criminal, Snap, with the integrationist impulse of social worker Sam Wilson. That the Falcon now embodies both Snap and Sam represents a vision of tensions within the black community that had been ignored previously for the broader interest of racial tolerance on a national level. Rather than offer the Falcon as representative of the potential for integration, the book leaves him unknown to himself or his white partner. The Captain America series, which began the decade playing with ambiguous identity, has seen that ambiguity explode into a full-blown identity crisis. The muddled identities of the Red Skull and Captain America in 1969 gave rise to and have been replaced by the multiple personalities of Sam/Snap Wilson.

The Marvel Philosophy Takes Form

By the mid-1970s Marvel had shed its strident anticommunism and lost the moral certainty of the high Cold War. Communists had all but vanished as the sinister other against which comic book America defined itself, replaced by growing distrust of domestic authorities, both political and economic. The stories were characterized by persistent identity crises for their characters, reflecting the breakdown of Cold War consensus and the growing ambiguity surrounding American culture and values. What emerged has been termed a passive liberalism, although that may not do it justice.[68] In a series of editorials known as "Stan Lee's Soapbox" Lee offered a "Marvel philosophy" that would, at times, be cited by readers in their letters to the magazines. In a December 1968 installment, Lee wrote, "Let's lay it right on the line. Bigotry and racism are among the deadliest social ills plaguing the world today. But, unlike a team of costumed supervillains, they can't be halted with a punch in the snoot, or a zap from a ray gun. The only way to destroy them is to expose them—to reveal them for the insidious evils they really are. . . . Sooner or later, we must learn to judge each other on our own merits. Sooner or later, if man is ever to be worthy of his destiny, we must fill our hearts with tolerance."[69] The March 1971 segment offered further outline, noting, "We support people everywhere—people striving to improve themselves and their lives—people working and praying for a better world, a world without war. Our heroes are your heroes—our villains are your villains—our problems your problems, as are our triumphs and defeats. We espouse no cause save the cause of freedom—no philosophy save the brotherhood of man. Our purpose is to entertain—to take the world as it is and show it as it might be—as it could be—and perhaps, as it should be."[70] Overblown and pretentious it might be, but there is still a core element here that seems to go beyond mere passive liberalism. The key elements are tolerance and responsibility. Tolerance is portrayed as an affirmative act, one in which people must take positive action to achieve equality. This notion would appear again in a reply to a letter from future Marvel writer Steve Gerber, who suggested (based on his reading of Marshall McCluhan) that nationalism was a fading anachronism in the age of the global media village. Lee wrote in reply that because of the decreasing relevance of nation, Marvel had "discontinued using any real foreign 'enemies' in [their books] . . . the world has become much too small a place for such a thing, and it is destined, obviously, to grow much smaller." He went further, to argue that Captain America was no longer a nationalist figure but "the idealization, the realization of the hopes and dreams of all freedom loving people everywhere—whether they be black, white, or any of the other million-and-one shades of a multi-hued humanity."[71] This vision of active tolerance is also an anti-ideological stance. The extremism of Firebrand, Rafe Michel, or the Captain America of the 1950s is contrasted in the stories to the tolerant pragmatism of Iron Man, Captain America, and the Falcon. Social problems exist, but to redress them through violence or ideological extremism always fails in the comic books.

Responsibility is also a key; everyone is responsible for their actions and their effects on the tolerant equality that is the goal. Captain America's return to uniform is the acceptance of that responsibility within a more sophisticated but less certain vision of what he had defined as the American dream; Tony Stark's recognition of his responsibility as a munitions manufacturer and narrow-minded Cold Warrior is made active through his rededication of both Iron Man and Stark International to the cause of peace. In short, an active, pragmatic, inclusive tolerance of difference and of uncertainties distinguish the Marvel political economy of the mid-1970s, just as active anticommunism and moral certainty had characterized it in the 1960s.

By the mid-1970s the idea of social relevance in comics had run its course. Some direct social commentary remained, but in general the stories turned to the fantastic and the nostalgic. Jack Kirby returned to Captain America in 1975 as writer, editor, and artist, and embarked on a two-year run that ignored continuity and generated much distress among the readers. Readers were dismayed at Captain America engaging in interdimensional travel and fighting space aliens. Iron Man similarly fought a variety of space aliens and even battled the Frankenstein monster. Monster and horror comic books returned to popularity for a brief period as well. Roy Thomas, who took over the editorial duties at Marvel, brought a fascination with World War II superheroes, who began to appear in various books—notably the Avengers series—and a new book set in World War II (the *Invaders*, first issue, June 1975), teaming Marvel's three great World War II heroes, the Submariner, the Human Torch, and Captain America. Frank Robbins (who also had a run on Captain America) was the artist who drew the book in a 1940s style. *The Invaders* lasted for less than four years. As the 1970s began to wane, Marvel went through four chief editors in three years and appeared to have lost direction. Sales, which had been in decline for much of the decade, fell off precipitously around 1978. Facing increased competition from a resurgent Hollywood, a declining presence at newsstands, and a new competitor for teenage leisure dollars with the emergence of video games, the comic industry suffered greatly and Marvel, along with the rest of the comic book industry, limped toward the 1980s.

4

Retreat into Privacy: 1977–1985

N JULY 1976, TONY STARK'S longtime secretary Pepper Potts and chauffeur Happy Hogan, now married, resigned from Stark Enterprises to remove themselves from the dangers they faced and would continue to face as allies of Iron Man. Wanting to enjoy their lives free from threat, they left the superhero world to enjoy private life.[1] Like many Americans, the Hogans had become exhausted by the constant social turmoil and seemingly pointless activities of the public realm and chose to focus on their personal lives.

Having weathered the Vietnam War, civil rights protests, and Watergate, and facing a stagnating economy beset by both rising prices and unemployment, Americans had lost faith in the government's ability to manage social change and retreated into privacy. Public opinion polls showed that after 1974 fewer than one-third of Americans indicated that they trusted the government. As the affluence that had made all things seem possible in 1964 turned into the stagflation of 1976, Americans came to believe in the limits to growth and sought to take care of themselves rather than to change the world. Phil Ochs, antiwar balladeer of the 1960s, once defined a liberal as "someone who is ten degrees to the left of center during the best of times, and ten degrees to the right of center when it affects them personally."

By 1976, rapid social change and a rapidly declining economy combined to affect most Americans personally, and they turned away from the public realm to focus on themselves, their families, and their local communities, apparently rejecting the idea of government-sponsored social change.

A Crisis of Confidence

This retreat into privacy and distrust of government fueled the 1976 presidential campaign of Jimmy Carter. An avowedly religious, family-centered, antigovernment candidate, Carter seemed to embody the growing concern with social morality. The deepening economic crisis and continued distrust of public affairs could not be solved by Carter. In 1979 he delivered his famous speech on the energy crisis in which he lamented the growing crisis of confidence in American society. Originally intended as another presidential message on the energy crisis, the speech was transformed into a jeremiad on the decline of confidence in American institutions. The structure of the speech reflected the ambiguities of the age. Carter begins by listing a series of comments he had received or solicited from people from a variety of backgrounds. This structure, which assumes that each position is unique, tacitly rejects the notion of a consensus concerning the American self. He follows this with a summary of the problem as he defines it, commenting, "I want to talk to you right now about a fundamental threat to American democracy. The threat is nearly invisible in ordinary ways. It is a crisis of confidence. It is a crisis that strikes at the very heart and soul and spirit of our national will. We can see this crisis in the growing doubt about the meaning of our own lives and in the loss of a unity of purpose for our nation. The erosion of our confidence in the future is threatening to destroy the social and the political fabric of America."[9] Carter thus laments the erosion of consensus—unity of purpose—and the decline in confidence in America, while the structure of his argument tacitly echoes that lack of consensus. He notes that this lack of confidence reflects a loss of faith in one of the key rhetorical elements that had defined the very language of the American self—progress: "We've always believed in something called progress. We've always had a faith that the days of our children would be better than our own. Our people are losing that faith, not only in government itself but in their ability as citizens to serve as the ultimate rulers and shapers of our democracy."[3] Carter clearly identifies and laments the weakening of the rhetoric of American national identity. He identifies the sources of this decline in the assassinations of the 1960s, the Vietnam War, Watergate, and the economic crisis of the 1970s. He notes the profound problems that could result from the loss of an accepted rhetoric of national identity:

> We are at a turning point in our history. There are two paths to choose. One is a path I've warned about tonight, the path that leads to fragmentation and self-interest. Down that road lies a mistaken idea of freedom, the right to grasp for ourselves some advantage over others. That path would be one of constant conflict between narrow interests ending in chaos and immobility. It is a certain route to failure.
>
> All the traditions of our past, all the lessons of our heritage, all the promises of our future point to another path—the path of common purpose and the restoration of American values. That path leads to true freedom for our nation and ourselves. We can take the first steps down that path as we begin to solve our energy problem.[4]

Ultimately, however, he can offer nothing save for a response to the energy crisis and a call for Americans to have faith. Carter's insightful identification of the loss of a rhetoric of national identity was received with at best a mundane response. The validity of his diagnosis, and the implications of this loss of faith, would play out over the next three decades. The energy crisis, economic stagnation, and apparent international drift would persist, and the ideal of American progress would continue to appear illusory.

Lacking faith in American progress and in American government to promote progress, citizens increasingly retreated into their own private worlds, rejecting an untrustworthy and impotent government and wary of calls for social reorganization. Rather than changing the power structure or developing new forms of social organization, citizens became active over taxes; the tax revolt seemed the only issue that Americans could flock to support, one which reduced the power of government while giving them more resources to feather their private nests. Even the cultural insurgents of the era, most notably punk rockers, dealt in the politics of private culture rather than public challenge. Their politics was restricted to anticorporatism, and their chosen mode of discourse was irony.[5] These responses reflect a distrust of public utterances and a fear of capitalist organizations' threats to private existence.

The retreat into privacy took several different forms as it spread across the political spectrum, often creating the strange bedfellows for which politics is famous. One aspect, common to the former countercultural participants, was a new concern with self-actualization and a therapeutic approach to emotional well-being that Christopher Lasch has termed the "culture of narcissism."[6] The popularity of self-help books such as Thomas Harris's 1076 *I'm OK, You're OK,* or Nancy Friday's 1977 *My Mother/My Self,* which purported to free the self from "dysfunctional" family relations, or of consciousness-raising seminars such as Erhard Seminars Training (more commonly known as EST), along with myriad other movements and ideas from Arica to Zen, represented a quest for inner tranquility, emotional validation, and self-awareness. This represented a significant change from the political engagement of the previous period and a vast distance from the liberal consensus of national politics that characterized the late 1950s and 1960s.

The growing importance of localized citizen action groups also represents a face of the retreat into privacy. While clearly engaged in public action, the movement for grassroots democracy tended to focus on small-scale local issues that emphasized blocking what was considered intrusive action into the private sphere by big government or corporations, ranging from urban revitalization in St. Louis, Missouri, to repealing state legislation that approved automobile insurance rate increases in Massachusetts, to blocking nuclear reactor construction in Montague, Massachusetts, and Seabrook, New Hampshire. The most famous of these, of course, was the California plebiscite Proposition 13, led by Howard Jarvis, which repealed and capped any future increase in property taxes.[7] Jarvis, a former John Bircher and insurgent conservative candidate for the U.S. Senate from

California in the early 1960s, would become a cult hero of the resurgent conservative movement that would give birth to the presidency of Ronald Reagan.

The lack of trust in big government and the failures of the economy that developed through the 1960s and 1970s, and which were the impetus behind this retreat into privacy, were shared by those who sought space for self-exploration and those who sought to limit the government's intervention into the economy. They also seem to have been central to the politicization of the new evangelical Christian movement that emerged during the 1970s. These new Christians saw the moral life of American society as coming undone, largely as a product of liberal government action. This may, as Bruce Schulman suggests,[8] be a nationalization of Southern Christianity, fueled by television's reach. Televangelists such as Jerry Falwell, Pat Robertson, Jimmy Swaggart, and Jim Bakker—all Southerners—garnered high ratings and preached a message of both Christian redemption and political education. Railing against pornography, the teaching of evolution, the Equal Rights Amendment, and, most important, the legalization of abortion in the Supreme Court's 1973 decision in *Roe v. Wade*, these preachers mobilized a significant minority to political action. Coming to national prominence in 1976 when Jerry Falwell organized his "I Love America" rallies, this group became formally organized as a political force in 1979 when Falwell formed the Moral Majority.[9] Linking the social concerns for morals of these groups with the antigovernment, antiregulatory forces that were revealed in the tax revolt would become a winning strategy for the Republican Party in the 1980s. The figurehead of this movement, a divorced actor with serious internal family problems, would become an emblem for a generation of conservatives.

All three of these trends—secular self-awareness, local citizens' action, and the new evangelicalism—represent a distrust of the institutions of the public realm—mainly, government and corporate capitalism. In the wake of the Vietnam War, Watergate, rising inflation, and growing Congressional scandals from Koreagate to Abscam, Americans increasingly looked on the government and economic firms as sources of threat rather than hope. After more than a decade of trying to reconstitute the American political economy, either through the political system or through extra-systemic action, many people saw politics and economics as futile avocations. Better to take care of one's self, or to create conditions under which one could take care of one's self, than to waste time seeking grand outcomes from a corrupt and ineffective political economy.

This retreat from public concerns was manifested in the popularity of escapist film and television, closing the door on the politically engaged and oppositional cinema of the "New Hollywood."[10] This is perhaps most obvious in the success of *Jaws* (1975) and *Star Wars* (1977) and the latter's film, television, comic book, and book progeny. It can be seen in the changes in popular television during this decade. In the 1972–73 season, three of the five top-rated programs treated contemporary political or social subjects—*All in the Family*, *Sanford and Son*, and *Maude*. By 1976, these had mostly vanished, replaced by the nostalgic teen visions of *Happy Days* and *Laverne and Shirley* or the escapist adventures of *Charlie's Angels* and the *Six Million Dollar Man*.[11]

In comic books it was represented by an increasing awareness of the domestic realm in the story line, an emphasis on the development of family and kin groups, and a growing psychologization of characters and problems, in which internal emotional states replaced ideology and politics as the sources of conflict. While the characters became more deeply drawn, they were increasingly domesticated and psychoanalyzed. This retreat into the private, while very much concerned with private identity, was a repudiation of the crisis of public identity that had characterized the books of the late 1960s and early 1970s.

The Comic Industry in Crisis

The end of the 1970s witnessed the comic book industry in crisis. Circulation was in sharp decline. Sales of Captain America books fell 48 percent between 1970 and 1978. Even the *Incredible Hulk*, buoyed by a popular television show in the late 1970s, saw a 28 percent decline in sales from 1968 to 1980. This was a result of several factors. The success of Marvel Comics in the late 1960s and early 1970s had led to a vast expansion of titles from both Marvel and National Comics, which meant that the books were increasingly competing with each other. Rising inflation increased the costs of paper and, ultimately, of the books, making them less economical for newsstands to carry in sufficient numbers. The rebirth of the film industry and the emergence of the video game meant that there would be increasing competition for the leisure dollars of adolescents. At Marvel this was combined with a loss of editorial direction after Roy Thomas left; Marvel would have five editors in chief between 1974 and 1978. These factors combined to create a loss of readers, declining sales, and an industrywide crisis.

This financial crisis would be solved through the mechanism of direct marketing. Comic books had generally been sold in supermarkets and drugstores and at newsstands where they were treated as any other magazine. Vendors would order on consignment and return any unsold books for a credit. This resulted in about 40 to 60 percent of all comic books printed being returned and destroyed. The margin of return was such that this was economical. As sales declined, however, first Marvel, and later National (which formally changed its name to DC Comics in 1976[12]), moved to create the direct market. Comics would be sold by the publisher to specialty stores dealing in comic books or collectibles. These dealers would buy the books without the opportunity to return them; instead, any unsold books were the property of the store and would be sold as back issues. The result was that the lost revenue from overproduction was passed on to the retailer rather than the publisher. To reach the same number of readers, publishers would need to produce only two-thirds the previous number of books, and thus save further costs. Direct marketing, however, reduced the visibility of comics to first-time buyers. With fewer books on display at drugstores and newsstands, and more in specialty stores, buyers would have to make a conscious attempt to find comic books. This recognized the increasing contraction of the market to those who already had an interest in the books.

With a smaller audience, but one that was intensely focused on the characters, Marvel comic books began increasingly to emphasize character development. Stories stressed the characters' history and private life rather than addressing social or political issues. This became particularly prominent in the Captain America series, where extended story lines centered on the protagonist's origin, his childhood before he was given the supersoldier formula, the events surrounding his twenty years in suspended animation, and the exploration of his Steve Rogers alter ego. For most of his career, Captain America's alter ego had mattered little; now his private life took on an extended role. Similarly, Iron Man comics developed story lines that added increasing details to his origin and emphasized the private life of Tony Stark; the most famous, perhaps, was his yearlong bout with alcoholism and the subsequent surrender of the Iron Man identity to his friend Jim Rhodes. Both series offered extended histories of the origins and activities of major villains, such as the Red Skull and the Mandarin.

While produced in part by the changing face of the consumer market, the focus on personal histories, families, and internal psychology in these stories represent a retreat from the public crisis of identity that had characterized the books in the 1970s into a private realm of self-exploration. Thematically in the stories, the concern with private affairs is linked to an increasingly untrustworthy government. Government is often portrayed as the source of social ills that create problems in the family. Rather than turn to government for solutions, help is generally defined as coming from private actors—friends and family, which are offered as the social institutions that need to be preserved.

Distrust of Government

By the middle of the 1970s, distrust in government had become ubiquitous. While Watergate was the clearest and most obvious source of disillusion, there were also revelations about the abuse of power under the guise of Cold War security needs that fueled discontent. Beginning in 1974, information about covert CIA activities began to emerge, ranging from complicity in the overthrow of Salvador Allende in Chile in 1973 to assassination attempts against Fidel Castro, Patrice Lumumba, and Ngo Dinh Diem (among others) to interception of private correspondence, counterintelligence programs against domestic organizations such as the Black Panthers, burglaries, wiretapping (including that of Martin Luther King Jr.), and the creation of hundreds of thousands of domestic intelligence files.[13] Sixty-nine percent of respondents to a 1975 poll reported that they believed that the country's leaders had consistently lied to them.[14]

Interventionist Government: The Commission on Superhuman Activities

This distrust takes several forms in the Marvel universe. In 1976 a new force appears, the U.S. government's Commission on Superhuman Activities, along with its agent, Peter Gyrich. Gyrich is specifically the liaison between the commission and the Avengers supergroup. In his first appearance he threatens them with the loss of government sanction because of their lax security.[15] Over the next decade, the commission and Gyrich would become increasingly prominent. Serving as government watchdogs on superpowered heroes, it appears that they serve the public interest. The commission may be a legitimate exercise of government's power to protect citizens from abuse by superpowered beings; one might see in them the same kind of restraints that were being imposed with the War Powers Act of 1973, or the restriction on covert CIA activities. But the books do not support this interpretation. Instead, the commission is portrayed as attempting to subvert the actions of heroes in preserving justice, an unwanted and counterproductive intrusion into the private realm. In *Avengers* 181 (March 1979), Gyrich informs the Avengers that if they wish to maintain their priority status with the government they need to reduce the size of their membership to seven—and he has selected which seven. Iron Man, chairman of the group, is infuriated. "You can't dictate our membership to us! Just who the hell do you think you are?" "I'm the government, mister," Gyrich responds. "Any more questions?" The roster he gives them omits longtime Avengers Hawkeye, Quicksilver, and Yellowjacket, and includes nonmember the Falcon. "If the Avengers are to be sanctioned by the government, they'll have to adhere to government policies," explains Gyrich, "and that includes equal opportunities for minorities."[16] The government's intervention, while ultimately accepted under threat of losing their official sanction, is challenged as illegitimate. The rejection of longtime members such as Hawkeye and Quicksilver, and founding member Giant Man (now known as Yellowjacket), to include a black hero seems clearly influenced by the case of *Bakke v. Regents of the University of California* (1978), which would have been receiving major news coverage at the time the book was written. That case treated the issue of reverse discrimination and became a touchstone in the white backlash against civil rights action in the mid-1970s. Thus, both in its structure and in its content, this story challenges government action as illegitimate, an intrusion into the private realm where it has no place, and as pursuing questionable racial policies. That becomes even clearer when, after serving on a few missions, the Falcon quits the Avengers because he does not want to be the token black member.[17] That civil rights and affirmative action were major products of the social reforms of the 1960s implies a specific repudiation of the government expansion of that period.

This differs considerably from the crisis of faith in the political system that Captain America suffered after Watergate. He could rededicate himself to preserving American ideals in the face of one man's attempt to subvert the system because he defined the source of the problems as individuals in government who were "every bit as bad as the Red Skull." Similarly, the distrust of government (the military in particular) expressed in the Hulk stories was largely defined as one man's obsession; General Thunderbolt Ross, the father of Bruce Banner's fiancée and overseer of the project that turned Banner into the Hulk, became a monomaniac in his attempt to capture the green beast. Neither the Hulk nor Captain America series defined the problem as inherent in the institutions of the system. The commission, however, is a legally established government institution; its mandate of protecting the public interest has a pedigree that reaches back at least to the Sherman Anti Trust Act. This is a truly governmental institution exercising the functions for which government is established. As its agent, Gyrich is not a corrupt individual seeking his own aggrandizement. He will, for instance, accept a weakening of his own authority when the Senate returns much of their autonomy to the Avengers.[18] He is a dedicated public servant, a bureaucrat. He may be rude and authoritarian, but he is a product of the government he represents. His is an institutionalized personality, and as such his rude authoritarianism reflects the institution that produced him. Throughout the next decade the commission will be portrayed as infringing on the actions of superheroes and undermining the pursuit of justice. It will easily be subverted by outside forces. In every instance it will fail to serve the public interest and will instead be the problem rather than the solution.

The Need for a Moral Politics: Captain America for President

The distrust of institutional authority is also represented in *Captain America* 246 (June 1980), in which a nameless superpowered villain begins attacking local politicians and a Social Security office. The villain is Joe, the father of a brain-damaged child who attends a facility at which one of Steve Rogers's neighbors works. The child had recently died after the city council had voted to cut special education funds and the Social Security Administration had rejected Joe's claims for benefits for his son. The rage out of which Joe attacks is not villainy; he is portrayed as a victim, although his attacks are clearly defined as wrong. He is a victim of a variety of social and political problems. He is a single parent whose wife left him because she could not deal with caring for their brain-damaged son. He is a victim of the economy, because he could not find work and money had become tight. He is a victim of government that sought to deny him funds that were necessary for his child's well-being. Family, economy, and government have all let this man down and are the villains in this story. "What happened to Joe is as much a tragedy as what happened to his son," Captain America explains to the paramedic who had attended to Joe's son; "and we've got to fight to save him just like you did to save Joey."[19]

Disillusionment with government will also surface in election-year politics. In *Captain America* 250 (October 1980) an upstart independent party (the New Populist Party) tries to get Captain America to run for the presidency. Seeking a real leader rather than "the same type of political idiots the Demos and GOP keep putting up," the party leaders convince him to think about it. At the Avengers' mansion, Iron Man tries to dissuade him from running because of the "red tape and corruption" he would face. He ultimately declines to run because he has "worked and fought all my life for the growth and advancement of the American dream" and the need for negotiation and compromise in politics would make him incapable of acting as president. "My duty to the dream would severely limit any abilities I might have to preserve the reality."[20] While Captain America does not directly express disdain for government, the comments from others such as Iron Man do. Further, the contrast between the American dream and American reality posed by Captain America here (and at the end of his retirement after Watergate) suggests that there is something fundamentally wrong with the reality of the American system.

Roger Stern (w), John Byrne (p), and Josef Rubenstein (i). October 1980. © 2006 Marvel Characters, Inc. Used with permission.

Figure 4.1. A New Nationalism?
"Cap for President" *Captain America* 250.

At the end of *Captain America* 267 (March 1982), the super-hero, having foiled an anticapitalist revolutionary group, walks off with one arm around a reformed female terrorist named Maggie, and another around a formerly disillusioned black man. Maggie says, "Maybe I won't be rich or famous . . . so what? Those things aren't America. People are America, ordinary people willing to help one another out of the despair, who are willing to share a little love along the way."[21] This is neither the progovernment message of the early 1960s, nor a restatement of the social commentary of the early 1970s. Government is not offered as a solution; "people helping people" is defined as the way to bring "this American dream of ours" to life. Government is not seen as the venue through which American values can be made real; it will instead be the private realm to which people turn to secure their dreams of America for themselves and for their families.

Preserving and Creating Families

Americans became increasingly concerned with family in the mid-1970s. The rising divorce rate, delayed marriage, and the increased number of people living alone, both seniors and young adults, seemed evidence that the basic infrastructure of American society was threatened. Critics from both the right and the left saw in this a source of the social conflicts that had characterized American society for the past decade. Christopher Lasch would see it is a loss of hope, as people no longer had a "haven in a heartless world."[22] This concern stretched beyond political calls for strengthening families. After the airing of the TV mini-series based on Alex Haley's book *Roots*, interest in genealogy exploded. The National Archives was receiving 2,300 requests for information per week.[23] Peter N. Carroll links the rise of interest in genealogy with a resurgent interest in American history, at least as commercialized nostalgia.[24]

In superhero comic books, the family becomes a central topic of concern throughout this period: the breakdown of the family is a frequent source of trouble for Captain America; Joe is driven to revenge against those he sees hurting his son largely because his own family had been under such stress. In *Captain America* 259 (July 1981) a neo-Nazi motorcycle gang has lured the son of a friend of Captain America into a life of crime. The weakness of the family is what gave the boy the potential to be led astray. "He had a rough time growin' up," his father explains to Captain America, "what with his mom dyin' early on, and I'm afraid I've never been too good at showin' affection. So while I tried to do right by him I guess we were never as close as we should've been."[25] When Captain America tells the son that his father loves him and wants him to come home, that is enough and the family is reunited.

Even when specifically political stories appear during this period, it is the issue of family that lies behind the conflict. In issue 267 (March 1982) an assassination attempt is made on Captain America by a revolutionary group that wants to overthrow the capitalist system in America. Everyman, a masked character armed with a tricked-out sword, offers to kill Captain America for the group. Meanwhile, while talking to some children in Harlem, Captain America is harassed by a group of unemployed men (only one of whom is black). The black man spits on the hero and tells him, "I've got your number, hero. You hung out in ghettos back when it was fashionable, but no more." After one of the children tells Captain America that this is his brother, the superhero takes them all to the Avengers' mansion. The black man tells him, "Instead of calling the cops or leaving the runts high and dry you decided to reach out a little, and that puts you in solid with us, if you can dig it." A news broadcast informs them all that Everyman has killed several police officers, and Captain America leaves in search of him. Meanwhile, Everyman is talking with one of the members of the revolutionary group, Maggie, whose brother was captured trying to assassinate Captain America. She and Everyman swap stories of their struggles against poverty and their abused childhoods. Everyman's father had been widowed, and he died poor. This led his son to "lead the revolution that would give all good men control of their lives" and make them aware of the falsity of the American dream. When he and Captain America fight, Everyman takes Maggie hostage and threatens to kill her, revealing that all he has wanted is television coverage because "I want to matter, I want to stand up above the crowd. I want to make all the rich pigs walk in fear of me . . . people are gonna remember me."[26] Like the black man earlier, he spits on Captain

America. After easily defeating Everyman, Captain America walks away with his arms around both the black man and Maggie. The revolutionary attitude is revealed as a sham, a way of getting attention rather than a means of achieving seriously held goals. That both Maggie and Everyman are products of poor families and that the black man is turned around by decent treatment of his brother suggests that if the family is healed then everything else will take care of itself. The children of poverty can achieve the American dream if they will simply work in the system and help one another out. This can heal both racial and class conflict, without any reference to government whatsoever.

During the depths of the Cold War in the 1950s, communists had been seen as attempting to subvert America by undermining the family. In the mid-1970s, the threat comes not from the communists but from the U.S. government. Familial dysfunction is linked to poor economic management by the government in *Captain America* 284 (August 1983), where Captain America intervenes when he finds a man threatening his wife and children with a gun. The gun turns out to be unloaded, and the wife pleads with Captain America, "Please don't call the cops . . . he's been outta work for close to ten months, we've barely been getting by on unemployment, an' with another baby on the way. . . ." When the husband goes on a shooting rampage in New York, Captain America again confronts him. "I gave this country all of myself that I had to give. Fought in Korea, worked my butt off for thirty years, never once leaving the straight and narrow, an' where did it get me? Nowhere!" the man yells at Captain America. "My kids are growin' up with less than I had. My whole life's a freakin' joke. I'm a disgrace!" When Captain America tries to calm him by telling him things will get better as they did after the Great Depression, he replies, "Bull! Ya' can't just make things better with a lot of stupid, empty words."[27] These two meetings bracket an interlude where Captain America as Steve Rogers attends a party with his friends in Brooklyn Heights and afterward watches *Yankee Doodle Dandy* in his apartment with his girlfriend, Bernie Rosenthal, preparing to tell her that he loves her (which he does on the last page of the book). The disintegration of the family in the story thus bookends and highlights the development of Captain America's own surrogate family, that which helps give him the strength to face the challenges posed by the difficult political economy of the early 1980s. That the shooter references the Korean War rather than the Vietnam War (although the age of his children would suggest that the latter should be his battle) discloses the degree to which the government policies of the 1960s are being rejected at this time.

Because government is no longer a trusted solution to social problems, family emerges in these stories as an appropriate venue for social service. The problems heroes face derive from broken or perverse families; the solution is often found in returning to a more functional family unit. Family, rather than government, is frequently offered as the solution to social problems. So, too, the superhero's family begins to become a central element of storytelling in this period. For Captain America, a new concern with the Steve Rogers identity will relocate him to an apartment building filled by twenty something singles who constitute a sur rogate family. Many of the stories will focus on his interaction with these people, with Captain America frequently acting to help them or others with whom they work.

Iron Man will similarly adopt several versions of the surrogate family. The first returns Madame Masque and Jasper Sitwell from the early 1970s, adding a novice superhero for Iron Man to mentor, Jack of Hearts. In this configuration Madame Masque becomes Tony Stark's lover, with Sitwell the jealous spurned paramour. This group will collapse when Madame Masque turns on Iron Man for battling her father, the evil Count Nefaria. Real family apparently trumps surrogate family. The second configuration includes Tony Stark's pilot, Jim Rhodes, who is introduced in a retelling of Iron Man's origin as a soldier in Vietnam at the time of Tony Stark's capture by the communists and his creation of Iron Man. There is also a potential love interest in the new director of security at Stark Enterprises, Bethany Cabe. The third group, emerging out of an extended, transformative story arc, will retain Rhodes but remove Bethany Cabe and add a brother and sister team of scientists who accompany Stark to California after his second bout with alcoholism. Some personal background is also offered for Tony Stark, presenting him as the brilliant child of wealth and privilege, whose parents never really understood him, and who is now isolated and alone from those around him. This isolation, a central feature of his character, is given psychological underpinnings and used to support the story of Tony Stark's alcoholism. During his period as an alcoholic derelict, Stark will befriend the pregnant Gretel, an alcoholic like himself. Only when she dies giving birth will he stop drinking, seeing the child as hope for the future. A central mechanism for nesting the heroes within families is the retelling of the heroes' personal histories. Adding increasing details to the histories and private lives of the superheroes is another feature of the domestication of the retreat into privacy.

Genealogies and Reinventing the Past

For both Iron Man and Captain America, retelling past histories is a key element of the late 1970s and early 1980s. Captain America, in particular, becomes obsessed with the history of his alter ego, and much time is devoted to offering extensive details of his history. The amount of space devoted to confrontations with supervillains will decrease. In 1969, the average issue of *Captain America* devoted over eleven of twenty pages (58 percent) to confrontations between superhero and villain. In 1981, the average issue devoted less than ten of twenty-two pages (44.3 percent) to such conflicts. This represents the increasing attention devoted to the private life of the hero and to the actions of the group of friends and allies created as a surrogate family for him. Conflict between superhero and supervillain will often be tangential to the story, thrown in as a necessary element of the genre but not central to the story line. Conflicts instead focus on individuals with personal problems or the hero's quest for emotional well-being.

This period begins by offering more details concerning the two lost decades in which Captain America was frozen in ice. In one story he finds that he was captured by a Nazi scientist who planned on flooding the United States with nerve gas in 1945. After defeating the scientist he was exposed to a low-level dose of the nerve agent; the interaction of the gas and the serum that made him Captain America is used to explain how he survived being frozen in ice. Subsequent to this he goes on a quest to find his familial history. Government documents reveal him to be the son of a diplomat who lived in suburban Maryland. Because this rings false to him, he enlists a psychologist to use regression therapy, through which he discovers that he was, in fact, a poor child from the streets of New York.[28] The regression, however, has an unintended consequence and reverts him, physically, to his weak condition prior to the administration of the super-soldier formula. During a battle, as his adrenaline begins to flow, he returns to his physical state as a superhero. In this sequence the emphasis is on psychology and internal dynamics rather than issues of ideology or cultural identity. Where the previous period had emphasized the social identity of the superhero, this period stresses his personal history, his psychological makeup, and his emotional state. It also links the concern with the hero's private life to a distrust of government; Captain America's past is obscure not merely because of the hero's poor memory but because the government falsified the records to keep his identity a secret during World War II. The result is that as Captain America seeks to find out more about himself from government records, those records are untrustworthy and intentionally misleading.

Having found himself to be a child of working-class New York, Captain America relocates himself within the city's working class. He moves from Manhattan to Brooklyn Heights, living in an apartment house in which several other blue-collar singles live. His interaction with his neighbors becomes a central element of the stories for the next several years. Frequently he is called upon to don his costume in order to help solve their problems, or they are drawn into his battles with supervillains as a result of their friendship with Steve Rogers. And, as Steve Rogers, he gets a job as a freelance graphic artist. Previously his only job had been as a police officer where he was working undercover for the commissioner to root out corruption within the force. Now with a new apartment (and a bit of a distance from Manhattan, super-hero central), new friends, and a new job, Steve Rogers begins to take form as a fully emotional character more important than Captain America.

Iron Man goes through a similar process, although the retelling of personal history is less an obsession than in the Captain America books. Because one of the main dramatic elements of the character has always been the isolation of millionaire playboy

Tony Stark, represented by his encasement in armor, it is more difficult to create a stable family for him. This, however, serves to highlight the link between declining family and social pathology.

Throughout this period a central story line will be attempts by various actors to take over Stark Enterprises, the industrial conglomerate headed by Iron Man's alter ego, Tony Stark. In each case Stark will fall into an ever deeper despair over his own place in the world. The first such attempt, by superrich super-villain Midas, will lead Stark to contemplate giving up his super hero life and role as corporate leader to retreat into a life of leisure with his new-found love, Madame Masque. He is drawn back to his corporate and social responsibilities by friends and agents of the Supreme Headquarters International Espionage, Law-Enforcement Division (SHIELD), who explain the threat Midas poses if he controls the government contracts of Stark Industries. Most signficantly Stark is led to return to his duties through an image of his dead parents telling him that he is a failure for rejecting his duties.[29]

The second attempt to take over Stark Enterprises comes from SHIELD itself, which sees Stark's unwillingness to pursue defense contracts and the increasingly threatening actions of Iron Man as detrimental to national security. In this case, Tony Stark retreats into self-loathing and alcoholism. The alcoholic story line exists for only one issue.[30] When Stark stops drinking through the help of his female security chief Bethany Cabe he finds a new resolve and regains control of his company.

The third attempt—by megalomaniacal industrialist Oba-diah Stane, who wishes to control the global economy and take power from political leaders—is much more involved. This story was written by Dennis O'Neil, the same writer who was credited with bringing political and social relevance to comic books with his run on *Green Lantern/Green Arrow* in the early 1970s. Those political concerns, fueled by the New Left ideology that O'Neil endorsed, have been transformed into private concerns with the character of Iron Man. This highlights the evolution of cultural concerns over the 1970s, from political engagement with social conflicts to a concern with personal issues.[31]

Running for over three years, the series begins with Stane creating a number of battles for Iron Man and blocking contracts for Stark Enterprises. He even hires a young woman to pose as a potential love interest for Stark, though she only rejects him at his weakest moment. When she does, Stark again retreats into the bottle and stays drunk for several months. Losing his company to Stane, Tony Stark ends up living on the streets as a wino while his pilot, Jim Rhodes, assumes the mantle of Iron Man. This story line, begun in issue 163 (October 1982), will continue until issue 200 (November 1985), when Tony Stark resumes his role as Iron Man. He begins drinking in issue 167 (April 1983) and stops drinking in issue 182 (May 1984). While most of the book will often focus on Jim Rhodes as Iron Man, the continuing story of Tony Stark is the gripping part of the tale that kept readers coming back month after month and dominated the letters page. Even when the emphasis was on Rhodes, the psychology of the narrative could not be neglected; much of the Rhodes story line stressed his growing addiction to the power of the Iron Man armor. Rhodes's reaction to the overwhelming power he possessed in the armor mirrored the hopelessness of Tony Stark as he drank himself into oblivion. These addictions reinforced one another and culminated in a battle between Rhodes and Tony Stark, both clad in different versions of the armor, one recovering addict fighting another. After Stark reassumes the role of Iron Man, he creates a different suit of armor for Rhodes, who will adopt the nom de guerre of War Machine, serve as Stark's sidekick for several issues, and ultimately gain his own, short-lived comic book title in the 1990s.

Captain America will also adopt a new sidekick. Jack Monroe, the Bucky from the 1950s who had fought Captain America in the early 1970s, returns. Now cured of his racist dementia, he has been released from suspended animation and set loose on the world. Unwilling to be Bucky, SHIELD and Captain America allow him to adopt the role of Nomad, the hero created by Steve Rogers after he quit being Captain America in the wake of the Watergate scandal. Nomad will appear for several months alongside Captain America but will ultimately strike out on his own. He will have his own short-lived title in the early 1990s.

Nomad and War Machine represent an increasing concern with the private lives of the human alter egos rather than the superheroes. Jack Monroe, like Captain America, is a man out of time, a 1950s-era teen released into the 1980s. Jim Rhodes begins as a friend and confidant of Tony Stark. Additional characters will emerge to people the stories. Captain America's girlfriend, Sharon Carter, herself a SHIELD agent, will be killed off, replaced by a civilian, Bernie Rosenthal. Arnie Roth will be introduced as a childhood friend of Steve Rogers, who appears on his doorstep and becomes a featured player in several stories. Roth, notably, is a homosexual, with a partner—Michael—although this is never stressed in the book. Tony Stark will acquire a third coterie of friends, as alongside Jim Rhodes and Bethany Cabe are added Morley and Clymenestra Erwin, two engineers who help Stark establish his new West Coast firm. This will also be true of villains in the stories. The Red Skull in Captain America will acquire his own family. While Iron Man's villains do not acquire as much history, they increasingly appear as private characters who attack Iron Man through his Tony Stark persona. All of this further demonstrates the retreat into the private realm of this period, the increasing concern with a psychologizing of the characters that reflects the popular desire for a retreat from public responsibilities in the twilight years of the Cold War.

Accepting the Hulk

Probably because of the success of the *Incredible Hulk* television show, the comic book was slower to exhibit the changes evident in other books during this period. The popularity of the character in the television medium may have frozen the character in a particular form to maintain its popularity. Also, the Hulk had, in many ways, retreated into the privacy of his alienation in the early 1970s, and thus he had fewer changes to make to adapt to the changed environment of the late 1970s and early 1980s. The Hulk had already been moderately psychologized, particularly with the addition of the character of Doc Samson, a psychologist brought in for consultultation (but who himself became infused with gamma rays, acquiring superstrength and green hair).[32]

By the early 1980s, however, even the Hulk begins to come ever more into the fold of the other Marvel heroes. Stories increasingly focus on the private life of Betty Ross, Bruce Banner's long-suffering girlfriend; her father, General Ross, the Hulk's tormentor; and Rick Jones, the boy whom Banner saved from the gamma blast that turned he himself into the Hulk. The Hulk's exploits also become domesticated and tend to involve private matters and personal stories rather than alien invasions and otherworldly exploits.

In one important story arc, the Hulk is infused by an alien raccoon (yes, raccoon) with more gamma radiation and gains the intelligence of Dr. Banner.[33] Now in control of the fury of the Hulk, Banner can stop the senseless violence of his alter ego. Captured by a villainous group known as the U-Foes, the Hulk's plight is televised. Seen by the television audience as a victim, the Hulk is granted amnesty by the president after he escapes and moves from uncontrollable force of violence to true hero. He is accepted by the world at large and revels in the end of his alienation. A New York City parade to celebrate his heroism is followed by a parade of Marvel heroes, all of whom express their joy that the Hulk can now "take his rightful place on this podium of power." With tears in his eyes, the Hulk states, "For once in my life the world is beside me instead of against me."[34] He is the prodigal son returned to his superhero family, and while the celebration is very public it is the private emotion of the Hulk and the idea of family that seems to dominate. While this acceptance will last for a time, it will soon fade as Banner's anger again releases the Hulk as a beast. Captured by other heroes he will be exiled to another dimension of existence by Dr. Strange to keep the world safe.

The Life and Death of the Red Skull

Steve Rogers's quest for a personal history culminates in a confrontation between Captain America and his nemesis, the Red Skull, in a story arc that runs almost two years (1983–84). Much of Steve Rogers's private life is brought into this tale, and the Red Skull is himself given greater personal background to match. The story involves not only Captain America but his new girlfriend, Bernie; his new sidekick, Nomad; his childhood friend Arnie Roth; the Falcon; and a minor character drawn from the mid-1970s, Dave Cox. The Red Skull acquires a daughter named Mother Superior and a henchman named Holst, and he is joined by Baron Zemo, the son of the same Zemo who caused the death of Bucky. The story begins with an attack by Zemo upon

Captain America through Arnie Roth, which results in the death of Roth's lover, Michael, and Zemo's recruitment to the cause of the Skull by Mother Superior. It culminates in a battle between Captain America and the Red Skull in which the Skull dies. The plot developments, character treatments, and arguments made during the course of this story arc reveal the degree to which the constant introspection of this period differs from and grows out of the earlier identity crises.

The use of characters reveals much about the period. The character of Dave Cox is particularly telling. Originally appearing in several issues in 1973, Cox was a Vietnam War veteran who had lost an arm and now declared himself a pacifist. In his original appearance he was a rival to Captain America for the love of Sharon Carter. His pacifist ideology was a foil against which the violence of Captain America could be played. The argument, as made by writer Steve Engelhart, was that both positions were valid and that both characters were noble and heroic in their defense of their beliefs. The ideological conflict was resolved as Captain America and Dave Cox recognized the validity of each others' beliefs and the common concern they shared for upholding their convictions.[35]

Cox's reappearance has him a victim of mind control by Mother Superior, who turns him into a violent serial killer known as the Slasher. While the argument of pacifism versus combating evil is reiterated briefly, the main object is not to demonstrate and reconcile conflicting ideologies but to suggest the psychological struggle within Dave Cox. Mother Superior has found within his psyche a tendency toward random violence and has made it dominant. The final denouement is not a resolution but a suppression, where the Slasher, in the midst of a killing blow against Nomad, stops himself and proclaims, "Whatever you've done to me, whatever filth you've untapped in me, I'm still a man and I will not kill!"[36] Having bested this violent streak with his own will and broken Mother Superior's mind control, Dave Cox appears to lie dead. The struggle to suppress his inner demon against the power of Mother Superior's mind control is too much.

As noted earlier, the dominance of the mental over the physical is stressed during this period, and the emphasis is on internal psychological struggles. The previous appearance of Dave Cox had revealed cultural conflicts between generations (those of World War II and the Vietnam War) and ideologies (pacifism and combat) and represented deep fissures within the American culture at the end of the Vietnam War. This conflict has now been displaced to an internal conflict between the violent and pacific nature of one man. Personalized, the tension becomes merely a psychological conflict, not representative of a cultural divide. While Dave Cox's apparent death is a bad thing—he leaves a wife and baby behind—it represents the costs of failing to control one's own psychological impulses and does not represent a major chasm in America culture.

The reduction of what had previously been portrayed as social conflicts into personal struggles is also demonstrated in the battle between the Red Skull and Captain America. Now an old, dying man, the Red Skull has launched his final plan to destroy Captain America. This is no longer a battle between competing ideologies—Fascism versus democracy—as it had often been in the past; now it is simply a personal conflict between two enemies. The personalization of this conflict becomes increasingly evident as the story progresses. Mother Superior has used her mind control on Nomad to get him to administer a serum to Captain America that will make him age so that he becomes an old man like the Skull. After this is revealed, Captain America is forced to relive the battle with Baron Zemo in which Bucky is killed, although this time he is able to save his young sidekick. This is as the Skull wanted it, for as he tells the younger Baron Zemo, "To be worthy of the Red Skull's hatred is to be worthy of his respect as well. And there is no man alive I respect more than Captain America. Our decades-long war is reaching its end. He will soon die by my hand alone and I wish him to face death with a heart unstained by guilt."[37] Not only are the importance of internal emotional states emphasized in this sequence (removing Captain America's guilt) but an identarian relationship is woven between Captain America and the Red Skull. This becomes more pronounced in the next issue, in which the personal history of the Red Skull is developed. His origin had been told before— how a poor, ignorant bellhop had been specially trained by Adolf Hitler to be the ultimate Nazi—but now extensive personal background is added. The Skull's mother died in childbirth and left him with a violent father who blamed the baby for her death. Left an orphan when his father committed suicide he becomes a street urchin, stealing to stay alive. As a teenager he rapes and kills the only woman who ever shows him kindness.

After the war the Skull, like Captain America, is caught in suspended animation, only to awaken in the 1960s. He meets a young woman whom he initially mistakes for his mother. He sleeps with her solely to produce a son to maintain his legacy of evil, but it is a daughter that is born, and the woman dies in childbirth. Initially planning to kill the child, he chooses instead to raise her to seek evil as he does. He concludes his story by noting, "My daughter was an able student, Captain, with an agile mind and a black heart. Yet, for all her wisdom and skill she was still a woman! And I realized at long last that no mere woman could ever hope to take my place."[38] Unbeknownst to the Skull, Mother Superior is listening to his tale. He then informs Captain America that he recently realized he is aging and dying and he intends to take Captain America with him. He locks himself in a bunker alone with Captain America so that they can fight to the death.

The Red Skull's story emphasizes psychology, rather than politics, in explaining his evil and deepens the identity being drawn with Captain America. Both were born poor children, but where Steve Rogers's youth was spent in a loving (albeit poor) family, the Skull is a product of the streets. The story suggests that if the Skull had been born into the same situation as Steve Rogers he might have turned out similarly. The oedipal imagery of the Skull's bedding someone he mistook for his mother suggests a profound psychological disturbance that might explain his penchant for evil. Where the previous versions of the Skull's history had emphasized the role of Hitler in his training, in this version Hitler appears on only one page out of eleven. The Skull is said to have surpassed Hitler in evil, and that during his suspended animation he had come into touch with a true cosmic evil. Minimizing the political elements that had been central to the Skull's persona in previous periods, this story emphasizes his social and psychological makeup, suggesting his evil is born less from politics than from his personal "dysfunctions."

The battle between the Skull and Captain America lasts for two issues but never becomes a political or ideological battle. It

instead remains a conflict between psychologies and social enti-
ties. As Captain America and the Skull duel in a bunker, Captain
America's friends come to search for him. Mother Superior, who
has seen the Skull reject her as unfit to follow him, begins to battle
Baron Zemo, whom she sees as a rival for her father's affections.
While Captain America duels the Red Skull, Mother Superior
battles Zemo, and Captain America's friends approach, Captain
America relates these three events to himself and the Skull, showing how they are different. The result of the Skull's grand plan
is the possibly fatal injury to his subordinate Zemo, inflicted by
his daughter, who now looks on him with hate. Captain America
points to a monitor showing his friends searching for him and
defines that as hope. Not a battle of politics, not freedom versus
tyranny, but whether one has friends and family is the central element of conflict defined here. What had been a political conflict
for nearly four decades has now been domesticated and brought
within the private realm. As Captain America and the Red Skull
battle for what seems to be the last time, the Skull weakens and
Captain America is poised to kill him. Refusing to do so, he holds
the Red Skull as he dies. At that moment, a comatose Dave Cox
awakens to tell his wife that Captain America had been helping
him fight for his life. As the story ends, Captain America carries
the dead body of the Red Skull sans mask out of the bunker past
Nomad (dressed as Bucky) who asks who the old man is. "He's
yesterday," replies Captain America (also sans mask). "He's the
past. And it's time, at long last, to bury the past, for good."[39] Having found his own personal history, Captain America now seems
to be divorcing himself from his public, ideological past. Along
with the Red Skull and the past, he seems to suggest, are buried
World War II, Nazism, the Cold War, and public duty.

Throughout this story the retreat into privacy is very pronounced. Whether it is the enhanced personal and psychological background of the characters, the redefinition of conflict as
personal rather than political, or the emphasis on family and
friends rather than on fascism versus democracy it all points to a
concern with private life rather than public responsibility. In an
era of discos, tax cuts, and shady financier Michael Miliken and
his film counterpart Gordon Gecko, the American public was
ready for a break from thirty years of the Cold War. Having lived

through the social turbulence of the late 1960s and early 1970s, and having experienced the crisis of confidence Jimmy Carter identified with the growing belief in the limits to growth, Americans seemed more concerned with feeling good and exploring internal states rather than framing issues in the broader political economic context. The Red Skull, from uber-Nazi into victim of oedipal conflict, is emblematic of the domestic trend of the retreat into privacy.

The Rebirth of Iron Man

The story of Tony Stark's alcoholism (*Iron Man* 167–82) culminates in his sobriety and his move from New York to California. This is part of a migration of several Marvel stories from the East Coast to the West Coast, most prominently in the creation of a new supergroup, the West Coast Avengers (a series that would last for 102 issues). As noted above, Stark does not resume his Iron Man identity until issue 200. Instead, he is part of a group of Stark International refugees from Obadiah Stane, which includes Jim Rhodes as the new Iron Man and scientist Morley Erwin and his sister Clymenstra. They make the journey to California to start anew in Silicon Valley. This also represents the growing interest of Marvel Comics in business in California—particularly the translation of their comic book characters into television and film.

In the context of the period, this move represents the creation of a new family for Tony Stark. The main supporting characters of previous incarnations, most notably Pepper Potts and Happy Hogan, have long since vanished, retreating into the privacy of married life. Within this new family Stark is willing to play the role of older brother. While they try to get their new electronics firm (Circuits Maximus) off the ground, Rhodes as Iron Man will confront a series of minor villains, several of whom are agents of Obadiah Stane, whose obsession with the destruction of Tony Stark supercedes his goals of world conquest.

Rhodes begins early on to express jealousy of Tony Stark, the fear that Stark wants to resume the role of Iron Man, and to complain of headaches. For his part, Stark persistently denies that he wants the armor, suggesting that being Iron Man was one of the reasons for his drinking. His failure to achieve a fully realized self as Tony Stark was rendered impossible because of his dual identity; he sees the Iron Man identity as a means of evading the problems of Tony Stark. When in the armor he is nearly invulnerable, a condition that Stark cannot achieve, but wishes he could. This, he suggests, is one of the main reasons he became a drunk.[40] Yet the armor is the public self of Tony Stark, Cold Warrior. The rejection of the armor, offered for personal reasons, is also a rejection of a public self. Stark's unwillingness to be Iron Man is itself a retreat into privacy.

Increasingly Rhodes acts with violence and hostility toward Stark and others and seems uncaring about the effects of his superhero battles on civilians. This reaches a turning point in a conflict with Vibro, a supervillain who emerges just as the Stark refugees arrive in California. Escaping from prison, Vibro poses a threat to the community. Rhodes dons the armor and follows him, cutting a swath of destruction and refusing the request of a policeman to lure Vibro to an unpopulated area lest he get away and a make a fool of Jim Rhodes. Fearing the threat posed to civilians by Rhodes, Tony Stark puts on the first suit of Iron Man armor he ever made, and the old Iron Man (Stark) faces off against the new (Rhodes). Stark disables Rhodes and reiterates that he does not want the armor. Rhodes explains that the armor fulfills his lifelong desire to be a hero, describing it as "the only thing that means anything to me."[41] Stark suggests this is something they have in common, and they renew their friendship.

After this Rhodes goes in search of a cure for his headaches. This leads him to medical science, which fails, and ultimately to an Indian shaman who takes him on an introspective journey into his own mind. Again the emphasis on a personal emotional journey to solve a physical problem highlights the psychologization of problems. In what is portrayed as a conversation between Jim Rhodes and his own soul Rhodes reveals that he feels inadequate to be Iron Man, that he has stolen the armor from Tony Stark, and that this guilt is the source of his migraine.[42]

As both Stark and Rhodes come to terms with their relation to the armor, Obadiah Stane still lingers on the horizon. He kidnaps Stark's former director of security (and brief love interest), Bethany Cabe. Stane's father is revealed to have committed suicide in front of him as a child, who dedicated himself

Figure 4.2. Old Iron Man and New.
From "A Duel of Iron" *Invincible Iron Man* 192
(March 1986), 22.

to developing his mind and a fascination with games. What had originally been portrayed as a megalomaniacal desire to control the world (common enough throughout all superhero comics) is now reduced to a personal conflict between Stane and Stark, who are equated. Both were the orphaned children of wealth. Where Stark turned his painful youth into service through building weapons for the military and as Iron Man, Stane seeks wealth and power for his own ends. Stane is allied with Iron Man's long-time foe Madame Masque, who defines her conflict with Stark as highly personal—revenge for Iron Man's defeat of her father,

Count Nefaria. Stane turns on Madame Masque and brainwashes Bethany Cabe into believing she is in love with him. Rhodes and Stark, in the new and old Iron Man armor, respectively, try to save Cabe, but to no avail. Meanwhile, Stane has his men kidnap all of Tony Stark's old friends—his secretary, Mrs. Arbogast, Pepper Potts, Happy Hogan, even the child born to fellow alcoholic Gretel. Having captured all those Tony Stark had held dear, Stane attempts to kill Stark's new friends with a bomb that succeeds in killing Morley and wounding Clymenestra and Jim Rhodes. The kidnappings and death make Stark relearn that he has responsibilities to others as well as to himself. He comments,

> I was afraid. Not of Stane . . . of myself, of myself as Iron Man.
> I feared that if I put on Iron Man's armor, I'd become what I
> was . . . what I fought so hard to stop being . . . a drunk. Don't
> call me Iron Man . . . that's what I've been saying for months.
> I've denied my connection to that identity. Even when I put
> on a metal suit, I refused to let you call me that name. I've
> been a fool or a coward or both. My friend is dead, others
> may have been captured, taken who knows where. I could
> have stopped him before it got to this point but I didn't. But I
> will, I'll accept the responsibility that goes with who I am and
> I will stop Obadiah Stane.[43]

The question of identity here is not a public but a private one. Captain America's interregnum as Nomad was a crisis of public faith; his return to the role of Captain America was an act of renewing that faith and redefining the public sphere. Both Tony Stark's rejection and resumption of the Iron Man identity represent a personal identity crisis, resolved not through a reengagement with the public realm but with a connection to those who matter to him in his private life. The postalcoholic Iron Man is not a renewed public servant but a man who has now come to terms with his own private demons, a more emotionally secure human being.

Stark dons a new red-and-white armor and goes after Stane, who has built himself a more powerful armor, calling himself the Iron Monger. Stane's armor, however, is computer controlled, and Iron Man is able to defeat him by breaking the radio link between the armor and the computer. Defeated, standing in front of the burning building that had been Stane International (formerly Stark International), Obadiah Stane kills himself just as his father had.

The confrontation between a computer-controlled Iron Monger and a human-controlled Iron Man suggests the importance of the human identity within the armor shell. After three years of alcoholism, loss, and rejection of the identity that he feared controlled him, Stark is now firmly in control of Iron Man and is able to step forth as a fully realized self. This makes him capable of assuming the hero's mantle again and facing one-dimensional villains like Stane. But aside from his personal redemption from the bottle, there is no renewal of public faith here; there is no public identity to Tony Stark/Iron Man.

Abortive Nationalism

By the early 1980s, the Cold War appeared to be heating up again. The Soviet invasion of Afghanistan and the crackdown on the Solidarity movement in Poland were seen as evidence of the USSR reasserting dominance over its sphere of influence and again trying to expand it. Coming at the same time as the revolutions in Iran and Nicaragua, it seemed that Soviet expansion was taking advantage of American weakness. The apparent impotence of the United States in gaining release of U.S. hostages in Iran, the installation of a second communist regime in the western hemisphere, the second set of oil shocks in 1979, and the coincidence of double-digit inflation with rising unemployment all seemed to confirm the notion that America was in decline, becoming impotent, and would have to accept the permanence of the age of limits. Such a limited nation would seem ill-equipped to face a resurgent expansionary communism.

While serious attempts to reassert American control of the Cold War and the economy began during the presidential administrations of both Gerald Ford and Jimmy Carter, it was Ronald Reagan who breathed new life into Cold War rhetoric and actions. Carter had sought to punish the USSR for invading Afghanistan by cutting grain exports, withdrawing from the 1980 Olympics in Moscow, and pulling the SALT II Treaty from the U.S. Senate. The dismantling of the regulatory state that would be considered a hallmark of the Reagan administration had been begun by Carter. Carter had also appointed Paul Volcker as chair of the Federal Reserve Board, knowing full well the recessionary policies the radical inflation fighter would impose. But Carter had too much negative baggage to offer the optimistic assertions of nationalism that Reagan could scatter throughout his campaign and presidency. Having presided over the America of decline, Carter could not offer a vision of "morning in America" as could Reagan; nor did he have the actor's skills at communicating his message.

It was the symbolism of the Reagan administration more than its actions that garnered support and created the conditions for his 1984 landslide victory. In 1982, few would have predicted such a lopsided triumph. With unemployment at its highest level in fifty years and interest rates at unprecedented highs, homelessness was a growing concern in the United States for the first time in half a century. While inflation was coming under control, tax cuts and increased government spending ballooned the federal deficit. Between 1980 and 1986 the national debt would quintuple. But Reagan was able to maintain sufficient support throughout this period by challenging the Soviet Union at arms control, in Berlin and in Central America. Reiterating an earlier version of world politics that saw the Cold War as a Manichean struggle between good (democracy and capitalism) and evil (totalitarian communism), in which all evil came from Moscow (the "evil empire"), Reagan was able to offer a vision of the world that placed the blame for America's problems clearly on the external enemy and on those who had been naive enough to think America could ignore that enemy. This fit well with a vision of a country beset by social disorders produced by liberal economic and social policies that had undermined self-reliance and a Christian morality. By linking a nationalist vision with calls for a return to Christian values and limited government, and benefiting from a modest and short-lived economic recovery beginning in 1984, Reagan was able to turn his 1980 majority, based largely on rejection of Carter, into a stunning 54 percent majority in the 1984 election.

Reagan attempted to rebuild an American consensus using the rhetoric of progress, freedom, and individualism in much the same way that rhetoric was used in the 1950s. Arguing that communism was in decay in the face of man's inherent desire for freedom, he asserted a vision of democratic progress as long as Americans did not become cynical. Everywhere, he told the British Parliament, "man's instinctive desire for freedom and self-determination surfaces again and again."[44] In an other speech he posited that "[t]he self-doubts of the 1970s are giving way in America to a new era of confidence and a sense of purpose. Communism is not the wave of the future and it never was—freedom is."[45] Fostering this desire was the American mission. This would be done in part by demonstrating the strength of a free market in America and reasserting Christian values.

In asserting unending progress but linking the basis of that progress to "traditional" values, Reagan was rejecting twenty years of government activity as misguided and un-American. "[G]overnment is not the solution to our problems," he famously stated in his first inaugural; "government is the problem."[46] His call for a renewal of values, which included his antiabortion and antiwelfare positions as well as a stance in favor of prayer in public schools, all challenged the policies of the 1960s and early 1970s. Progress, for Reagan, would be made possible if America could erase the cynicism and secularism of those two decades. "Together we've chosen a new road for America," he told Americans in a national address in 1982. "It's a far better road. We need only the courage to see it through. I know we can. Throughout our history, we Americans have proven again and again that no challenge is too big for a free, united people. Together, we can do it again. We can do it by slowly but surely working our way back to prosperity that will mean jobs for all who are willing to work, and fulfillment for all who still cherish the American dream."[47]

His foreign policy rhetoric also returned to the language of the 1950s. In a series of speeches in Germany, Britain, and France commemorating the fortieth anniversary of the end of World War II, he never failed to link the allies' battle against Nazi Germany with the U.S. confrontation with the Soviet Union. This was most clear at a speech at Bitburg Airbase in Germany, where he told the assembled NATO troops that the lesson of the war against Nazism was that "freedom must always be stronger than totalitarianism and . . . good must always be stronger than evil."[48]

In his first inaugural address Reagan defined America as "this last and greatest bastion of freedom" and called upon Americans to "begin in an era of national renewal." This renewal would be made possible by reducing the size of government and advocating a Judeo-Christian morality. "Freedom prospers when religion is vibrant and the rule of law under God is acknowledged," he told the National Association of Evangelicals.[49] Quoting Whittaker Chambers on the equation of Marxist ideology and Eve's temptation in the garden ("Ye will be like Gods"), he moved from his opposition to abortion and support for prayer in school to opposing a nuclear freeze as a misguided stance in the "struggle between right and wrong and good and evil." The tide of history was against communism and in favor of freedom. The desire for freedom inherent in all humans was leading to the isolation of the Soviet Union; its own totalitarian system was generating economic decay. Soviet evil, he argued, would be defeated by the progress of freedom, led by America, if the country would only rededicate itself to "bedrock values of faith, family, work, neighborhood, peace, and freedom."[50] This would create a new American consensus, defined by opposition to the Soviet Union and support for the limited government, proreligious values advocated by Reagan: "When it comes to keeping America strong, free, and at peace, there should be no Republicans or Democrats, just patriotic Americans."[51] Opposition to the values defined by the president was representative of a lack of patriotism, or, in earlier (but now discredited) terms, *un-American.* Again asserting the centrality of progress to his vision, he concluded, "I've never felt more strongly that America's best days and democracy's best days lie ahead."

While Reagan clearly achieved the support of the majority of the American electorate in 1984, his policies had created a vocal minority of significant size. A large antinuclear movement spread throughout the United States and Europe, and opposition to his administration's aggressive policies in Central America led to widespread demonstrations. His controversial foreign policies were a major point of contention around the country.

The growing conservative ideology was apparent in the way readers were consuming Captain America. One letter writer applauded the turn away from social commentary and the search for identity: "Cap has thrown off the fads and the fallacy that morality is a transient concept. . . . In returning to the old values and representing what is best in America, Cap has once again become, for the first time in many years, truly worthy of being the rock-ribbed, John Wayne–style symbol of American solidarity."[52] While writer Roger Stern tried to assert that Captain America was not as conservative as the letter writer suggested, others saw the book trending in the same manner. A March 1982 letter describes a page in a battle scene in issue 263 as sending his "heart and adrenaline racing" with a "feeling of pride coursing through my body." With the hero buried under a band of evildoers, the reader sees "An arm and a clenched fist break free, bursting into view, crushing the enemy. Significantly it is the right arm. The third panel screams an image of good over evil, right over wrong (perhaps even, America over all else?), as your hero emerges from the oppression and repression. . . ."[53]

The symbolism of an optimistic and resurgent progressive nationalism that leant such support to Reagan was partly a co-opting of American symbols to partisan ends. The preemption of such American symbols, from flags to the military to Bruce Springsteen's song "Born in the USA," found its way into Captain America comics briefly with the creation of "Team America," a group of flag-clad motorcycle stunt riders. Introduced in *Captain America* 269 (May 1982), they had their own short-lived (twelve-issue) series. Captain America would himself be used by conservative moralists in several issues (277–280, January–April 1983). When he discovers that his image appears on a poster stating "America as It Once Was. America as It Could Be Again" he confronts the group behind it, the Coalition for an Upstanding America, a "group of concerned citizens—men and women of considerable wealth—who have banded together to speak out against the erosion of moral values in our country."[54] Captain America orders them to remove his image because he stands for all Americans and not one sectarian group. As the story unfolds it is revealed that the leader of the group was hoping to make money from the campaign, but is thwarted by his own son, who has gone mad and, calling himself the Scarecrow, is now murdering members of the group and their families. The attempt to usurp American symbols for nationalistic ends is thus offered as illegitimate, serving the interests of the wealthy, and ultimately is undermined by their own familial dysfunctions. The attempt to reassert a Cold War nationalism, while reflecting the growing conservatism of the moment, never approached the level of hegemonic discourse and was thus aborted in the face of continuing distrust of public action.

As the mid-1980s approached, the obsession with self, personal history, and the retreat into domesticity began to recede. Having weathered a crisis of public identity in the early 1970s, comic books retreated into escapism and self-involvement but began to return to a public concern in the mid-1980s. Tony Stark had rediscovered his private identity and could resume his heroic role as Iron Man. Steve Rogers had acquired a history and had been domesticated; Captain America was now grounded in a real society, no longer an anomic ideal in search of a people. The liberal consensus was long dead, and battle lines had been drawn in the politics of identity. This conflict would be different than the past, though. Thirty years of Cold War policy, of seemingly unchecked executive power, of covert activities, of extensive government intervention into the private sphere, had placed the belief in American virtue and the virtue of American institutions at risk. Distrust of government was part of a general questioning of a basic theme in the rhetoric of American identity. Thus the reengagement of citizens with the public realm that would come in the 1980s was of a different ilk than that of the 1960s or 1970s; the reborn Cold War of Reagan's America did not have the same cultural power and could not generate the same kind of hegemonic consensus as the Cold War of the 1950s, even with the attempt at monopolizing American nationalist symbols to do so. The weakened rhetoric of virtue would mean that no public utterance would be completely trusted. Irony and order would have to sit side by side as the Cold War was reborn and ended.

5

Betrayal in the Mirror: 1986–1996

THE 1980S WERE A PERIOD OF VAST TRANSFORMATION in the American political economy. The Fordist industrial structure of large firms tied to strong unions that guaranteed lifetime job security and provided extensive benefits was coming undone. It would be replaced by the leaner, more mobile firms of the era of globalization, which did not provide such benefits nor guarantee such job security. The decline of Fordism also heralded a changing political landscape. Without strong industrial unions and the large-scale firms with which they worked, there was decreasing support for New Deal liberalism, a trend already apparent in the tax revolt of the late 1970s. The economic underpinnings of the Democratic Party's ideology and electoral base were thus vanishing. The creation of the Democratic Leadership Council, chaired at different times by both Michael Dukakis and Bill Clinton and seeking to create a probusiness economic ideology within the Democratic Party, gave rise to intraparty tensions that would become very apparent during Bill Clinton's first term as president.

For their part, the Republicans were also facing a transformed base of support. The emergent economic reality saw manufacturing industry declining in importance. Rather than producers, the new economy was driven by stockholders and investors. Increasingly, the Republicans found their support among financiers and stockholders. The decline in employer-provided pensions and the deregulation of the securities indus-try created the conditions for a massive explosion of middle-class investment in equities. For millions of Americans in the mana-gerial and professional classes, this meant that the pocketbook issues that concerned them were no longer being served by the Democrats but by the Republicans, who based their economic policies on controlling inflation and decreasing income taxes. While most Americans still adhered to a civil libertarian inter-pretation of government social involvement, there remained a significant population who saw society on the wrong moral track. As the new managerial class migrated to the suburbs to start their families, they became receptive to a message about the need to protect society from the threats of moral decay, evident in the rising crime rate, the epidemic of crack cocaine in urban areas, and the growing incidence of sexually transmitted disease, of which the new scourge AIDS was the most frightening. These moral threats could easily be defined in terms of stereotypical identity, as blacks sold crack and homosexuals were most likely to get AIDS. The manner in which moral decay was defined had an unsubtle identity subtext.

As the American economy groped toward a new reality, nei-ther political party seemed capable of offering a dominant vision that would capture a majority of Americans. Instead, presidential elections turned on personality, and Congressional elections were unable to offer definitive outcomes. Between 1980 and 2000 this resulted in only two years in which both houses of the U.S. Congress and the presidency were controlled by the same party. With elections unable to define a clear winner, the parties resorted to what Benjamin Ginsberg and Martin Shefter call "politics by other means."[1] Congressional investigations, court battles, ideological fights over presidential nominees, media attacks, and scandal-mongering became regular occurrences.

The material and cultural changes of the 1980s left Americans anxious. The economic recovery begun in 1983, coupled with an optimistic vision of the American future, propelled Ronald Reagan to his stunning win in the 1984 presidential election, but it did not give him a united government. Nor was the economic recovery received with the exuberance that growth in the 1960s had been. Instead, it was received cautiously and with trepidation. Rather than heralding a bright future, the economic growth of the 1980s was seen by many as a blip on the downward spiral of economic decline. Linking American economic woes to Cold War interventions, Paul Kennedy compared the United States to imperial Britain and saw inevitable economic decline as a consequence of imperial overreach.[2] Political scientists focused on the end of U.S. hegemony as a consequence of economic decline.[3]

As the Cold War approached its entropic end, the international stability provided by the bipolar division of power began to wane, and new, unexpected national security threats loomed on the horizon. International terrorism seemed to be on the rise in the 1980s, and it increased greatly after the collapse of the Soviet Union. Ethnic and regional conflicts seemed to be ubiquitous and unending, from Sierra Leone to Somalia, Cambodia to Colombia, and Baghdad to the Balkans. The reduction in tension between the United States and the USSR, and the ultimate end of the Cold War, seemed to open a Pandora's box of ills upon the globe, and the hope of security and a peace dividend seemed frail and ephemeral.

The actual bipolar conflict of the Cold War had vanished from comic books well before the Cold War itself ended. Between 1971 and 1986 there were only ten issues of the Captain America and Iron Man series that hinged on communists as enemies. The era of détente, the lessening of tensions between the United States and USSR, had rendered that conflict less omnipresent. Increasingly preoccupied with personal lives, and increasingly aware of the excesses of government action, often justified by Cold War security needs, Americans lost their obsession with communists and retreated into privacy. Even the reinvigorated Cold War of the Reagan administration did not bring the communists back as the major enemy. Only after 1986 did the communists start to reappear, but not as enemies bent on destroying the United States. Between 1986 and 1996, twenty-eight issues of the Captain America, Iron Man, and relaunched Nick Fury series would focus on communist threats; twenty-one of those came after 1991 and focused on the potential threats of held-over Soviet technology (often superheroes) falling into the hands of international terrorists, or unreconstructed Soviet leaders attempting to recapture past Soviet glory. Secret organizations, now defined as terrorist or anarchist organizations rather than totalitarians bent on global domination, were more common; thirty-eight stories in the three books had the heroes battling Advanced Idea Mechanics, Hydra, or other secret global organizations between 1986 and 1996. An equal number of stories (thirty-nine) cast as the source of threat an overly interventionist or corrupt U.S. government. The decline of the bipolar conflict brought to the fore concerns over global security and threats from unknown sources for unclear goals. This, however, was tempered by continuing distrust of government; the Reagan Revolution, built as it was on presenting government as the problem rather than the solution, could not bring back trust in institutions of authority even while garnering support for the new Republican coalition.

Anxious to see the social liberalism of the 1970s rolled back, conservatives became more vocal and militant after Reagan's second inaugural, while opponents entrenched themselves in their positions to block further rollback. The stagnation of movement on civil rights and rising immigration by non-European populations meant that racial and ethnic issues remained unaddressed while they became more politically salient. Reductions in social programs meant that the poor faced an increasingly deprived existence; declining opportunities for the urban poor were countered by the increasingly lucrative crack cocaine market and an apparent epidemic of violent crime.

All of this generated a profound unease in American culture and politics. The consensus identity of the Cold War had been shattered, and no one knew exactly what was to take its place. Americans had reemerged from their retreat into privacy, but they were not sure into what they had emerged. These concerns about the lack of cultural cohesion informed an academic quest for answers that ranged from Allan Bloom's criticism of cultural relativism on college campuses to E. D. Hirsch's list of things every American should know.[4] Robert Bellah and his colleagues conducted a study in the early 1980s seeking "how to preserve or create a morally coherent life."[5] Reagan's campaign slogan of 1984, "It's Morning Again in America," implied that after the era of limits to growth, it was possible to reestablish a notion of

American virtue reminiscent of the early 1960s. This, however, proved illusory. The new engagement with the American scene could not be achieved with the consensus arguments of the 1950s nor with the traditional comic book heroism of truth, justice, and the American way. A decade after the Watergate scandals and the fall of Saigon, readers would not accept such pat answers. Instead they responded to stories in which institutions were not accorded full trust, ulterior motives abounded, and irony was the dominant voice. In this context, heroes became darker, more sinister, and less easily discernible from villains.

While the Reagan administration had attempted to reconstruct the myth of American progress as the centerpiece of a new modal identity, the growing fractiousness concerning his economic and Central American policies, the antinuclear movement, and ultimately the Iran-Contra scandal had rendered that reconstruction problematic. With increasing income inequality and homelessness, an economy beset by junk bonds, leveraged buyouts, and massive layoffs, and apparently increased domestic and international violence threatening security, people did not necessarily see progress. Instead they saw looming security threats, economic uncertainty, and social disruption. The world of the mid-1980s was a dark place with an uncertain future, even if, for the moment, things were going well. The looming darkness, many believed, was produced by America's own actions, overextending itself economically and militarily during the Cold War, permitting the growth of a controlling and uncontrollable national security state, and promulgating an ideology of tolerance that had given rise to epidemics of drug use, sexual promiscuity, abortion, and social violence. When Americans looked at the world in the mid-1980s, they feared. When they looked at the institutions of authority—government, business—and in the mirror, they saw betrayal.

Betrayal is a major theme of comics of this period. Nick Fury will have to destroy the Supreme Headquarters International Espionage, Law-Enforcement Division (SHIELD) because he is betrayed by several of his agents. Captain America will find himself betrayed twice by the very source of his powers, the super-soldier formula. The first time is in an antidrug story line; in the second the formula will kill him. Iron Man will be betrayed by his technology, engaging in two sets of "Armor Wars," and will ultimately betray the Avengers, the supergroup to which both he and Captain America belong. These betrayals are especially significant because in each case the betrayal is linked to the Cold War. In most cases, it is some form of self-betrayal, in which America is seen as betraying itself in pursuit of Cold War policies. In this period, the Cold War will come full circle, and the ideas and tropes that had justified U.S. action in the 1960s will be used to deny the validity of those claims. America will be portrayed as the betrayer of America as the Cold War comes to its conclusion.

To face a world characterized by betrayal, heroes need to be more willing to take action, even at the expense of legalities. In the face of a more threatening world of betrayal, the American people seemed to want someone to do more than uphold ideals of tolerance, justice, and fairness to which they could aspire. They sought someone to defend them from these threats no matter the cost. Hence the world of betrayal also becomes the world of vigilante justice.

Vigilantes

On December 22, 1984, thirty-nine-year-old electronics specialist Bernhard Goetz shot four young black men on a New York City subway. Goetz claimed they were trying to rob him. Three years later, a jury acquitted him of attempted murder and assault, finding him guilty of carrying an unlicensed firearm. The national debate surrounding "the subway vigilante" reflected the continued racial tension in the United States and the growing fear of violence in American society and the desire to see something done. This is reflected in the emergence of a new vigilante style of comic book hero. Such characters as the Punisher, originally cast as a villain in Spider-Man comics in the mid-1970s, emerged as a hero beginning in 1986, bent on vengeance for the brutal murder of his son and daughter. That the Punisher learned his killing skills as a soldier in Vietnam testifies to the link between the perceived breakdown of order in the 1960s and 1970s and the newer, more vicious heroes of the late 1980s and early 1990s. Similarly, Daredevil, a character who had been on the fringes of Marvel comic books for years and in danger of cancellation, was reinvigorated by writer/artist Frank Miller in the early 1980s; Miller turned him from a blind lawyer seeking justice into a ninja warrior, and then into a brutal vigilante.

Nor was this trend limited only to Marvel comics. Frank Miller and colleagues' reimagined Batman in *The Dark Knight Returns* (1986) presents the hero as a psychotic, ruthless agent of Thanatos, bent on a career destroying criminals to make up for his perceived failure to save his parents. Miller sees the existence of a creature such as Batman as a catalyst for the existence of villainy; Batman's villains are portrayed as existing only because he exists. Alan Moore and Dave Gibbon's seminal *Watchmen* (1986–87) also shows a dark side both to the world and to the costumed heroes. These would be followed by ever more violent and vicious vigilantes.

The art of the books became increasingly challenging. Due in part to the popularity of the work of Frank Miller, many books came to be drawn in a similar style. Gutters all but disappeared as panels abutted one another and were ordered in nonlinear ways with insets, varied shapes, and multiple-page spreads. Lines became less distinct and images bled into one another. The result was a somewhat more chaotic visual expression, with the distinctions between images increasingly obscure. This mirrored the more porous moral boundaries between heroes and villains as vigilantism became dominant and the heroes and villains were increasingly equated within the stories.

Both Captain America and Iron Man would undergo some revision to render them compatible with the more sinister version of the superhero that was becoming popular. In both cases, this took a specifically ideological form. With thirty years of narrative and ideological continuity that rendered these characters specifically political creatures, this move could only go so far. To touch the darker mood of Americans it was necessary to create darker versions of these characters. In the mid-1980s, Steve Rogers would, for a time, be replaced as Captain America by John Walker, who would ultimately become the hero U.S. Agent. Also, the Bucky from the 1950s, now cured of his dementia and released as Nomad, turned increasingly dark and got his own book title. So too would Jim Rhodes, the replacement Iron Man from the alcoholism story line, and now designated War

Machine, get his own title. These more violent heroes would come to be less concerned with the constraints of legality than their predecessors and represent the darker notion of justice that characterized this period.

The Return of the Gray Hulk

Similarly, a grimmer version of the Hulk develops during this period. The emergence of a darker, more sinister version of the Hulk coincides with a complete psychologizing of the character that transforms the monster from a product of technology gone wrong to a mental illness. Revealing the Hulk to be a product of Banner's split personality, psychologist Doc Samson and SHIELD agents try to cure him. In so doing they unleash a new version of the Hulk, a gray beast.[6] The original Hulk had been gray, but the color did not work well with the inks and papers used in comic book publishing, so the color scheme was changed to green. Now, the original color returns, along with a smarter but less moral Hulk who becomes an enforcer for a casino operator, and romantically involved with a young lady of questionable morals, in the mob infested Las Vegas of the Marvel universe, taking the name of Joe Fixit.[7] Throughout this extended story, Joe battles to keep Banner from asserting control over the Banner/Hulk persona. Frequently images of Banner and Joe talking are offered, representing the internal battle for control of Banner's brain and the body of the Hulk.

This sequence blends the elements of the two previous periods. In the 1970s, the Hulk was transformed from unleashed emotional fury to alienated victim of society, now he is a mental disease. This privatizes the transformation of Banner into the Hulk completely. At the same time, by making the Hulk a more sinister, less virtuous figure he is brought into the "grim and gritty" texture of the mid-1980s. This suggests the proximity of the threats perceived by Americans in the 1980s. No longer is the threat from outside the nation, nor now even from public authorities. It is much closer, internal to the self, threatening from within; something inside the American self is the major source of insecurity.

In the early 1990s the source of Banner's transformation into the Hulk is defined as specifically psychological, as a "split personality," a manifestation of Bruce Banner's psychosis. A common narrative element in the Hulk stories is the separation of Bruce Banner and the Hulk, or the ability of Bruce Banner to control the Hulk persona. In each case, this had been triggered by physical means; even the psychologist Doc Samson had twice separated the Hulk from Banner through physical means in the early 1970s and in the 1980s. This physical characterization of the Banner/ Hulk relationship in which an external agent (gamma radiation) created the transformation is now replaced by one in which an internal state (multiple personality disorder) is the source of the transformation.

After the gray Hulk stories (nearly four years, issues 330 to 376) the gray and green Hulks battle with Bruce Banner within Banner's mind. Doc Samson brings this confrontation about in an attempt to "integrate" the Hulk personas with Banner. The story reveals that Banner was abused as a child by his father, who also killed his mother.[8] After working through the repressed memories a new Hulk persona emerges who will be known as "the professor," where the Hulk body exists but is controlled by Banner's mind. This "integration" of Hulk personas, however, is premised on the new knowledge of the familial dysfunction that created the psychosis in Banner. Family, which in the former period had been offered as the means of achieving progress and virtue, is cast as a source of the insecurity that Americans face. The abusive family of Bruce Banner's childhood is the basis of his rage, of his transformation into a monster, the betrayal that creates the Hulk.

The Captain and the Superpatriot

Between 1986 and 1987, Captain America faces several new villains, each of which draws him into a darker and more violent mode. The first is a murderous vigilante called the Scourge who kills supervillains. When Captain America defeats and unmasks him, he finds that the Scourge is merely a vengeful individual who claims, "The American justice system is far too lenient. I have to compensate for it."[9] Learning of justice and morality from the B-movie Westerns his director-father made, the Scourge could not stand that his brother had become a criminal. He killed his brother and then moved on to deliver his brand of justice to other criminals. His gray hair and reference to Westerns suggests that he is a child of the 1950s; again the Cold War through which Captain America slept has come back to haunt him, this time in the guise of murderous violence. While the brand of justice meted out by Captain America is counterposed to the murderous, fratricidal violence of the Scourge, the end of the story suggests that it is the Scourge's methods that are the trend of the future. The Scourge, captured, unmasked, and bound by Captain America, is shot by an unseen sniper from a clump of bushes as the sniper calls, "Justice is served." Captain America stays with the critically wounded Scourge while the assailant gets away but wonders. "Who could it have been? . . . Is there more than one Scourge?"[10]

Captain America next faces an international terrorist group led by the anarchist Flagsmasher. The terrorists have hijacked an airplane and taken the passengers as hostages in some nameless European country. Infiltrating the terrorist group, Captain America begins to defeat them when a desperate terrorist opens fire on the hostages. Seeing it as the only way to stop the bloodbath of innocents, Captain America picks up a gun, shoots, and kills the terrorist.[11] The cover of the book does not mirror the anguish expressed by Captain America in the story, but depicts him with a vicious snarl, firing an automatic weapon toward the reader, implicating her in the violence and breakdown of order against which the hero wages his battle.[12]

The growing violence continues, as Captain America is next forced to confront a superpowered hero who calls himself the Superpatriot and fights a band of strong men wearing Captain America masks calling themselves the Bold Urban Commandoes, or Buckies. While this confrontation turns out to be staged to draw Captain America into a fight with the Superpatriot, it creates continuing ambiguity about the virtues for which Captain America is supposed to stand. The Watergate story line from the 1970s had portrayed the enemy as an evil empire, albeit one that had grown up inside the American government. Its evil was clear, and its contrast with the virtues of Captain America was obvious. Here it is a private scheme with no connection to the government; nor is the Superpatriot necessarily a villain. He is overzealous and more violent than Captain America, but he is not necessarily malicious.

Mark Gruenwald (w), Paul Neary and John Beatty (p). © 2008 Marvel Characters, Inc. Used with permission.

Figure 5.1. The Answer to Our Disorder
From "Ultimatum" *Captain America* 321 (September 1986).

The confrontation between the two reaches a zenith when a terrorist parachutes onto the Washington Monument with a nuclear weapon. That same day Captain America is called before the secret government Commission on Superhuman Activities, which oversees the government's superpowered agents. Asserting government copyright over the costume, shield, and name of Captain America and claiming that he was never formally discharged from military service, they seek to force Captain America to be an agent of the U.S. government. While Superpatriot stops the nuclear-armed terrorist, Steve Rogers debates what he should do. Ultimately deciding that he cannot serve the ideals of America and a specific regime, he turns in his uniform. Accepting his resignation, the commission selects John Walker, the Superpatriot, to be the new Captain America with a black sidekick named Bucky (who will later change his name to Battlestar).[13]

In a world populated by murderous vigilantes and international terrorists, the values of democratic tolerance that had characterized Captain America in the 1970s and early 1980s seemed inadequate. His own resort to murder led Captain America to extensive soul searching about what he had done; such regrets needed to be put aside to face the more sinister world of the late 1980s. Hence, John Walker the Superpatriot is given the mantle of Captain America. Where Steve Rogers used only appropriate force, practiced patience, and never started a fight, Walker is violent, short-tempered, and aggressive. When a former associate who had supplied him with the drugs that gave him superstrength tries to infringe on his new government role, Walker steals some powered military body armor and beats him to a pulp (*Captain America* 334, October 1987). In subsequent adventures, Walker frequently uses too much force, and on several occasions he kills his opponent in a fit of rage. He realizes that this is wrong. After his actions he will claim, "This is not what Captain America would have done" and vow to do better. Nonetheless, he continues to be driven more by rage and violence than by reason and necessity.

The real Captain America, meanwhile, has donned a black costume and adopted the name of the Captain. With his various partners from over the years (the Falcon, Nomad, and a new ally, Demolition Man) he travels across the country, frequently doing battle with the members of an international terrorist group, the Serpent Squad, while keeping tabs on the "new" Captain America. In one bizarre story, he returns to Washington, D.C., to battle the leader of the Serpent Squad, the Viper, who is dosing the capitol's water supply with a chemical that turns people into lizards. Drinking a glass of water before going to bed, President Reagan is affected by the chemical. Issue 344 sports a cover of the Captain under an American flag in combat with a lizardly President Reagan and sporting the words "The Captain vs. the deadliest snake of all."[14] After battling the president and foiling the Viper's scheme, Captain America becomes the object of a government search led by the commission. Having apprehended his allies, they now seek to capture him because they "cannot permit someone with such a blatant disregard for national security to remain at large." This disregard is evidenced by his continued actions as a superhero, despite the commission's stripping him of his Captain America title. The issue ends with a presidential address, assuring the American people that everything is safe and that the president and his wife were never in any danger. The final image, however, is of President Reagan making this speech and sporting the fangs of a snake.

In the next issue,[15] several features of the previous stories come to a head. John Walker is ordered by the commission to find Captain America, continuing the vision of the government as bent on squashing American values. Before he can get started, however, he is contacted by members of a vigilante group he has been battling called the Watchdogs that espouses a racist nativism tinged with a Christian rhetoric. The group bears a strong resemblance to other racist groups, such as the Sons of the Serpent, who had been a staple of the Marvel villainy for several decades. The religious overtones of the Watchdogs are, however, new to the 1980s and may represent a commentary on the emergence of the Christian Right. The Watchdogs, in an attempt to force Captain America to leave them alone, have discovered his secret identity and taken his parents hostage. When he arrives at his boyhood home, the Watchdogs prepare to lynch him. Breaking away from the noose he battles the group's members, who fire their weapons indiscriminately, killing his parents. In a fit of rage he kills the entire group. He is arrested and taken back to Washington, where the head of the commission suspends him and chastises him, telling him that he was told to stay out of the Watchdogs' business. Walker continues on a spree of vengeance. Finding the two former associates who revealed his identity to the Watchdogs, he burns them alive.

The story arc moves to its inevitable conclusion as Flag-smasher returns and defeats John Walker. He holds him hostage, demanding that the real Captain America face him. After being saved by Steve Rogers, John Walker confronts the head of the commission, who is killed during their conversation by a poison that shrivels the skin and turns it red, creating a Red Skull face on the victim—the trademark of the now dead Red Skull. When tracing the source of the poison, he finds himself face-to-face with Steve Rogers. It is revealed, however, that this is in reality the Red Skull. The rise of the Superpatriot and the removal of Steve Rogers from the role of Captain America is explained as a plot of the Red Skull. The Skull, whose mind was preserved when he died several years earlier, inhabits a cloned body of Steve Rogers, wearing a face he claims is appropriate for decadent America.[16] As Rogers and Walker battle (as they must) the Red Skull watches. After Rogers defeats Walker, the Skull comes to speak to him, intending to kill him with his "dust of death" hidden in a cigarette. As he gets ready to deliver the toxin, Walker throws his shield, forcing the Skull to inhale rather than exhale. Without killing him, it returns his face to its normal Red Skull appearance as he escapes. Confronting the commission afterward, John Walker states that he no longer believes he should be Captain America, and he returns the uniform and shield to Steve Rogers, who will again become Captain America.

While this multiyear story arc culminates in the return of the virtues of the traditional comic book superhero, it exhibits the elements of the darker tone that characterize comics during this period. The government is not trustworthy and may be insidiously involved in the schemes of villains. Referring to President Reagan as the deadliest snake of all, leaving him with fangs even after he has been cured of the lizard toxin, and having the commission strip Steve Rogers of his uniform, all are evidence that the government will go to any lengths to assure its own agenda, and that the agenda is likely to run counter to national interests. While the commission is ultimately portrayed as having been manipulated by the Red Skull, the Skull manipulates only one member. The others went along and were actively involved in the whole John Walker project. The one bad apple did not spoil the bunch; it was already rotting. Linking the government to the Watchdogs, a high-tech version of the Ku Klux Klan with the rhetoric of the moral majority, comments directly on the relationship between the Reagan administration and the Religious Right. Most stunning is the return of the Red Skull in Captain America's body. While the identarian link between the Red Skull and Captain America had been asserted during the period of the retreat into privacy, here it is made with less subtlety. In the previous period its function was psychological, to demonstrate the effects of emotional development on the propensity to good or evil. Here it is a direct comment on the American political economy of the 1980s. Neglecting the poor and civil rights while decreasing economic regulation and promulgating tax cuts that favored the richest segments of society, American policy could be seen as an economic eugenics. The rich get richer and the poor disappear.

By 1989, the comics seem to be suggesting that the world is more sinister and less safe than previously thought. The security that permitted the retreat into privacy is gone as the very providers of security have become America's betrayers. The orderliness that the Cold War had spawned has also begun to unravel. Both the Serpent Society and Flagsmasher are anarchists, bent on destroying all government and order. The emergence of such threats anticipates the collapse of the Soviet Union and the end of the stability that the bipolar Cold War conflict had brought. With new kinds of international threats, and a renewed belief in the potential of betrayal by the government, the comics seem to be sending a message that new actions, new behaviors, and perhaps new heroes are needed to provide for the safety of the world.

Corporate Raiders and the Evolution of Iron Man

Having barely survived alcoholism, losing his business and fortune, ceding his heroic armor to Jim Rhodes, and finally battling to get it back during the retreat into privacy of the previous period, Iron Man falls victim to himself in profound and repeated ways during this period. Betrayal is the only word that fits the story lines that run from the late 1980s into the mid-1990s, both in the Iron Man books and in other books in which Iron Man appears, most notably the Avengers series.

The cycle of betrayals in *Iron Man* 225–231 (December 1987 to June 1988) begins to unfold in a series called Stark Wars (although it will become known as the Armor Wars among followers of the book). Tony Stark discovers that technology that he has developed for his Iron Man suit has been stolen by his business rival, Justin Hammer, and sold to both superheroes and villains who have incorporated it into their own suits.[17] Taking on the guilt for all the evil committed by these villains ("If I hadn't developed the technology, they could never have hurt anyone"), Iron Man begins a vigilante war on all armored supervillains who have pirated his technology. While these actions are viewed as extreme by his superhero compatriots, nobody seems to get too upset about it. When Iron Man begins attacking a government superagent who might be using his technology, and later takes on agents of SHIELD who use armor with this technology, opinion begins to turn against Iron Man. The opposition is so great that Tony Stark must hold a press conference in which he fires Iron Man as spokesperson for Stark Enterprises (an interesting act since, of course, Tony Stark *is* Iron Man).[18] The opposition reaches its heights, however, only after Iron Man flies to the Soviet Union to confront the two Soviet armored heroes, his longtime foes the Crimson Dynamo and Titanium Man. Crimson Dynamo, a Russian nationalist, will battle Iron Man out of duty; the Titanium Man armor, now controlled by Soviet supervillain the Gremlin, is being operated solely for the Gremlin's power. In the conflict among these three Titanium Man is destroyed and the Gremlin killed.[19] The killing of a Soviet villain in an attempt to regain control of his proprietary technology makes Iron Man a pariah in the United States to such an extent that Tony Stark must feign the death of Iron Man, pretending that the person wearing the armor is a new Iron Man.

Several things stand out in the series. The first is that conflict between superhero and supervillain is not driven by their crimes but by successful industrial espionage and pirating of proprietary technology. The vigilante war fought by Iron Man may be justified by Tony Stark's guilt at having this technology leak out, but it is still an attempt to recapture a copyright that is the heart of the action. Iron Man is willing to go to any extreme in this endeavor; while he does not seek to kill Titanium Man, there is no soul searching after his death at Iron Man's hands. The capitalist impulse that underlies the Iron Man character and had been seen as benign through most of his history has now emerged as a central element of an increasingly malignant structure.

The second thing that stands out is how the elements of this story, all familiar from previous periods and story lines, have acquired profound new meanings. Beating the Crimson Dynamo and Titanium Man had been a staple of Iron Man's anticommunism in the 1960s and a symbol of misguided loyalties in the 1970s and '80s. Now Crimson Dynamo is offered as a nationalist hero, doing what he must even though he is on short time (his term as Crimson Dynamo is up in a week), behaving with the honor and nobility that is clearly lacking in Iron Man. Iron Man is more akin to the Titanium Man/Gremlin, who flouts the orders of his party superiors and is motivated solely by self-interest rather than ideology or national security. The killing of Titanium Man renders Iron Man a pariah and symbolizes the death of the nobility within Tony Stark. He is not good enough to kill Crimson Dynamo; he kills Titanium Man and then must have Iron Man feign death, a symbolic murder-suicide. This presents a second familiar element of the Iron Man stories, which is the role of masks and identity. In the 1970s the multiple maskings of the many characters had symbolized a crisis of national identity. Here, however, the maskings are no longer subtle, unintentional elements but are instead conscious subterfuges employed by the character himself. Previously the ambiguity surrounding identity and masks was forced upon characters by circumstance rather than actively manipulated to the self-interest of the hero.

By the end of the Stark Wars series Iron Man has become much less of a hero in the standard comic book sense of the word. Nor has he become the vigilante for justice, as have Daredevil and the Punisher. He has, in fact, become what he had all along pretended to be—a private soldier and shill for a very large capitalist transnational corporation. He fights company battles, engages in industrial espionage, punishes those who spy on his company or benefit from that spying, all the while flouting whatever law stands in his way. There is no longer a pretense to serving a larger political cause or even a larger context beyond the corporation. A sequel series (Armor Wars II[20]) leads into another confrontation with the Mandarin,[21] in which Iron Man's origin is retold. This time, rather than being injured while surveying how well his weapons' systems functioned against the communists in Cold War Vietnam, Tony Stark is injured while investigating sabotage at one of his plants in Southeast Asia. Rather than being captured by a communist general, Stark is captured by a warlord allied with the Mandarin, a superpowered villain who is Iron Man's nemesis.[22] Everything becomes part of the corporate tale of Tony Stark, and thus the story becomes internally driven with no reference to outside context. By the 1990s Marvel's most political of characters has become devoid of politics, a mere cog in the capitalist machinery. Defending democracy, promoting national security, and securing some notion of justice is no longer relevant in these tales. Justice, for Iron Man, is whatever benefits Tony Stark. This is a very different kind of superhero.

Incomplete Avatars: Nomad, U.S. Agent, and War Machine

For several Marvel characters replacement players were created. Thor was to be replaced by Thunderstrike, Iron Man by War Machine, and Captain America by either Nomad or U.S. Agent. War Machine was Jim Rhodes, Tony Stark's friend and pilot who had taken over the mantle of Iron Man during Stark's alcoholic recovery. His short-lived series began with him going to work for an international agency that sought to improve conditions in developing countries. This led him frequently to involve himself in civil wars and other forms of localized global conflict. Picking sides in such conflicts was perceived by other heroes as anathema—an imposition of values by force on people who should be permitted to design their own fate. This led him into direct conflict with Iron Man and other heroes of long standing. Beyond this willingness to go where other heroes felt they should not, and his use of violence to solve political disputes, there was little interesting in War Machine. The book quickly lapsed into a world of interstellar fantasy and was canceled.

U.S. Agent was John Walker, the Superpatriot and replacement Captain America from the mid-1980s who became a member of the Avengers West Coast and appeared in one four-issue miniseries. U.S. Agent was a direct representative of the U.S. government, and thus he frequently found himself at odds with the more independent members of the superhero community. He often used excessive force and held a rigid set of ideological beliefs. He retained the attitudes of Superpatriot even if he was now a U.S. Agent. His major role was to serve as foil rather than to be an interesting character in his own right.

Nomad, the most interesting of the three, was Jack Monroe, the Bucky from the 1950s. Originally resurrected in the early 1970s, he had been driven mad by the supersoldier formula he had ingested in the 1950s, becoming a paranoid, commie-hunting super-McCarthy. Defeated by Captain America, he was returned to SHIELD, where he was given both psychological and chemical therapies that supposedly cured him. He returned in the pages of the Captain America stories in the early 1980s, taking on the role of Nomad—the identity assumed by Steve Rogers when he quit being Captain America in the 1970s—and served as Captain America's sidekick for several months before striking out on his own. He returned periodically, each time a bit more jagged and vengeful. Finally, he would receive his own series in the early 1990s, first a four-issue limited series, then followed by an ongoing series that lasted for nearly two years.

Several aspects of the Nomad character are interesting. Because of his twenty-year history with Captain America, the ideological center of the Marvel political economy, Nomad is himself a comment on the American ideology. Second, Fabian Nicieza, the writer of the two Nomad series, had a taste for controversy and challenge that placed the character at the center of several debates. Finally, the book was clearly conscious of both the political and fictional histories of Captain America and made solid use of both to make its own commentary, generating a small but cultishly loyal fan base.

The chief eccentricity of the Nomad series is the introduction of a character named Bucky, the infant daughter of a drug-addicted prostitute who is rescued by Nomad. Given the mother's condition, Monroe decides to raise the child himself. Dressing her in the red-and-blue outfit of Captain America's sidekick (complete with domino mask) Nomad carries her on his back as he fights crime from the underground. As unsubtle a symbol for innocence as the child is, dressing her in the Bucky outfit that Nomad himself had worn during his days as a true believer renders it absurd. It is this absurd need for innocence that actually is the key to the Nomad character. Clearly more cynical than Captain America—he is willing to break the law to get the criminals, is willing on occasion to kill, and carries a shotgun— Nomad is also more romantic and thus more innocent than

Captain America. Unlike the other violent heroes of the 1980s Marvel universe such as the Punisher, Nomad clearly dreams of a better place, a golden age that might have once existed. If it never existed he is still sorry that he had to learn the truth about the world. Exhibiting this innocence in the wake of cynicism, Nomad travels through a multicultural world for the twenty-five issues that his series runs. During that time he deals with the Los Angeles riots in the wake of the trial finding the police officers who beat Rodney King innocent of criminal charges, with gay-bashing and hate crimes, with fears of HIV, with government–Native American relations, and with drug trafficking. The world of Nomad is primarily nonwhite, poor, and outcast, not at all the kind of story lines one would see for Captain America. Save for its happening in the early 1990s rather than the 1970s, this quasi-leftist vision of society would offer little more of interest if it were not for where it leads.

The last four issues, however, transform everything.[23] The last story tells of Jack Monroe's youth. He was born in Clutier, Indiana, on D-Day. His parents, as well as most of the town, were German expatriates and members of a terrorist, pro–German Bund group working to sabotage the American war effort. Young Jack bragged outside the house of what was going on, which led to the whole ring being captured by the FBI. He was sent to a foster home and had no recollection of this until his memories are recovered by the evil Dr. Faustus. He returns to Clutier to find that neo-Nazis have resurrected the Bund organization and are now linked to the militia movement in the United States. His own long-lost sister has returned to join this group. The organization is linked to a U.S. senator who had been a classmate of Nomad's in the 1940s in Clutier, and who is trying to use the group to overthrow the U.S. government and has ordered Jack Monroe killed by the FBI. Nomad ultimately defeats the movement, exposes the senator, and is placed back in suspended animation by a friendly FBI agent rather than killed.

Nomad's history, in which he is a teenage anticommunist patriot obsessed with Captain America and becoming a paranoid anticommunist in the process, is linked here to the Nazis of World War II. His parents were Nazis; his sister continues to be a Nazi. The comics of the 1960s linked the communists and

Figure 5.2. Nomad (Jack Monroe) Confronts His Past
From "American Dreamers Part 2: Favors Paid in Blood"
Nomad 23 (March 1994), 11.

Nazis as a major trope to identify objective good and evil. Now that identification has shifted; here the rabid anticommunist is identified with the Nazis, linking him to the foundational evil of the superhero comic. Where the trope had once been used to justify unquestioning faith in American virtue, now it is turned on that vision of America. It is the nationalists, the Nomad story seems to suggest—the zealots who want America for Americans (whomever they actually are)—and not the communists who are the true heirs of Adolf Hitler. The same trope that had given the 1960s comics their ideological identity is resurrected in the 1990s, but with a different object. Rather than offering a definition of the world around and outside America, it now offers a vision of the American self. The consensus self, the myth of the Cold War, is the problem for Nomad; that myth makes possible the evils of totalitarianism that the Nazis represent. With that myth gone, Nomad, wandering aimlessly to find a national identity to replace the myth he has lost, finds the opportunity to construct a multicultural world, with nuances of color and ideology that would be impossible to achieve with eyes clouded by the myth. Nomad seems to assert, in the midst of betrayals, doubts, and fears, that the collapse of the myth of American consensus is not a tragedy but an opportunity to see the nation for what it is rather than what we might wish it were. Rather than a window onto the past, Nomad becomes a mirror of the American present.

In these various stories the superheroes become more violent, and less constrained by legalism in defense of a notion of justice that is less clear but more desperate. Recasting the hero as vigilante is often linked to some form of betrayal. For Captain America, it is the attempt by the government to use him for partisan concerns, portraying politics as a betrayal of American values. Iron Man's own technology is being used for criminal acts, and this leads him to engage in violent corporate warfare. Nomad and War Machine adopt violent methods because of domestic and global problems that have been left unaddressed, a betrayal of the people by their governments, ultimately made very clear in the denouement of the Nomad series. The idea that the American government had betrayed the American citizen is common outside of comic books by the early 1990s. Extreme libertarianism is the source of much of this, from the antitax movement of Randy Weaver to the freedom of religion argument proposed by David Koresh to the revivalism of eighteenth-century political rhetoric by the militia movement. Betrayal of this eighteenth-century legacy is a seminal theme of the early 1990s, as Weaver met his fate at Ruby Ridge, Idaho, in 1992; Koresh in Waco, Texas, in 1993; and the militia movement emerged at its most popular around 1993. Betrayal is also the common theme of comic books at the end of the Cold War.

Captain America and the Betrayal of Self

In two significant Captain America stories the protagonist finds himself betrayed by the very thing that gives him his power, the supersoldier formula. In the first, Captain America finds one of his civilian allies has become addicted to a drug called ice, similar to crack cocaine. In trying to break the drug ring that supplies the dealers, Captain America accidentally ingests the drug, which bonds with the supersoldier serum in his blood.[24] Now permanently high on ice, Captain America becomes a brutal hunter of drug dealers, ignoring the pleas of his allies to help. Finally realizing what is wrong he concludes that the serum that gave him his strength is the equivalent of a steroid, and he has a complete transfusion in which the serum is removed. He retains his strength and skill but has lost the enhanced powers the serum gave him. Over time, the serum returns, having bonded with his marrow, but he is now free of the ice. The very elements that give Captain America his abilities to serve as the embodiment of the American dream also render him highly susceptible to the drug.

This minor betrayal is challenged later by a larger betrayal. Captain America finds himself becoming lethargic and easily tired. He discovers that the supersoldier serum is actually killing him.[25] He will have to adopt an armored costume to keep fighting crime, but he will ultimately succumb to the serum and die. The very thing that made him Captain America kills him. He is resurrected, but only by a complete transfusion of blood and marrow from the one person who is his true genetic match, the Red Skull, who inhabits a body cloned from Steve Rogers.[26] Betrayed by the supersoldier serum, Captain America owes his life to his nemesis, with whom he now shares a strong identity. He battles alongside the Red Skull to retrieve the Cosmic Cube, into which the Skull had placed the mind of Adolf Hitler, which has now become aware and is trying to remake the world into a Nazi utopia.

Adding to the sense of betrayal in this story, Captain America is reunited with his love interest from the 1970s, Sharon Carter, a SHIELD agent whom he had presumed dead. Instead, she had been on an undercover operation that went sour and was abandoned by SHIELD somewhere in the Caucasus Mountains. She survived by becoming a mercenary and has now returned, bitter and angry at her betrayal by SHIELD and, apparently, by Captain America. When finally the cube is retrieved and the Skull defeated, Captain America is called before President Clinton. To retrieve the cube, Captain America had to infiltrate a secret U.S. military base; security cameras revealed him attacking American soldiers alongside the Red Skull. Branded a traitor, he is stripped of his uniform and exiled from the United States. For several issues he fights alongside Sharon Carter to clear himself of the charges, ultimately saving the president from assassination and blocking an attempt to steal U.S. nuclear codes. An apologetic Clinton returns his shield and uniform.[27]

The series of betrayals in this story—Hitler by the Red Skull, Carter by SHIELD, and Captain America by his body and by the government—present a bleak vision of America in the mid-1990s. The Skull's betrayal represents the continued presence of evil, the clear villainy that Americans still see in World War II. That clear villainy, however, is represented as coursing through the veins of the icon of the American dream, because the Skull rejuvenated Captain America. Carter's bitterness at having been abandoned represents a betrayal that can be read on several levels. In one version she can be seen as a soldier abandoned by her government when missing in action. In another she is simply a casualty of the Cold War, abandoned to maintain U.S. deniability of covert actions against an enemy. In either case, her betrayal represents the human costs Americans paid to win the Cold War; her bitterness suggests the costs may have been too high.

The betrayal of Captain America by the supersoldier serum is most fundamental and most problematic. That which made him Captain America killed him. The suggestion might very well be that that which gives America its uniqueness is also causing its problems. That this is followed by the government seeing Captain America as a traitor compounds the interpretive dilemma. Captain America, undone by that which makes him who he is, reborn with the help of the evil that is his antithesis, and joining that evil to fight against American troops to defeat a greater evil makes it impossible to draw clear lines between good and evil, us and them. At the end of the Cold War, the quest for the "meaning of America" or a national identity is portrayed as empty.

Too many Cold War betrayals have intervened. While Captain America is cleared of charges, reborn and ready to defend the American dream at the end of the sequence, the journey to get there has not been a reeducation in the politics of virtue, as it was in the 1970s. It has simply been a sequence of betrayals that will, in all likelihood, recur. Perhaps the meaning of America in the post–Cold War world is simply to survive the inevitable betrayals and continue on. This Captain America will not do; for after one more issue, the series would be canceled and restarted along with several other titles under the Heroes Reborn story line.

The Betrayal of Nick Fury

Nick Fury vs. SHIELD (1989) tells another story of Cold War betrayal.[28] In this six-issue series, Nick Fury becomes a fugitive from SHIELD. The council controlling the organization since its inception in 1964 has become corrupt. Infiltrated by a Life Model Decoy (LMD) that has achieved sentience, the council has developed a secret plan to replace all SHIELD agents and corporate leaders with LMDs. They have created a religion surrounding this program, with the final goal of controlling the world to bring sacred order.

Again religion and politics are linked in the service of subverting the ideals of freedom and equality. The government is again easily manipulated by the very resources it has used to achieve its goals. As in the Captain America story line (albeit more symbolically) the Religious Right is linked to the subversion of fundamental political ideals for which the superhero is supposed to stand.

The indictment of the Cold War in this process is explicit in the Nick Fury series. One of the tactics of the council is to decide which agents will be more easily replaced by LMDs and turned to serve the new order. The agents are each posed the same question: If ordered by the council, would you kill Nick Fury? The two agents who were also members of Fury's World War II commando team, the Howlers, refuse. The agents recruited during the Cold War who had peopled SHIELD stories since the early 1960s all agree that they could. Trained by Fury to follow orders and the chain of command, they have been turned into automatons by the bureaucratic machinery of the Cold War. Replacing them with android replicas is almost unnecessary and goes unnoticed by other SHIELD agents. The only exceptions to this change are Fury's longtime girlfriend and SHIELD agent, Contessa Valentina di Allegra, and agent Clay Quartermain. Quartermain was introduced in the 1960s as a classic hero against which to portray the gruff, blue-collar heroism of Fury. Tall and blue-eyed with a flow of longish blond hair, Clay Quartermain was intrepid and brave, a classic adventurer with an innate sense of justice. In this story, his replacement by an LMD occurs before the attack on Fury. His is portrayed as the perfect replacement, the achievement of machine perfection. However, the LMD fails to see itself as a replacement and believes it is the real Clay Quartermain. The timeless heroism that his character represents cannot be undone; having been turned into machine he cannot be dehumanized. This contrasts with the Cold War SHIELD agents, whose heroism is bound by time and motivated by anticommunism rather than innate notions of justice. Having already been dehumanized by the machinery of Cold War bureaucracy, they easily become agents of the machine religion while Quartermain does not.

The Contessa's love for Fury also represents something outside of the ken of the machines and the Cold War agents. She is deemed a likely candidate by the council and turns Fury into them when he contacts her seeking safety. Still, she fights against being replaced and battles beside Fury in the end. Like the heroism that is embodied in Clay Quartermain, the love represented by the contessa transcends the limited scope of the Cold Warriors. Quartermain and the World War II agents represent a deep sense of justice and heroism that goes beyond the boundaries of national security, as the contessa's love goes beyond the realm of organizational duty. That all of the other agents, whose experience is limited to Cold War national security, are corrupted by the machines implies that the blinders of the Cold War continue to betray Americans into serving a false notion of justice.

This represents an interesting modification to the use of World War II in comic book mythology. In the 1960s, the Nazis and Soviets were equated to identify the USSR as an enemy, blurring the lines between World War II and Cold War opponents of the United States. In this version, only those who had fought in World War II can identify the enemy clearly, while those who were Cold Warriors only cannot see the true villain and are thus susceptible to subversion. The lack of moral clarity is identified here as a specific product of the Cold War, rendering U.S. actions themselves suspect. Apparently Nick Fury is not the only character who has suffered betrayal.

SHIELD Reborn

The success of the Nick Fury versus SHIELD miniseries gave birth to a new monthly Nick Fury title. *Nick Fury, Agent of SHIELD* would last fewer than four years, but it would demonstrate how much the Marvel universe had changed. Like the Nomad series, it attempted to resurrect the 1960s trope that equated evil with the Nazis, redefining the Cold War as largely a product of World War II. Letters from readers found this unconvincing, and several specifically rejected the connection.

The reborn SHIELD, now responsible to the United Nations rather than the United States, also stood for something else. Where the SHIELD of the 1960s was about law enforcement and espionage, international criminals as well as communists, the new SHIELD stands for Strategic Hazard Intervention Espionage Logistics Directorate. This sounds more like an environmental emergency relief agency that engages in some spy activity; sort of a global FEMA. The Directorate term suggests a managerial role rather than action. This new SHIELD consists of only seven agents, and of these only Fury has connections to World War II.

Beginning in issue 7, Fury and SHIELD face off against a global terrorist named Leviathan.[29] Leviathan is clearly meant as a mirror for Fury. Missing his right eye and sucking on lollipops (Fury has a patch covering his left eye and sucks on cigars) Leviathan corrupts army officers, enticing them to join his fanatical cult through charisma and brainwashing. He uses the connections of his military followers to locate a missing Soviet submarine whose secrets he seeks to gain. Locating and raising the submarine, he tries to sell its secrets on the black market, giving the lie to his claims of being a politically motivated terrorist, an anarchist. Instead, he seeks merely to reap the monetary reward of the sale, being in fact, a mere criminal. Fury defeats him by breaking his hold over the officers by presenting them with Captain America, an icon of all they believed in and loved. This reminder is strong enough to break Leviathan's hold over their minds, and they turn on him and defeat him.

The object of the tale is to offer the still faithful Fury as a foe of the faithless Leviathan, and to reinforce that message that all that stands between order and chaos is the faithful defender of order, Fury. The use of Leviathan as foil creates as many moral ambiguities as it suggests moral clarity. First, several references are made to Fury's commitment to SHIELD and the indoctrination

Figure 5.3. Competing Mind Controls
From "A Matter of Faith," *Nick Fury Agent of SHIELD* 10 (April 1990), 14.

of his agents. This can be taken as equivalent to Leviathan's brainwashing of his "converts." Leviathan's coven is cultish, its beliefs ultimately an empty charade covering Leviathan's plans for black-market riches. The beliefs that Captain America articulates to break the hold of Leviathan over the officers is, however, equally cultish. The battle is not one of faith versus infidelity but of counterfaiths cultishly maintained and sinisterly promulgated. This is reinforced by the imagery, with narrow panels linking Captain America's eyes to the eyes of the converted officers, suggesting a countermesmerism to Leviathan's mind control.

The series ends with the destruction of SHIELD. The centerpiece of the security apparatus of the Marvel universe had been destroyed and reconfigured as a globalized rapid response team. The destruction of the original SHIELD presaged the unraveling of the entire political economy of the Marvel universe. Built as it was on a foundation of Cold War conflict, the strategic configuration of the Marvel political economy came undone as the Cold War wound to an entropic end in the late 1980s. Nick Fury would hang around with SHIELD for four years until the title was canceled, and make periodic appearances in other titles, but he was always portrayed as an anachronism, a throwback to a different era. The other key figure to face such destruction and betrayal is Tony Stark/Iron Man, benefactor of both SHIELD and the Avengers, now lodged on the West Coast and struggling to come to terms with his own post–Cold War identity. Central as Stark had been to the Cold War configuration of the Marvel universe, even more central was his role in its undoing; rather than being the betrayed, Tony Stark will become the betrayer.

Closing the Loop: Iron Man's Betrayal

The Nomad series, which saw itself as a sociopolitical commentary on American society in the early 1990s, consciously resurrected a 1960s trope legitimating America's Cold War position and used it to criticize that very position. The Avenger's stories "The Crossing" and "Timeslide" less consciously used the continuity of the Avengers series to provide a similar criticism of Cold War America.[30] In this story the Avengers Mansion, which had been destroyed several years earlier, suddenly reappears in

Manhattan, but with an odd door located in the basement that cannot be opened. A series of strange occurrences involving the door culminate in the murder of one member of the Avengers and one ally. These murders are committed by an unnamed assailant who seems to have intimate knowledge of the Avengers. The betrayer is none other than founding member Iron Man. Iron Man has been a sleeper agent for the longtime Avengers' foe, Kang the Conquerer, who is now allied with former Avenger Mantis. Ultimately to defeat Kang, Mantis, and Iron Man the Avengers must find someone of the same genius level as Tony Stark. The only person they can think of is Tony Stark himself. They go back in time to find Tony Stark before he became Iron Man and bring him to the future to kill his future self and help them defeat Kang and Mantis.

Several elements of this story arc are relevant. The betrayer is the Marvel hero with the most intimate links to the Cold War. Tony Stark initially was an arms manufacturer who was captured by communists in Vietnam. As Iron Man he fights a multitude of Soviet agents, including Titanium Man, Crimson Dynamo, and the Black Widow. He is the chief technological supplier for Marvel's Cold War spy agency SHIELD. He helps found, and bankrolls, the Avengers. In many ways, Iron Man is the linchpin of the political economy of the Marvel universe. His betrayal of the Avengers suggests that at the core of society something has been profoundly disrupted and tainted.

Bringing the character of Mantis into this story deepens the link to Cold War history. Mantis was the first specifically Vietnamese hero in comics, created in the mid-1970s by Steve Engelhart in one of the most celebrated Avengers story arcs. That story, as well, included Kang the Conquerer, although he was defeated, and Mantis supposedly ascended to a cosmic entity known as the Celestial Madonna. Still, her presence in the book in the 1970s was clearly meant as a reference to American involvement in the Vietnam War and to the price paid by the Vietnamese people for that involvement. To bring her back in the 1990s as a villain linked to Kang, whom she helped defeat twenty years earlier, signals a reference to that famous story arc by the most political of Marvel's writers and deepens the connection between "Timeslide" and Cold War Marvel.

The solution to the betrayal—retrieving an earlier version of Tony Stark to defeat the current version—cements this as a Cold War commentary. Bringing forth Tony Stark from an earlier time creates a new innocence, untainted by thirty years of Cold War adventurism, the Vietnam War, the Central American conflicts of the 1980s, Stark's own history of alcoholism, selfish corporate wars, and spoiled relationships. Instead, at the heart of the Marvel political economy exists something sui generis, a Tony Stark without the history, without the baggage of the Cold War dragging him down. He can help fashion a post–Cold War world without having to carry the weight of Cold War responsibility and what it did to Americans.

Cultural Confusion and Industry Disarray

The end of the Cold War, the collapse of the Soviet Union, and the reunification of Germany could have brought great exuberance to Americans, a positive affirmation of the Cold War American self. Instead, it brought skepticism, doubt, and fear of the future. The stability of the bipolar world gave way to the ethnic cleansing of the Balkan Wars, terrorist attacks in Oklahoma City, and New York City, and war and perpetual but unsatisfying engagement in Iraq. The continued darkness of the images and the parade of holdover Soviet villains and weapons in the comic books attest to the fears that the post–Cold War world would be more frightening than hopes of a peace dividend suggested.

While the Cold War was over, its legacy for the rhetoric of American community persisted. Four decades of international adventurism, replete with limited wars, covert operations, and support for regimes that might be anticommunist but were far from democratic had rendered untenable a description of America's global role as progressive and virtuous. The excesses of executive power, from Watergate to Iran-Contra, further weakened belief in American virtue. The lack of movement on civil rights since the 1960s, growing inequality, and the continued fragility of the American economy, still in the throes of post-Fordist transformation, challenged the vision of a progressive America. The weak economy, experienced in the early 1990s as a deep recession, seemed more relevant in the 1992 presidential election than the apparent success of the dominant U.S. foreign policy issue of the past fifty years—containing communism. The Cold War definition of the American self had proven a sham. No longer could freedom, progress, and providence form a coherent description of the American without irony born of self-betrayal. Reconstructing a coherent American national identity in the post–Cold War period would prove difficult.

The comic book industry would be strongly affected by the changing economic landscape. The decline in circulation had seemed to steady by the early 1980s, but a boom period came in the early 1990s. Fueled by speculators who saw a potential high return in comic books as investment instruments, sales exploded for a period. New companies entered the market—Image, Malibu, Wildstorm, Vertigo, and both Marvel and DC catered to the investors with multiple covers of various issues, special collector's editions, and other sales events. In the wake of this economic boom, Marvel was purchased by Ron Perelman, who sought to turn the company into a media powerhouse via comic books, toys, collectible cards, and movie deals. His creative financing, including taking the company public, and the collapse of the investors' market (it was lost on many—but not for long—that scarcity was what made comics collectibles) would drive Marvel into bankruptcy. Its stock went from over thirty dollars per share to under two dollars in less than a year. A corporate war broke out over control of the company between Perelman and Carl Icahn, a major stockholder. Marvel would finally be purchased by ToyBiz, a smaller company that manufactured action figures and saw the characters as a potentially lucrative asset for film and television. The result was much disarray at the company by the mid-1990s.[31]

By 1996 Marvel had declared bankruptcy and was in the midst of a corporate battle between Perelman and Icahn. Under the editorship of Bob Harras, Marvel attempted to reinvigorate several of its titles, including *Captain America, Iron Man,* and *The Avengers,* by ending and restarting the series. This permitted both the publication of several books with a number 1 on the title, which catered to the investor market, and to clean up complications of continuity. The yearlong Heroes Reborn titles would be followed by the restarted Heroes Return series, which would bring the books back into Marvel continuity. The teen-aged Tony Stark would be forgotten, along with several other complications of continuity. This new, post–Cold War Marvel universe would have much looser continuity, but would still offer an interesting window into post–Cold War America.

6

The New World Order: 1996–2007

B Y THE MID-1990S a divisive partisanship and ideological "culture war" suggested that the consensus identity of Cold War America had long vanished. During the previous three decades, Americans had replaced the external enemy with an internal enemy and had become disillusioned with the public sphere and retreated into privacy. Emerging from that retreat in the 1980s, they had found themselves betrayed and themselves as the betrayers. The ideological legacy of the Cold War seemed increasingly a loss of national identity that had created a space for political compromise; partisan polarization and an increasingly acrimonious political discourse between neo conservatives and interest-group liberals marred the political landscape, obscuring the centrist positions of most Americans.

In a speech at Georgetown University in 1995 President Bill Clinton specifically identified the loss of a consensual vision of the American self as a major problem facing the United States:

Politics has become more and more fractured, just like the rest of our lives; pluralized. It's exciting in some ways. But as we divide into more and more and more sharply defined organized groups around more and more and more stratified issues, as we communicate more and more with people in extreme rhetoric through mass mailings or sometimes semi-hysterical

messages right before election on the telephone, or 30-second
ads designed far more to inflame than to inform, as we see politicians actually getting language lessons on how to turn their
adversaries into aliens, it is difficult to draw the conclusion that
our political system is producing the sort of discussion that will
give us the kind of results we need.[1]

Clinton describes a politics of acrimony that was produced, in
part, by the inability of the electoral politics to produce a definitive choice for leadership. So difficult was it for parties to muster
a majority that the first Democratic president since Franklin
Roosevelt to win a second term was never elected with a majority of the popular vote, and the Republican president who followed did not win the plurality of the popular vote in the most
contested election since that of Rutherford B. Hayes and Samuel
Tilden. From 1968 to 2002 a single party controlled the presidency and both houses of the U.S. Congress for only eight of
thirty-four years, and Congressional majorities grew increasingly
close during the period. One consequence was the substitution of
congressional investigations, lawsuits, and media campaigns for
the electoral arena as means of deciding political outcomes. This
"politics by other means" emergent in the 1980s would dominate
the political landscape as the old century ended and the new one
began, with the last president of the twentieth century beset by a
seven-year congressional investigation of financial dealings that
ranged widely beyond its original charge and the first president
of the twenty-first century being certified as president only after a
lengthy court battle to determine the validity of his election.

The myth of consensus stood as just that—a myth. Attempts
to re-create it in the 1980s had failed. The very elements of American rhetoric had seemed to lose their power. The celebration of
the individual was still heard, but it no longer seemed a certain
good. The anchoring values of progress and virtue had been lost
during the Cold War. While economic affluence returned in the
1990s, it did not affect all equally. The disparity in wealth was
getting larger. Income inequality rose at least 9 percent between
1991 and 2001, reaching its highest ever recorded mark at the
start of the twenty-first century.[2] Anxiety about job security and
the transforming economy was widespread. Where nearly one in
four workers had been employed in manufacturing in 1967, with

the job security, health benefits, and pensions that went along with big labor and big business, by 2005 only 11 percent were so employed. This reflected long-term transformations in the American economy that had become increasingly rapid during the last two decades as production became a truly global process. President Clinton identifies the anxiety of the American worker in the global economy in the 1995 speech, noting, "Millions of American people go home at night from their work and sit down to dinner and look at their children and wonder what they have done wrong, what did they ever do to fail. And they're riddled with worries about it. Millions more who are poor have simply given up on ever being able to work their way into a stable life-style."[3] While affluence was rekindling a sense of complacency in some, it was leaving many others behind. Progress, if measured at all, was measured solely in consumption levels, and those were growing increasingly uneven.

Not only had progress lost its power to assure but the role of the American leadership as the providential agent of progress had also come into question. The virtue of the American mission and the political economic agents who pursued it were questioned at every turn. Trust in government had never recovered from the body blow it took in the 1970s, dropping to a low of 26 percent in 1994.[4] Government action always came with a question; public utterances were distrusted *because* they were public.

Postconsensus America

In the last decade of the twentieth century the culture wars that had been simmering since the 1970s boiled over into the public consciousness. With the election of the first president born during the Cold War taking office as that conflict ended, the twin impulses of American ideology—the left-leaning economic equalitarian and social libertarian and the right-leaning economic libertarian and moral regulation tendencies—became the dominant mode of political discourse. As these tendencies came to dominate the two political parties' core leaderships the parties increasingly seemed polarized, while the mass of the American public seemed lost somewhere between these extremes. From the right, partisan writers, particularly of the neoconservative movement, criticized the Left as fostering a politics of entitlement or for their lack of religious virtue.[5] From the Left, the Right was characterized as a tool of big business and Christian conservatives, threatening civil liberties while championing private property to the detriment of the middle class and poor.[6] Between these extremes lay the majority of Americans, apparently unrepresented by the partisan extremism and triviality that seemed to dictate public policy.[7]

The divide between these positions was bridged by an apparent return of affluence unseen since the 1960s. The 1992 presidential campaign was conducted under the shroud of economic recession and the prediction of government budget deficits as far as the eye could see. By 1997 the economy was booming and the government budget showed the highest surplus since the 1950s, and trust in government was rising.[8] Fueled by the fiscal savings brought about by the end of the Cold War and the overly optimistic estimate of the profitability of computer-based technology companies, this affluence created the conditions for a national optimism that papered over the ideological divide. Without the external push of the Soviet Union, and without the disciplining action of the House Committee on Un-American Activities or Senator Joseph McCarthy, Americans seemed to conform out of desire rather than fear; conformity returned with affluence, and everyone seemed poised to benefit from the new economic prosperity of the global economy.

Everyone, that is, except the comic book companies. The end of the investor-spurred surge in comic book sales of the early 1990s brought vast changes to the industry. Marvel Comics went public in the early 1990s and sought to expand its role in the comic book and collectible industry. The company expanded into the production of trading cards and action figures and attempted to monopolize distribution of comic books. This backfired, and when the investor-spurred sales boost ended, Marvel fell into bankruptcy.[9] While Spider-Man, Daredevil, and the X-Men still sold well, the other titles saw sales drop.[10] Declining quality led even die-hard readers to protest, and a fan-based boycott of Marvel books added to Marvel's problems. Additionally, forty years of continuity had begun to take its toll, with characters being written into corners from which they seemingly could not emerge.

To address the problems of slumping sales and continuity dead-ends Marvel staged a universal crisis—a battle with a creature called Onslaught—in 1996 that brought about the end of several titles and permitted them to be restarted with new continuity. This affected all of the books under discussion here— Captain America, Iron Man, the Avengers, and the Hulk. Initially, the reconfigured Marvel universe seemed a combination of the moral certitude of the early 1960s with the fantastic emphasis of the mid- to late 1970s. This was, in part, the influence of writers heavily influenced by the products of these eras, such as Kurt Busiek and Mark Waid, and artists such as Andy Kubert and Ron Garney, who saw themselves as reviving a classic vision of the "silver age" comic. This "neoclassical" interpretation, however, could not offer itself with the same clarity as had the books of the early 1960s; within these stories something seemed amiss. The very rhetoric of American identity—the language of virtue, progress, and freedom—had lost its power, a victim of Cold War events. Rising interest group pluralism, loss of trust in government, and international adventurism had rendered that language suspect, and it could not be reasserted without irony. Nor could a single template of America serve to capture the reality of the multicultural milieu within which American comic books existed.

By the start of the twenty first century, with the terrorst attacks of 9/11 and the subsequent so-called War on Terror, the changed world order of comic books became increasingly apparent. With the politics of interest as the dominant form of politics in the United States, the War on Terror growing increasingly to resemble the Cold War, and the virtue of American leadership continually at issue, the pillars that had sustained a myth of American national identity into the 1960s could not serve as foundation for the reassertion of that myth. The new political economy of the Marvel universe, like that of the United States, is one where the government is increasingly untrustworthy, every group has a private and often sinister agenda, and global threats need to be faced but often lead to the realization that the source of these threats emanates from those who are supposed to be defending against them.

Three moments of the post-1996 period demonstrate the failure to re-create an American consensus. The first is the difference between the post-1996 Marvel tales and the tales of the 1960s that they sought to emulate. Captain America is cast as a reminted icon, a paragon of the American dream, and reunited with the government agencies with which he had worked in the 1960s. Iron Man returns to his form as playboy industrialist, facing a string of villains from his earlier tales. The Hulk becomes a beast of rage again, and the fractured psyche that had been the key to the character since the 1980s is linked to politics and the Cold War. Perhaps most telling is the creation of a new superhuman team, the Thunderbolts, who reiterate the tropes of the 1960s but with neither conviction nor certainty.

The second moment is the almost immediate questioning of the moral position of the United States in the wake of the terrorist attacks of September 11, 2001. With Marvel headquartered in Manhattan, and its tales generally taking place there, these events elicited a strong emotional response from the comic book producers. Marvel, for instance, released a short-lived series celebrating emergency response workers titled *The Call*. Almost immediately, however, the nationalistic and sympathetic response was conditioned by a series of stories that placed the United States' position vis-à-vis the terrorists in a complicated and conditional light. This would be related directly to the terrorist attacks in the Captain America stories, but ranged more widely, raising questions about the culpability of the U.S. government in the Avengers and Iron Man series.

The third moment builds on the specific culpability of the government to raise questions concerning the virtue of power in general. Iron Man will be forced to engage the government directly as Tony Stark seeks to become secretary of defense. The Mighty Thor will take over the leadership of Asgard after the death of Odin and will succumb to the hubris of power. Both stories not only raise questions concerning the possibility of moral action by government but render problematic the very possibility of heroism in the modern world. Each of these moments demonstrates the continuous engagement with the question of American identity and illustrates the difficulty in asserting consensus in the wake of the Cold War.

Back to the Future: Neoclassical Marvel

Marvel's attempt to reinvigorate its comic book line in 1996 was an attempt to return to the sources of its success in the 1960s. The company literally tried to start over. To do this, it developed a story line that crossed into most major titles involving a super-villain named Onslaught. Onslaught was so powerful that in defeating him, most of the major Marvel heroes had apparently been destroyed. Those destroyed included Captain America, Iron Man, the Fantastic Four, Thor, and the Avengers. All of these titles were canceled by Marvel. These books (except for Thor) were restarted at issue number 1 under the title Heroes Reborn. The Heroes Reborn story—in which the heroes were not dead but merely relocated to a pocket universe where they could survive Onslaught—lasted for a year. Those titles were again ended and restarted at number 1 under the title Heroes Return. Even those titles that had continued during the Heroes Reborn interregnum—Spider-Man, Daredevil, Hulk—would be stopped and restarted within a year as the rebooted Marvel universe began to emerge.

This convoluted process had several benefits for Marvel. It offered the opportunity to produce several major titles with the number 1 on the cover, making the books attractive as potential collectibles to the investor market. This would escalate sales for these titles, for a short period at least. It also offered Marvel the opportunity to begin fresh, ignoring some of the continuity that made stories hard to tell, or even starting with a new continuity. For instance, prior to Heroes Reborn, as noted in the last chapter, Iron Man had proven a traitor and been replaced by a teenage version of himself. In the Avengers, the Wasp had literally been turned into a bug. Captain America was dwelling in a body cloned from the Red Skull. All of this could be imagined away with a yearlong break in continuity.

The stories of the rebooted Marvel universe reiterate themes and tropes from the heyday of Marvel's success. This is quickly apparent in the very look of the books, which return to the bright colors, clear lines, and firm contrasts of the earlier period. Gone are the impressionistic and ambiguous images of the early 1990s. Instead, the books have a more contained look, with gutters separating panels, characters firmly distinguished from backgrounds, and a color scheme that accentuates bright backgrounds and primary colors. While the panel arrangement is more challenging than was common in the 1960s and 1970s, with more insets and diverse shapes, it is also more common for there to be multiple splash pages with greater focus on visual rather than verbal narrative. The clear and distinct images give a strong sense of certainty to the ideas being portrayed while the bright colors and stark contrasts suggest a positive message of a pleasant world. Within this visual assertion of positivity and truth, however, the re-creation of the earlier epoch's themes and certainty fails. After the Cold War, American virtue and unquestioned progress cannot be asserted without irony or question.

Iron Man: Reconstructing Family

The first two years of the Iron Man series—retelling his origin as it was constructed in 1962, with the hero in an armor design reminiscent of the mid-1960s—have him battling a sequence of his oldest enemies, including Whiplash, the Controller, Firebrand, and the Mandarin. There is even the return of his earliest consorts, Pepper Potts and Happy Hogan, now divorced and replicating the romantic subplot of the mid-1960s. The stories remain pointedly apolitical, unlike those of the early 1960s. Firebrand may mouth anticapitalist rhetoric, but he is offered as mentally deranged. The Mandarin retains his anticapitalist rhetoric, but seeks merely to conquer Russia where a strong man might rule.

The backdrop to the stories is the new global economy. There is some language that offers concerns about global capitalism. Tony Stark has lost control of his company to a Japanese firm and must contend as well with another global corporation, Bain Electronics. As chief of his new company, Stark Solutions, Tony Stark will travel to Europe, Asia, and the Pacific Islands as a global consultant and face his enemies, who now pose global threats either through their own desires for conquest or as agents of international corporations. The villains now represent either the potential for global threats (Firebrand works for an international crime syndicate) or strive against global capitalism. The Mandarin refers to corporate leaders as the new feudal lords, and he calls workers the new peasants. Behind this series of conflicts, however, there is something more sinister. Iron Man's enemies are being organized by some force that seeks to defeat Iron Man and Tony Stark. Initially believing it to be the Mandarin, Stark is stunned to find that he is not the source of threat. The threat comes from Sunset Bain, director of Bain Electronics, who is a spurned paramour of Tony Stark. While this subplot becomes increasingly intricate, it ends in issue 24 without ever being resolved. Iron Man stories for the next year would focus on his armor, which becomes sentient (reiterating a story from the early 1970s), and a reemergence of the Vietnamese warlord Wong Chu, who was responsible for his building the first Iron Man armor.

In this period the Iron Man series reflects the attempt to recapture the narrative power of 1960s Marvel comics but does so with very little political awareness. The emphasis on the private life of Tony Stark, his relations with Sunset Bain and Rumiko Fujikawa, daughter of the man who took over his company, and the return of Pepper Potts and Happy Hogan all reflect the most basic elements of the Iron Man character—the isolation of the rich playboy and his attempt to create a family around himself. They also indicate that the private life of the individual is still dominant over the public life of the hero, as had been the case since the 1980s. The independent life of his armor may raise the question of identity, but the armor is never mistaken for Stark, never assumes his role with his friends. There is no mistaken identity as there had been in the earlier version of the story. This seems an attempt to retrieve the engagement of the early 1970s, but never achieves it. Ultimately, Iron Man of this period represents the inability to recapture that sense of community and hope that existed in the days before the Cold War disillusion.

Captain America and Totalitarian Icons

The rebooted Captain America series drew heavily on the themes of the early 1970s. The first sequence focused on battles with the secret society Hydra and involved confused identities.[11] The Hydra leader was in reality a Skrull, an extraterrestrial shape-shifter who had used Hydra to run a media campaign boosting Captain America's celebrity only to take his place and to use his popularity to take over the world. He did this by convincing

Americans that one in twenty people were shape-shifting aliens. Believing the accusation of the Skrull as Captain America, Americans turn on their neighbors, friends, and even family, attacking anyone who seems different as a potential Skrull. The twinning of the cult of celebrity and the social paranoia reminiscent of the anticommunist crusade of the 1950s offers an interesting portrayal of the 1990s. In the earlier period there was a consensus about the virtue of American leadership in pursuit of a progressive mission around which the consensus was formed. That created a space for opposition to the paranoia fostered in the anticommunist crusade, and ultimately its downfall. In this story it is the worship of celebrity rather than virtue that ties Americans together. The cult of celebrity, with the inherent narcissism it implies, renders Americans susceptible to the Skrull's attempt to turn them into violent paranoids. The ease with which the Skrull is able to manipulate Americans suggests that there is nothing to which to anchor an American individualism. Similar stories in the early 1970s had focused on political manipulations, which had always been greeted with skepticism by the public. In this case the response is near universal and apolitical. The 1970s had seen the public sector discredited, and the American people had retreated into privacy. Now the private sector, worshipping celebrity rather than virtue, is portrayed as deficient.

A subsequent series has Captain America confront a supernatural creature, Nightmare, who can invade dreams.[12] Nightmare is subverting believers in the American dream, turning their visions into nightmares in order to gain power over the waking world. A baseball hero known for his generosity with fans beats a group of autograph seekers with a baseball bat; a philanthropist becomes obsessed with keeping his money; an architect of public housing and community centers blows up his own construction site—all those possessed by Nightmare become selfish and self-centered. Even Captain America becomes possessed, concerned only with his own strength and power. Sharon Carter, self-styled cynic and unbeliever in the American dream, feels herself immune to Nightmare's power, but even she is subverted. Nightmare is ultimately defeated by a populist army who have been awakened by Captain America, the strength of whose dream gives him power in Nightmare's realms.

While Nightmare's defeat offers some hope that there is still a common identity to Americans, this particular transformation reflects the reliance on a language of individualism, of freedom, without the context of a progressive vision or a call to virtue. Absent these companion rhetorical elements the American dream becomes a nightmare of selfishness and greed. The ease with which Nightmare is able to subvert the American dreamers, as with the Skrull's manipulations in the earlier story arc, suggests that at the core of the American identity there may be a void. This is challenged by the corruption of Sharon Carter by Nightmare. Her cynicism represents the lost faith in government, that fear of a vacuous cult of celebrity that had empowered the Skrull earlier. That her cynicism masks a deeper idealism suggests that while there is doubt about progress and virtue there is still a thirst for the romantic vision of America that defeats Nightmare. A void there may be, and this may generate cynicism, but even the cynics still believe in the dream somewhere.

Throughout its fifty-issue run, *Captain America* volume 2 returned to the visual and verbal narratives of the 1960s and 1970s. Captain America was reunited with his partner the Falcon and his love, Sharon Carter. While their relationship was placed in question, it provided an underlying tension for the run of the series. Captain America would develop an alternative love interest, Brooklyn lawyer Connie Ferrari, but the Sharon Carter text was always dominant. The creation of a love triangle, a new element for the Captain American character, continues the emphasis on private lives from the 1980s and increases the ambiguity of goals defining the character. Again, as in *Iron Man*, the continued emphasis on private over public lives, particularly in this most ideological of books, implies that no true reengagement with a public American self has yet occurred. Captain America has also begun working closely with SHIELD again, as he had in the 1960s. But even with the return of these characters, the stories of mistaken identity and assertions of American dreams, there cannot be a statement of value rendered as certain, spoken as surely, as those of the early 1960s.

In each of the stories the character of Captain America is treated more as a nationalist icon than has been true of the character since the mid-1960s. Jeffrey S. Lang and Patrick Trimble's seminal article on the character notes that Captain America's humanity renders him an ambiguous hero, unlike his character in the 1940s.[13] Beginning with the death of Captain America sequence that was the penultimate story line in volume 1, though volume 2 writers attempted to return Captain America to the stature of nationalist icon within his own narrative. This would become a key tension in the "Civil War" story of 2006–7, as this nationalism would generate tensions within the idea of the hero.

The Hulk: The Psychology of the Cold War

Having been transformed from a force of unbridled rage to an alienated victim of government conspiracies and then to a sufferer of multiple personality disorder, the Hulk entered the post–Cold War period with a lot of baggage. This baggage would be reconfigured by Paul Jenkins and Ron Garney into a commentary on the Cold War and conspiracies in a telling story, "The Dogs of War."[14] In this story Bruce Banner discovers that he has Lou Gehrig's disease and seeks help from neurophysiologist Angela Lipscombe, an old flame from his graduate school days. She and gamma-irradiated psychologist Doc Samson attempt to help him reintegrate the various personalities, revealing that there are in fact thousands of potential Hulks in Banner's brain. The Hulk is also being sought by General Ryker, a shadowy military figure who heads a secret government program to create gamma-irradiated soldiers. One successful experiment on a Gulf War veteran has produced a creature called Flux, who battles the Hulk.

Ryker represents the darkest side of government. He operates outside the chain of command on a series of covert operations. To learn about Ryker, the Hulk consults with Nick Fury, who describes him as a "psycho with resources" involved in testing biological weapons on illegal immigrants and drug smuggling. He continues,

> But that's nothin' compared to the big one. . . . Hypothetical story: It's a nice, sunny day in a Texas town—a beautiful day for a drive. The birds are singing and all the crowd are out for a very special person visiting that day. Only not everyone is happy to see the VIP. Some people are mad at him because he's shut down some of the more expensive black ops waged

against the Vietnamese. So they make sure that his open-top limo slows down right at the most vulnerable part of the parade route, and they put the VIP in the crosshairs, and they blow his brains out."[15]

This story is told over a series of inset panels in black and white, revealing a rifle muzzle pointing up from a sewer grate rather than down from a book depository window. This recounting of the assassination of John F. Kennedy is bookended by a

Figure 6.1. Nick Fury Recounts the Kennedy Assassination

From "The Dogs of War, part 3" *Incredible Hulk* 16 (July 2000), 18.

confrontation between Dr. Angela Lipscombe and Doc Samson in which she accuses him of lying to Banner—that the Hulk personality called the Professor is not an amalgam of Hulk and Banner, as Samson has told Banner, but instead merely another Hulk personality. The lie by Samson, told back in issue 377 (January 1991), is equated with a supposed government conspiracy to kill Kennedy. This link of a lie about Banner's psychological state to government lies underscores the theme of this story—the link between the fracturing of the American self and the Cold War. Lies private and public abound in this story. Ryker is not operating for the government but trying to heal his wife from cancer using gamma-irradiated blood. Ryker himself claims Kennedy was killed by Cubans, and that he concocted the conspiracy story to cover his own tracks in other areas by misdirecting the attention of the American public. Lies are Ryker's stock in trade. "Lies are useful," he says. "Every other word I speak is a lie, Doctor Banner. People are so busy trying to connect me with this and that they miss the point. I lie to you and the President and even my own people on an hourly basis because that means the only person who knows what's going on is me."[16] The truth is hidden, manipulated in this story, both by the government and by those who are supposed to be Banner's friends. The young soldier who has been turned into Flux is the product of a lie; he thinks his condition was the product of an enemy biological attack during the Gulf War, when in fact it was an attack by Americans under Ryker's orders to create a gamma-irradiated monster.

As a representative of the government, albeit a rogue, Ryker represents a Cold War history that is untrustworthy, plagued by government deception. The very deception of the government that runs back in this tale to Kennedy's assassination has produced a fractured truth and the fractured American self that is represented by the many Hulks that occupy Bruce Banner. Throughout the story Banner falls into a mental reflection in which he dwells in his brain, conversing with the various manifestations of the Hulk that have appeared over the years— particularly Joe Fixit and the Professor. They form an alliance to contain the worst of the Hulk personas, portrayed as the devil.

That Ryker is motivated by personal rather than public concerns does not exonerate the government. The weight of the story suggests that the government is untruthful, manipulative, and often malign. There is no virtue here, nor any progress. Ultimately there are merely self-centered people who foster conspiracy theories to save the economic costs of war, who turn on those they are supposed to protect for individual goals. Bruce Banner's psychological disorder that manifests as various Hulks is thus relinked to the Cold War that gave birth to the Hulk forty years earlier. This time there is no external enemy to give it identity, no progressive mission to give the Hulk meaning. Instead there is just one fractured man who stands for all Americans in the face of government that "lies on an hourly basis."

The Impossibility of Redemption: Thunderbolts

One of the more interesting narrative developments during this period is the creation of a new group of superheroes, the Thunderbolts. Claiming to have come together to replace the heroes who had gone missing after the battle with Onslaught, the Thunderbolts are in fact a group of supervillains masquerading as heroes to gain the opportunity to take over the world.[17] Led by Citizen V (really Helmut Zemo, longtime Captain America villain), the Thunderbolts were a group of B-list villains, including Songbird (formerly Screaming Mimi), Mach 1 (Beetle), Atlas (Powerman), Techno (Fixer), and Meteorite (Moonstone). They will be joined by two teenage heroes, Jolt and Charcoal, who believe the Thunderbolts are real, and later will be led by Hawkeye, formerly of the Avengers. Several of the villains—Songbird, Mach 1, and Atlas—actively seek redemption. They are being manipulated by Zemo, who, along with his lackey Techno, is using the Thunderbolts for his own nefarious ends. Moonstone is the most ambiguous of the lot; she is even more manipulative than Zemo, but her goals are never made completely clear.

For the first several issues the tension between the heroic role the Thunderbolts play and the evil ends they seek is merely a background element. Soon, however, the Thunderbolts are discovered to be hiding their villainous identities, and they move from heroes to antiheroes. While some seek actual redemption, others feign the desire to pursue their own agendas.

The story resembles the transformation of the Avengers in 1965, as most of the major heroes resigned, leaving Captain

America to recruit a group of new Avengers. This group was composed of three former villains, Hawkeye, the Scarlet Witch, and her brother Quicksilver.[18] This connection is directly made when Hawkeye quits the Avengers to lead the Thunderbolts, remembering how important and difficult his own redemption had been.[19] The earlier Avengers story never questioned the desire of the former villains for redemption; the issue was primarily one of public perception and willingness to follow orders. In the case of the Thunderbolts, which actors seek redemption and which merely feign that desire is a constant element. Where the Avengers story from the 1960s was a clear narrative about the possibility of redemption, the Thunderbolts narrative is more ambiguous. Who is a hero and who a villain remains a question throughout; the possibility of redemption is never assured.

Another element of the Thunderbolts that connects the book specifically to Marvel's stories of the 1960s is the character of Citizen V. Originally a hero of the World War II era, Citizen V appeared in the Marvel (then Timely) Comics title *Daring Adventures*. Dressed as a soldier and based in Britain, Citizen V fought the Nazis. Citizen V of the Thunderbolts is a new incarnation of this World War II hero, fighting the same fight in the twenty-first century. This resurrects the trope of the 1960s, asserting the moral virtue of the hero by placing him in the context of World War II and simultaneously asserting the immorality of the foe by equating him with a Nazi. Citizen V serves to connect the battles of the Thunderbolts with the antifascist forces of the 1940s and thus lends them an aura of moral certitude and virtue that would otherwise be lacking.

This trope is rendered questionable from the start because Helmut Zemo is masquerading as Citizen V. Zemo is, along with the Red Skull and Baron Strucker, one of the three sustained connections to the Nazis in Marvel's stories. Zemo is the son of the Baron Zemo who was a Nazi scientist and agent in World War II, the man who killed Captain America's sidekick Bucky. He has fought Captain America by himself and also been a staunch ally of the Red Skull, affirming his own connections to the Nazis and their racial prejudices. Thus, from the first issue of the Thunderbolts story, in which hero and villain are rendered ambiguous in this redemption tale, the very morality of the project—of the whole rebooted Marvel universe—is brought into question because the architect of the Thunderbolts is a Nazi masquerading as an Allied hero. The very trope that had given Marvel comics a clear definition of virtue in the 1960s is resurrected in the Thunderbolts, but rendered incapable of clarifying anything other than that there is no clear definition of virtue.

The ambiguity of the heroic identity becomes even more complicated in an intricate story in which the Thunderbolts are being assassinated by the Scourge of the Underworld. Originally a character in Captain America comics of the mid-1980s (see chapter 5), the Scourge now returns wielding an impressive arsenal of weapons and great physical prowess. He first kills Jolt, then fights Zemo, apparently killing him in his own castle in a shrine to his father that includes a Captain America shield and the tattered costume of Captain America's sidekick, Bucky, whom the older Zemo had killed.[20] Scourge is finally revealed to be Jack Monroe, the Bucky of the 1950s and later Nomad, released from suspended animation and controlled by Henry Gyrich of the Committee on Superhuman Activities. Gyrich's hatred of superheroes has led him to force Nomad to kill them, beginning with the Thunderbolts. Gyrich, however, is not in control of his own actions; he, too, is being controlled by an unidentified external force. While he truly hates superheroes, he would never act so violently.[21] In the wake of these revelations of government-supported assassination against superheroes (albeit under external influence) Hawkeye demands that all the Thunderbolts be given a full pardon. This Gyrich grants, but Hawkeye must go to prison for his vigilantism. Hawkeye thus sacrifices himself for the redemption of the remaining Thunderbolts Songbird, Mach 1, Moonstone, and Atlas.[22]

The redemption tale, a particularly common motif for the antihero narrative, was a major element of Marvel's success in the 1960s. The countering of great power with great tragedy meant that most Marvel heroes were at some level seeking redemption—for the death of a sidekick or loved one (Captain America, Spider-Man, Daredevil), for a wasted life of privilege (Iron Man), or for hubris (Thor). The return to the theme of redemption in this case is an attempt to recapture the fire of the early Marvel success. The inability to offer the redemption narrative without complicating it, however, demonstrates how much the world had changed during the last half of the Cold War. The pursuit of redemption is initially false, a lie told to the public by villains in a masquerade. Some of these villains—the least successful of the lot—do ultimately seek such redemption; others do not. This problematizes the process of redemption, its attractions, benefits, and even its desirability. Redemption becomes an ongoing process with no discernable outcome, no moment when one can say, "This character has been redeemed." There is no progress to the process, merely one individual's movement. Nor is redemption a process of clear virtue. While it is presented as such in the late-1990s version of the Thunderbolts, that virtue is not given without question.

September 2001 and the War on Terror

The twenty-first century brought a revival of direct political commentary to comic books. While there had been reference to political and social issues over the previous two decades, comic books had not engaged the political world so directly since the early 1970s. With the polarizing effects of the contested 2000 presidential election and a growing political engagement by Americans in general, comic books began increasingly to treat current political events and personalities. In so doing they revealed the weakness of the rhetoric of community to describe contemporary America and pointed to both the problems and possibilities this posed for twenty-first-century America.

The conclusion that the language of American community, particularly the vision of a virtuous, progressive America, has been seriously weakened is nowhere more apparent than in the reactions to the terrorist attacks of September 11, 2001, and the subsequent so-called War on Terror. While a sense of paranoia reminiscent of the early 1950s invaded American popular culture, the identity of the threats has not been identified as clearly as in that earlier period, and frequently has been seen to emanate from within American society rather than from without. The explosion of television dramas that explore the destructive secrets and lies underlying a facade of normalcy, ranging from *Desperate Housewives*, *24*, and *Alias* to the comic book–inspired *Smallville*, has been married to the continued quest for security at all costs that has been the staple of the popular police procedurals of the last fifteen years, *Law and Order* and *CSI*, which have spawned a growth industry in their spinoffs. The best-seller lists continue to be dominated by serial-killer fiction, in which seemingly random and brutal violence is given a scheme and form by police profilers, bringing order to the chaos of the modern world. The popularity of these books and of their television and film progeny further indicates the degree to which security and order in the face of cultural chaos and unclear threats is on the minds of American cultural consumers.

The two major producers of superhero comics, Marvel and DC, headquartered in Manhattan, responded to the 9/11 attacks quickly. Both produced special books, the proceeds of which went to the families of the victims of the attacks. Marvel, whose stories were largely set in New York, had stories in which their heroes would confront the attacks, most famously *Amazing Spider-Man* 36, which has Spider-Man swinging over the smoldering World Trade Center. Generally, the books reflected a more ominous tone, a greater sense of insecurity and moral ambiguity in the wake of 9/11. The artwork, for instance, underwent a drastic change. Having returned to a presentation of bright colors and sharp contrasts during the neoclassical phase of the reboot, the books now took on a much darker background and less distinct contrasts. The stories also offered plots of a more insidious nature. So began a Hulk series that ran until the book went on hiatus in which the Hulk was pursued across the country through dusky, barren landscapes by a variety of actors, none of whose motives were clear. The Avengers were "disassembled" and reconstituted with a more morally ambiguous roster, including Wolverine, the dark mutant assassin from the X-Men, and Luke Cage, former criminal and "hero for hire."

These darker contexts, more ominous and ambiguous threats, and more morally questionable heroes imply that an undefined but dangerous enemy confronts Americans, but the sources of that threat and the proper means to respond to it are unclear. Without a clear definition of national mission, and with a continued questioning of American virtue, there was no clear sense of how the nation *should* approach the War on Terror. Unlike earlier national security crusades, such as World War II or the Cold War, there was significant ambiguity from the start not only about how the United States should respond but the extent to which the nation might be culpable in the emergence of this threat. In part this was a response to globalization; nationalism seemed a limited idea in confrontation with a threat that seemed truly global. This issue would emerge in the stories of the post-9/11 era, as would issues of American responsibility for terrorism and whether a military response of the War on Terror was a reasoned action of responsible power or whether it was the hubris of imperialism.

Captain America: "Enemy"

Marvel Comics' Captain America series (volume 2) ended in 2001 and was restarted in its more adult-oriented Marvel Knights line (as Captain America volume 4).[23] While the decision to do this was not related to the terrorist attacks of 9/11 (it was a contingency in case Marvel lost a legal battle with one of the character's creators, Joe Simon) the new story lines that emerged when volume 4 began were heavily influenced by those attacks and the subsequent War on Terror. Writer John Ney Reiber notes that he had already drafted the first three issues of the new series when the terrorist attack occurred. He had intended to make the book about contemporary concerns, and the terrorist attacks forced a rewrite: "I feel like now is a really good time for us as Americans to consider how this happened, how it could happen . . . Americans are becoming conscious of the world beyond our shores in a different way because of this. And I'd like for a lot of good to come out of that."[24]

The very look of the book provoked questioning. The covers of the first six issues, which contain a story titled "Enemy,"[25] invoke nationalist images from American crusades of the past such as World Wars I and II, or ask the reader, "Are you doing your part?" Perhaps most revealing is the cover of issue 6, which has Captain America at the center of a seemingly fascistic display of American national symbols, standing atop a plinth on which are carved the words "Liberty and justice for all." Symbolically, the American values for which Captain America is supposed to stand are being used to construct an image that evokes visions of Nazi ceremonies. As central as the Nazis have been to define good and evil in the Marvel universe, this melding of ideological ideals and symbols creates an unsettling projection, problematizing the ideal of virtue without ever uttering a word.

The story contained in these books is equally challenging. In "Enemy," Captain America confronts an Arab terrorist, Al Tariq. The story begins with Captain America's alter ego, Steve Rogers, sifting through the debris of the World Trade Center on the day of the attacks, hoping to find survivors, linking Al Tariq to the 9/11 attacks. Al Tariq has taken a small Midwestern town hostage, seeding the area with land mines and cluster bombs

Figure 6.2. Liberalism with a Fascist Aesthetic
From "Enemy, part 6" *Captain America* vol. 4, no. 6 (December 2002).

and threatening to kill all citizens unless the icon of American power, Captain America, comes to him. When Captain America comes to the town he battles a group of youthful followers of Al Tariq, all of whom have prosthetic limbs. They were all victims of land mines and cluster bombs left behind by the American army in various military actions. As he battles them, Captain America finds that they are being controlled by Al Tariq through a device called a CAT (Casualty Awareness Tracking) tag, a piece of American technology that Captain America has refused to wear.

To stop Al Tariq from destroying the town Captain America must kill him. After doing so he unmasks himself on camera to reveal his secret identity to the world, telling them that America did not kill Al Tariq, he did. He then confronts the U.S. secretary of defense to find out how the terrorists acquired the CAT tags. This leads him to Dresden, Germany, where he discovers that Al Tariq used the CAT tag to transfer his mind to another body. In a bloody battle he defeats Al Tariq and destroys his CAT tag. The device, it is revealed, was devised by Al Tariq and sold to the U.S. military. As Al Tariq tells Captain America, "You can rely on a militaristic government to embrace a new technology before its repercussions are explored and understood."[26]

Several elements of the story undercut nationalism and moral certainty. The soldiers of Al Tariq, his prosthetic-wearing victims of American weapons, are offered to suggest that U.S. militarism may well be a prime cause of the terrorist threat. Al Tariq describes his own history as a product of U.S. anticommunist military actions that killed his parents and left him disfigured. Al Tariq challenges Captain America to identify his nationality based on this story:

> [Al Tariq:] You know your history, Captain America. Tell your monster where he's from. You can't answer me. . . . You played that game in too many places. . . . The sun never set on your political chessboard—your empire of blood. In Africa, Asia, South America, we died, and your people . . .
>
> [Captain America:] My people never knew.[27]

This interlude not only suggests that American Cold War militarism was a major factor in the emergence of terrorists but also that there is a lack of openness and transparency on the part of the U.S. government. This is further revealed in Captain America's attempt to see the secretary of defense. Locked in an underground bunker in Virginia with U.S. superspy Nick Fury, the secretary criticizes Captain America for revealing his identity, claiming that he has compromised his usefulness. Nick Fury responds that no one has ever accused Captain America of compromise. The moral purity of the hero is contrasted with the impurity of the political appointee. In the previous three issues, Captain America repeatedly questioned his own moral certitude in the face of the army of amputees, rendering him a morally ambiguous hero. The secretary tries to keep Captain America from getting into the bunker, claiming he is not cleared for this room. When the hero enters the room and demands to know where the CAT tags came from the secretary replies, "That's privileged information, a matter of national security, which Colonel Fury is not at liberty to discuss with you, Mister Rogers."[28] Fury gives Captain America the information he needs, and Captain America sets off for Dresden, although he must foil another terrorist attempt on his life (on the Fourth of July) to get there.

Captain America's visit to Dresden evokes the firebombing of that city during World War II, which Captain America sees in retrospect as an act of terrorism:

> Dresden. You didn't understand what we'd done here until September the eleventh. Before then you would have said that we were doing what we had to do to defeat Hitler and the Nazis, crush the Axis, end their evil. But now, what do you see? February the thirteenth and fourteenth, 1945. They huddled in the dark, trapped, while the fire raged above them. Faces pressed to the broken walls that locked them in. Clawing at the cold earth until it grew too hot to the touch. And when there was nothing left to breathe there in the dark, they died. The city's firemen fought the blaze for days before they could begin the search for survivors. There were no survivors. History repeats itself like a machine gun.[29]

The equation of the U.S. firebombing of Dresden with the 9/11 attacks against the United States undermines the moral certainty of U.S. policy by implying both U.S. complicity in the rise of terrorism and a lack of moral purity to the nation's government.

Figure 6.3. On the Origins of Terrorism
From "Soft Targets," *Captain America* volume 4. #5
(August 2002), 22.

The structure of the story suggests the reader transfer those virtues to the superhero (who does not compromise his morals),
but he has already defined himself as equally complicit in the
moral failure.[30] As the icon of American power, Captain America
also suffers from the same moral impurities and inadequacies of
the nation in the face of a global problem. His quest for solutions
is the nation's quest, and his failure to find certainty is the failure
of nationalism in a global environment.

This element of the story also resurrects the trope of World War II, equating villains with Nazis; in this instance, the villain in Dresden is not the objectively evil Nazi but the objectively virtuous United States. The trope that had defined U.S. moral certainty in the 1960s is not merely rendered ambiguous here but completely inverted.

This story shows the major problems of U.S. culture confronting a postnationalist conflict such as the War on Terror. Four decades of Cold War global activity have removed from the United States any vestige of its moral superiority to other nations. Attempts to develop national explanations for or national responses to terrorism prove inadequate. Lacking a moral core, the United States is generally portrayed as complicit in terrorism or incapable of confronting it. Superheroes, frequently offered as morally superior to politicians and therefore capable of bearing the national burden with more virtue, are rendered morally problematic themselves, and they are thus unable to save America from itself. The complicity of the United States in spawning terrorism is also frequently related to U.S. adventurism during the Cold War, further undermining the moral position of the United States. The loss of virtue, identified in part as a legacy of the Cold War, makes it difficult for the United States to assert a morally sound position in the War on Terror. Instead, that position is frequently portrayed as self-interested, overbearing, and imperialistic.

The Hubris of Power: Iron Man and Thor

In 2003 the War on Terror came to Iraq. A controversial action, the U.S. invasion of Iraq had been opposed by several longtime allies of the United States and by a large segment of the American public.

President George W. Bush, while justifying U.S. action in Iraq, articulated anew the American progressive mission, reminiscent of the Cold War Truman Doctrine, stating, "America believes that all people are entitled to hope and human rights, to the nonnegotiable demands of human dignity. People everywhere prefer freedom to slavery; prosperity to squalor; self-government to the rule of terror and torture. America is a friend to the people of Iraq."[31]

This vision, of an America promoting the progress of freedom and prosperity around the globe, reflects the call to defend free peoples of the world in President Harry S. Truman's famous speech of 1947. Also, as in the Cold War, it is linked to a low-intensity war against terrorism that will be of long duration. The 2006 National Security Strategy specifically states, "The United States is in the early years of a long struggle, similar to what our country faced in the early years of the Cold War." The doctrine lists as the first objective of U.S. national security "championing aspirations for human dignity."[32]

This reassertion of a progressive American mission, however, was couched within a framework that seemed a significant departure from previous policy. In 2002 the White House issued a new national security policy that authorized military action against states or other actors which might at some point in the future pose a threat to U.S. security interests.[33] For the first time, preemption was the specific policy of the United States. Additionally, while U.S. policy for the previous two administrations had emphasized a multilateral approach to international relations, the United States seemed more willing to act even in the face of opposition from its allies. While strengthening alliances was another objective of the National Security Strategy, U.S. action in Iraq had been sanctioned by neither the United Nations nor longtime allies such as France and Germany. Unilateralism and preemption combined to suggest that the United States would act not in the interests of a progressive mission of freedom and prosperity but in its own interest, wherever and whenever it occurred. The term imperialism was used by both supporters and critics of U.S. policy. Neoconservative supporters of unilateral U.S. global activity argued that the United States was the strongest power and had a moral duty to impose a Pax Americana on the world. Critics argued that this was counterproductive and that such actions would promote a backlash against the United States as a hubristic and imposing power. [34]

The new political economy of the Marvel universe was a fertile ground on which such debates could be addressed. One of the key factors of the hero is his inner direction that renders him a moral actor above the law and above politics. Marvel's heroes of the 1960s were guided by the moral certainty that they served a virtuous cause in opposing communists, even more so than the government. In the 1970s and 1980s, this inner direction was turned against the government, which had proven unvirtuous. It led Captain America twice to give up and then reassume his role, first in the face of the Watergate scandal and second in response to government interference. It led Tony Stark to quit producing weapons for the government in pursuit of peace. In the early 1990s, Iron Man became a fugitive from the government in the attempt to regain his proprietary technology to protect people from its use by evil men. While there is some question in this latter case of whether Iron Man had gone too far, in general the inner moral compass of the hero is portrayed as superior to that of the politician or of the law. Increasingly, the strength of the moral compass of the inner-directed hero was weakening throughout this period, representing growing doubts about the virtue of the American system.

The inner direction of the hero has the potential to become a fascistic control by the superpowered actor. When virtue becomes hubris, inner direction is lost. Two stories from Marvel treat the subject of the potential of the hero to become a totalitarian force of control. John J. Miller and Jorge Lucas offer one treatment in "The Best Defense,"[35] in which Tony Stark is approached by a representative of the Bush administration to take on a consulting role with the Department of Defense because of difficulties soldiers are having with new weapons systems. No longer a weapons manufacturer, Stark resists, citing his moral commitment to peaceful technologies. On a mission with Captain America to rescue some sailors trapped in a submarine, Stark finds that the weapons systems being used have been pirated from his own designs. Further investigation reveals that the Pentagon subverted the contracts that they have signed with him in order to pirate the technology. Seeing that the genie is out of the bottle, Stark decides to deal with the problem by becoming not merely a consultant but secretary of defense. The U.S. Senate is about to reject Stark as nominee for secretary of defense when, as Iron Man, he saves Washington from a missile attack (launched by our own Department of Defense). In the wake of this action, the Senate confirms him unanimously. The story ties the pirating to one person within the defense department, but also implicates politicians, defense contractors, and other members of the military.

Several elements of the story question the moral role of the superhero. References are made to several earlier stories that were significant to Iron Man's development as a political actor—his earlier testimony before the U.S. Congress (which is paralleled directly in this tale), his decision to stop manufacturing munitions, and his attempt to regain control of his technology in the "Armor Wars." These decisions, which were treated as moral within their contexts, are problematized here. In a discussion with Stark about his decision to stop making weapons Captain America refers to his World War II experiences to suggest that making weapons is not an immoral act. He refers to women working in munitions factories in 1944 who "didn't seem conflicted at all about the machines they were building. I don't mean they were working in some patriotic fervor. Honestly, they just felt they were working to get their husbands and sons back sooner." Discussing mechanics who worked to maintain combat battalions in France he notes that "they never complained. Because they saw the poor guys coming back from the line, needing a working rifle, or jeep, or whatever so desperately—and they did what they had to do."[36] Both of these instances remove the moral certainty that surrounded Stark's earlier decision to purse "peace industries" rather than munitions. Those decisions are placed in the arena of "abstract," and thus not considering the real world. These earlier decisions, derived from Iron Man's inner-directed moral compass, are now implicitly a product of his hubris. Rather than consider what everyone wanted, he did what he thought was right and attempted to impose his will on the world.

This issue is specifically raised during Stark's Senate confirmation hearings. He does very well in the hearings, too well for his opponents. Senator Zimmer, working closely with the undersecretary of defense who is pirating Stark's technology, attacks Tony Stark:

> You think the smartest guy should be in charge—and you think that guy is you. We've got new weapons technology? You don't think our forces are smart enough to use it safely. We've got deadlier weapons than before? You don't think our leaders are smart enough to use them morally. We've got criminals

running loose? You don't think our police are smart enough
to catch them on their own. Mr. Stark—you're a time bomb.
We can't let you loose in the Pentagon. You'll turn it into a cult
of personality and you'll never listen to this body again. You're
too smart for school, Mr. Stark. You make up your own rules.[37]

Facing the charge of hubris, of not being the hero but the potential totalitarian threat, Stark explodes in a rage. His nomination
is rejected by the Senate committee, although after he saves
Washington from the missile attack he is unanimously confirmed
(much as his earlier testimony before Congress was terminated
after his battle with Titanium Man). But the charges of hubris
cannot be erased, nor can the discussion with Captain America
that casts earlier decisions in a new, unflattering light. The hero's
moral compass, so accurate in the 1960s defending against communists and in the 1970s against a distrusted government, no
longer points to true north. Even the earlier decisions are now
questioned, retroactively challenging the moral certainty of the
earlier age.

Dan Jurgens offers a more direct questioning of the moral status of heroic hubris in *The Mighty Thor*. In a story line beginning
in 2002, and which would run until the series was canceled, Thor
has taken over as ruler of Asgard after the death of his father,
Odin. Deciding that humans are incapable of addressing their
own problems without destroying themselves, he moves Asgard to
the skies above New York City and proceeds to interfere directly
in the affairs of humans. This leads to conflict among the gods of
Asgard as well as between the Asgardians and the humans. While
Thor sees himself as aiding mankind by providing clean energy,
assuring everyone's economic well-being, improving health care
through Asgardian magic, and putting an end to war, humans are
angered at the loss of their freedom. Thor is chastised by members of the United Nations who see his actions as infringing on
national sovereignty. Proud, independent workers are reduced
to worshipping Thor as they are unable to make a profit without
accepting his benefits because of the disruption to markets. Even
his allies, the Avengers, intervene to keep him from stopping a
war. In a telling story, he faces Iron Man, in the midst of his own
crisis of morality, who sees the thunder god stepping far across
the line of acceptable behavior.[38] Thor finally realizes his own

limits when he tries to restore life to a dead child using the power of Asgard, only to create a soulless zombie who cannot recognize her own mother. As humans turn against Thor's intervention a military attack is launched against Asgard, with a nuclear explosion destroying the city. In an anger-filled response, Thor attacks, leveling New York.[39]

A central element of Thor's character has always been his moral purity and his struggle with pride. He was bound to the Earth by his father, Odin, and forced to share a body with a frail human doctor to learn humility. In this series (volume 2) he is bound initially to a human named Jake Olsen, but has broken that bond. He has thus lost part of the humanity that tempered the pride of the god. Thor wields a war hammer that can only be lifted by one whose soul is pure. After Asgard has been destroyed, Thor states, "Earth must change. Man must change. Those who caused this think I went too far when in reality I did not go far enough."[40] At this point, Thor unleashes his power over the elements and destroys New York. His anger and his pride have taught him that even though everyone counseled against his actions, he still should have gone further. Absolutely certain he is right, Thor turns to pick up his hammer, only to find that he cannot lift it. Thor has lost the ability to raise the hammer, indicating that his hubris has rendered his motives impure and himself unworthy.

The story then jumps several decades into the future; Thor is master of the Earth, a totalitarian tyrant unwilling to brook any opposition. His own son is recruited by an underground rebel movement to defeat him. Thor will later regain his ability to master the hammer, but only after his son is nearly killed and Thor, realizing that his own actions, derived from the hubris of his moral certainty, have set in motion the chain of events that led to these tragedies, goes back in time to stop himself from leveling New York City. He is reunited with his human host to restore his humanity and takes Asgard back to the realm of the immortals, shunning intervention in human affairs.[41]

In both the Thor and Iron Man stories the very essence of the hero is brought into question. Thor claims to know what is best for humans; Tony Stark is motivated by the belief that only he knows how to deal with military technology in an appropriate way. In the Iron Man story even the claims to moral certainty in past decades are problematized and rendered suspect. Both characters need to learn that they cannot take free will away from those they seek to protect. Thor loses control of his hammer, and Stark is rejected as secretary of defense nominee by the Senate Armed Services Committee. Only when they regain their sense of the hero as servant of others do they regain their stature as heroes. Any assertion of moral certainty in the twenty-first century, it appears, must be questioned as an act of hubris.

After 9/11, a nationalist response offered a sense of unity, of a possible return to the consensus of American identity of decades past. Absent an acceptable rhetoric with which to articulate that identity, however, it could be asserted with neither conviction nor acceptance. The very tropes that had been used to project that certainty were subverted well before the terrorist attacks on the United States. The nation's goals could not be defined in black and white; even the terrorism that was supposed to be the enemy was offered, in part, as a product of U.S. global adventurism. In this context, any claim to moral certainty could only be read as hubris, an attempt to impose one will on another with no true standard to measure the relative worth of differing values. Without a convincing assertion of American moral superiority, the American identity could not hold together; it would remain fractured into the plethora of self-interests identified by President Clinton in 1995. Nor would a plea to nationalist sentiment be sufficient to maintain a unified American self.

The Limits of Nationalism

The limits of nationalism are a constant theme in *Captain America* volume 4. Following the "Enemy" story comes "The Extremists,"[42] in which Captain America must face a threat posed by a Native American shaman, Inali Redpath, who controls the weather and seeks to return America to Native Americans. When faced with Redpath's argument that America was forcibly taken from the natives and built with slave labor, Captain America responds, "I'm tired of people trashing this country," and hits Redpath. Yet even in what seems a clear chauvinistic turn, Captain America must doubt his cause and his moral role. Government superagent Nick Fury tells him, "Ever since 9-11 you've been challenged to be something you don't want to be and it's making you nuts."[43] After defeating Redpath, Captain America muses, "I remember a time when it was easy to feel pride in 'this' country. When 'this' country celebrated the victories of its loyal soldiers. When 'this' country was my country right or wrong—and most of the time it was right. But times have changed haven't they. The battles are less clear, the wars less noble, the cause less right, even in the shadow of 9-11."[44] While he reasserts his pride in his country, he also recognizes the complexity of the context, the issues and the responses. As the avatar of the American mission and the American creed, Captain America must be plagued by doubts, and this again dominates the story line. Torn between the chauvinistic nationalism of his costume and his history, Captain America is not sure who he is, what he wants, or where he is going.

In the Avengers story "Red Dusk," a bioweapons attack is made on Mount Rushmore. It is revealed that the weapons were designed by the U.S. military and released by an order given by Secretary of Defense Dell Rusk, who is, in fact, Captain America's World War II nemesis the Red Skull (of which Dell Rusk is an anagram). When revealed, the Red Skull notes that he has given up his dreams of reviving the Nazi regime, claiming, "I have a new dream, a new vision. Freedom must feel fear, and fear leads to control. I was wrong about this country. This wonderful 'United' States of America. It has all the resources already in place. It has the right attitudes laced within. They just need to be exploited. To become the perfect nation America just needs a little push in the right direction."[45] This story presents a vision of political failure that permits the evil to grow within the bosom of government. That the evil is a fascist demagogue who describes the United States as ripe for a fascist movement if only Americans can learn to fear suggests that Americans are impure and morally degenerate as fear turns "freedom" into fascism.

In all of these stories the nation is indicted as incapable of dealing with the terrorist threat or as complicit in it. The argument extends beyond the government to the citizens of the United States, indicted by the Red Skull as willing accomplices in his rise to power. It extends to all nations that are willing to cede power to someone who looks like a hero but who, in fact, wants only to create a personal empire. The complicity of nationalism

Figure 6.4. The Secretary of Defense: The Red Skull
From "Red Zone part 5: The Great Escape" *Avengers*
vol. 3, no. 69 (September 2003), 13.

and of the national government makes it impossible for the
United States to claim itself virtuous. Less than three years from
the attacks on the World Trade Center, superheroes cannot
seriously view the United States as virtuous victim nor can the
United States raise nationalist arguments in support of its actions
without causing more destruction than before.

At a moment when a national mission has been articulated—
a War on Terror—and actual combat continues to take place
in Iraq and Afghanistan, comic books might be expected to

articulate support for that mission and those actions. Were there a defined American self to place in these contexts, were there an accepted rhetoric with which to make the case for such support, it might be there. That rhetoric, however, had been discredited. The assumption of a global role to contain communism had led the United States to engage in international activities—the Vietnam War being the most prominent—that led people to doubt the virtue of the American mission. The imperial presidency created a "credibility gap" that, when coupled with other evidence of government misdeeds (and again the Watergate Scandal stands out), rendered untenable claims to the virtue of American leaders. The costs of pursuing a Cold War strategy of containment and expanding social programs put great strains on the American economy; structural transformations associated with economic globalization increased those strains and undermined belief in the open-ended progress that the virtuous American mission was supposed to achieve. The affluence that had papered over the rising ideological conflicts in the 1960s thus came to an end, and those conflicts came into the open, defining the "culture wars" that would characterize politics in the 1990s. Now they would be expressed largely in terms of the individual, without reference to virtue or progress. Without a common language of progress and virtue, only individualism remained as an American value to be asserted; this proved insufficient to sustain an idea of the national community that would support missions such as the so-called War on Terror. Within two years of the attacks of 9/11 comics were questioning U.S. cupability. Americans could no longer define themselves as a virtuous nation in pursuit of a progressive global mission. Within a year of the invasion of Iraq, hubris and deception were attributed to both government and superheroes.

7

Civil War and the Death of Captain America

I N 2007, CAPTAIN AMERICA DIED. It was not Steve Rogers's first death, but it may well be his last. While earlier deaths had been brief narrative moments, reimagined back story, or fakes, this latest death came in the wake of Marvel Comic's "Civil War," a story that crossed over into nearly all Marvel titles and that was an allegory of the War on Terror and the USA Patriot Act, raising the tale from closed narrative to cultural commentary. It was treated as such, and reported in major news outlets, including the *New York Times*.[1] While Marvel editor in chief Joe Quesada refused to interpret the death of Captain America, he repeatedly claimed that it was meant to be allegorical and open to interpretation.[2]

The unwillingness of Quesada to interpret the narrative may have been an attempt to avoid alienating his audience, which was heavily divided over political issues. By 2007, popular support for U.S. military action in Iraq was meager. A CNN–Opinion Research Corporation poll found that not only did 67 percent of Americans oppose the U.S. presence in Iraq, but 54 percent did not believe the war was morally justified.[3] Positions on the war were heavily polarized along partisan lines, with 62 percent of Republicans still supporting the action and 90 percent of Democrats opposing it. That a military action justified by a claim to the progressive mission of America would have such weak and partisan support indicated the extent to which the American self was fractured. That a majority doubted that the United States was acting morally indicated a loss of faith in the virtue of the nation and the government. The death of Captain America may well symbolize a decline in the power of rhetoric of American national identity, particularly of the belief in the virtue and progressive mission of America, and the death of a particular construct of the American self.

Setting the Stage: Secret Wars and Winter Soldiers

A new version of grim and gritty Marvel seemed to emerge in 2005. As the economy began to take a turn for the worse and the public turned against the war in Iraq, all within the context of continued fears of terrorism, Marvel's comic books turned darker, the stories more ominous. Color schemes lost the brightness that had characterized the previous decade; backgrounds became darker, contrasts less distinct. In yet another summer crossover event, Marvel killed off the Mighty Thor, disbanded the Avengers, and destroyed most of the population of mutants who had emerged over the many years and manifestations of the X-Men.[4] Both the Iron Man and Captain America series, as well as the Avengers titles, were restarted at number 1 yet again, and the Hulk was placed on hiatus. When the books were restarted, they exhibited this new, darker aesthetic of counterterrorist America.

The Iron Man series restarted with a tale reminiscent of the origin, in which Tony Stark is injured while observing the operations of weapons systems. The context, however, is not the Vietnam War, as it had been for the previous forty years, but Afghanistan in the post-9/11 world.[5] The first story arc treats a stolen biological weapon, the Extremis virus, that enhances human power.[6] To capture the villain, whose powers have been enhanced by the virus, Tony Stark will expose himself to it. As a result, his power as Iron Man is no longer limited to wearing the armor but is now infused within his bloodstream, internalized into his body rather than externalized in the machine. What had been a shell, a protective coating, has now entered the blood. Defending against the threats of the twenty-first century, this suggests, has necessitated the development of a power that is more invasive, intrusive, and interventionist than previously used. The greater power of the Extremis virus allows Iron Man to defeat the new, more powerful threat, but only by transforming his own body with this biological agent. Allegorically, defending against the threats of the contemporary world may lead to a major transformation of the American body politic. As the Cold War transformed the American self, so too would the postnational conflict of the twenty-first century.

This theme, of new threats, both within and without, is echoed in the next story, "Execute Program,"[7] which deals with mistaken identity and internal subversion. The Extremis virus has made Iron Man vulnerable to external control by the son of Hu Yinsen, the man who helped Stark develop the first Iron Man suit in Vietnam. Under this control, Iron Man is being used to kill all whom the son considers responsible for the imprisonment and death of his father. Believing Iron Man to be responsible for the deaths, Strategic Hazard Intervention Espionage Logistics Directorate (SHIELD) and the Avengers try to subdue him. Tony Stark becomes a fugitive and must disguise himself to avoid capture. The new power needed to defeat these new threats has made the hero vulnerable to subversion and rendered unclear the source of the danger. The story opens with Iron Man easily defeating the Crimson Dynamo, a major, superpowered Soviet foe from the Cold War days, whom Iron Man refers to as an "old school pain in the ass." This signals a transformation of threats; the nationalist Soviet agent is easily defeated and cast aside. The new threats, however, will need a more powerful, less nationalistic, and less obvious hero.[8]

The Captain America series was also rebooted, in 2006, but without a retelling of the character's origin. Instead, the first fifteen issues included a series of flashbacks to World War II, reconstructions of moments in the development of the protagonist. The threat he faces also involves terrorists, but in this case it comes from Russia rather than Afghanistan. The Red Skull is shot by Russian capitalist and international criminal Aleksander Lukin, so that Lukin can gain control of the Cosmic Cube. Using the cube, the Skull transfers his mind into Lukin, although this will not be apparent immediately. Instead, the Skull's longtime henchman, Crossbones, will team with the Skull's daughter to seek revenge on Lukin for killing her father, only to find that the Skull and Lukin are one and the same.[9] Lukin's quest for world dominance will thus be linked to the Nazis, resurrecting the trope from the 1960s with greater vigor, a dark threat for a dark world.

The flashbacks also render problematic the history of Captain America. The Red Skull/Lukin uses the Cosmic Cube to alter Captain America's dreams such that he is misremembering the events of his life during World War II. As Iron Man has redefined the threats facing the nation in the twenty-first century and the implications of the self-altering response to these threats, the Captain America books render mutable the American self as defined by the past.[10] By asserting a trope of continuity between the threats of the past and the present but unmooring the past to make it changeable, the Captain America narrative creates greater ambiguity about the present and the American self that occupies it.

These transformations entail another major change for Captain America's continuity. One of the key features of the character had always been his regret at the death of his young sidekick Bucky Barnes at the end of World War II; but in a major twist, Bucky returns.[11] Found near death in the North Atlantic by a Soviet submarine, he was taken to the Soviet Union, nursed back to health, and brainwashed into becoming the most lethal assassin the USSR had. He would later be placed in suspended animation, revived only when there was a particularly thorny assassination to carry out. Code-named Winter Soldier, he became a figure of myth and legend. Now, with the USSR no longer extant, Bucky is awakened by Lukin and comes to the United States. Believing himself a communist assassin, Bucky kills Jack Monroe, the Bucky from the 1950s who was revived in the 1980s and became the hero Nomad, and is confronted by Captain America, who uses the Cosmic Cube to reawaken Bucky's memories.

At this point in comics history, the political economy of the "Marvel universe" has been almost completely reconfigured. Iron Man is no longer tied to the Cold War but is instead a product of the War on Terror and is once again involved in the development of munitions for the U.S. military. Captain America is connected deeply to World War II (although the meaning of that connection is now less clear) both through his confrontation with the minions and avatars of the Red Skull and through the resurrection of Bucky, removing a major feature of the character's Cold War persona. The flashbacks to World War II often show Captain America on the Russian front, making a direct connection between the pre–Cold War USSR and post–Cold War Russia. Similarly, the revival of Bucky removes Captain America's guilt, but it also brings a character whose history is dictated by pre–Cold War America and Cold War–era Soviet Union. The American Cold War has almost vanished from this book, and Captain America is dislodged from his standard narrative.

Nick Fury is immune to neither the new, darker world nor the need to delink Marvel from the Cold War. In the 2004–5 miniseries *Secret War*, Fury becomes aware that third-rate criminals are using very expensive technology to commit crimes. The technology is provided by a criminal engineer called the Tinkerer, who is backed by the government of Latveria. Formerly ruled by Fantastic Four villain Dr. Doom, Latveria is now a fledgling democracy being supported by the United States. When Fury informs the U.S. president that Latveria is engaged in terrorist actions in the States, the president tells him to drop it, that he himself will deal with it. Fury, realizing that nothing will be done, recruits a group of heroes, including Captain America, to take down the Latverian government. Unknown to the heroes this is a rogue mission without government sanction. After the mission, Fury erases their memories of the mission, but these memories return a year later when the Latverians retaliate by mobilizing technologically advanced criminals to try to destroy New York City with a nuclear weapon. With the villains defeated, Fury becomes a behind-the-scenes actor in several stories, remaining largely unseen for some time.[12]

Removing Nick Fury and making him a shadowy presence moves one of the key figures of the Cold War Marvel universe from active agent to background feature. His influence, like the Cold War legacy he represents, is no longer active and direct. The Cold War is over, and there is no longer a place for him. Fury represents the moral certainty of the Cold War; he knows who the enemy is, and he wants to take decisive action, but these absolutes do not serve the post–Cold War world, where enemy states may help fight against terrorists and friendly states may harbor them. The complex reality does not comport with the Cold War myth, and the Cold War certainties that guide Fury's actions have no place in a world where the American government is allied with a Latverian state that sponsors terrorism, so he must vanish.

Fury's absence, Iron Man's relocation in time from the Cold War to the War on Terror, and the problemetizing of Captain America's definition of self through a mutable history and the resurrection of Bucky set the stage for the Civil War series that dominated the books in 2006 and into 2007. This civil war pits hero against hero, particularly Iron Man against Captain America, in a contest to define the American self and the very idea of the hero in the twenty-first century.

Civil War: Captain America versus Iron Man

Marvel's Civil War series is an allegory of the War on Terror and particularly the USA Patriot Act.[13] The story begins with a twenty-first-century tragedy. The New Warriors, a group of young superheroes who are the subject of a reality television show, engage with a supervillain named Nitro in Stamford, Connecticut. In this battle, Nitro, a human bomb, explodes and kills more than six hundred civilians, including children. As a consequence, the government enacts the Superhero Registration Act, a law that requires all superpowered heroes to become licensed agents of the government or risk arrest as outlaws. The act is masterminded by Tony Stark, Reed Richards of the Fantastic Four, and Henry Pym of the Avengers—three of Marvel's maverick scientist-cowboys of the 1960s. Opponents of the act are led by Captain America. The story follows the conflict between the proregistration forces led by Iron Man and backed by SHIELD (absent Nick Fury) and the antiregistration underground led by Captain America. It culminates in a battle in which the antiregistration forces appear to be winning, until Captain America realizes the level of destruction the heroes are bringing to Manhattan and surrenders.

The Civil War series is a clear commentary on the USA Patriot Act and post-9/11 U.S. government actions and includes a variety of specifically allegorical moments. Reed Richards designs a special prison for supervillains (including heroes who fail to register) located in the Negative Zone, away from the prying eyes of the media or civil liberty attorneys, a reference to U.S. intelligence renditions to overseas detention camps or the detaining of "enemy combatants" at the U.S. Naval base at Guantanamo Bay, Cuba. One of the New Warriors is arrested and charged with the murders of all the citizens of Stamford who were killed in the confrontation with Nitro; he is denied legal counsel and tortured during his interrogation.

The central focus of the story remains the Superhero Registration Act and the conflict between the traditional vision of the hero as above politics, operating under a self-directed moral code, and that of the hero as an agent of the government. Iron Man's argument—that heroes need to be trained and properly regulated—suggests a vision of moral certainty for the established authorities. That the Registration Act is masterminded by three of the paradigmatic scientist-individuals of the 1960s directly confronts the individualistic rhetoric of the Marvel comics of the Cold War.

The debate is voiced on the two sides by Iron Man and Captain America. In *Civil War: Rubicon,*[14] Captain America and Iron Man meet to discuss the conflict that has rendered them enemies. They recount their shared history. Referring to events that occurred in 1964, Iron Man states, "Those were the days, when we could almost kill each other and smooth it over with a couple of words." The reference to a period of shared values that served as a ground for compromise even amid dire conflict suggests that the current crisis is sourced in that loss of common ground. The civil war of the superheroes is a product of a lost rhetoric that permitted compromise. Unsurprisingly, both heroes accuse each other of hubris. Captain America recalls several events from Iron Man's past, claiming that, in each case, "You've always thought that you knew best by virtue of your genius, and once you decide that's it." Iron Man accuses Captain America of being blinded by his own iconic stature: "You can't see things from my perspective because it's predicated on the premise that superheroes make mistakes. And you're Captain America. You don't make mistakes." Both are absolutely convinced of their rightness, and neither can find the ground for compromise that had existed for them forty years earlier. They have no language of compromise, no rhetoric of community with which to allow them to resolve their dispute short of civil war.

A significant subplot is the role of several key heroes in determining the fate of the superhero community. Tony Stark and Reed Richards, along with several other prominent Marvel heroes (Namor, the Submariner, Professor X of the X-Men, the Black Panther, Dr. Strange, and Black Bolt of the Inhumans), are given a new status as the Illuminati, a self-appointed group of overseers for superhuman action. While not created until the twenty-first century, the story claims that they have played this role throughout modern Marvel comics history.[15] Simultaneous with the events of "Civil War," the Illuminati decide that the Hulk is too powerful and destructive to be left on Earth and conspire with SHIELD to maroon him on another planet. This inaugurates a two-year story "Planet Hulk" and "World War Hulk," which casts the Hulk as Spartacus on this new planet and offers a strong argument in favor of the power of individual liberty.[16] Running simultaneously with "Civil War," "Planet Hulk" reveals the hubris of the Illuminati, particularly Stark and Richards, who are responsible for both the Hulk's exile and the Registration Act, and renders their ideological position problematic.

Again, distrust of government and fear of public authority are linked to a betrayal of American ideals. The actions of the government in the Registration Act reduce the heroes of the Marvel universe to government agents, removing the internal direction that once defined their heroism. No longer living by a moral code that is more stringent than that of the legal system, the heroes have become officers of the latter, superpowered police officers enforcing governmental law. The subordination of the hero to government, the rendering ignoble of the noble, is produced by those who forty years earlier were the noble heroes—Tony Stark and Reed Richards. The actions of the government via the Registration Act and in exiling the Hulk are questionable, acts of hubris that run counter to the moral values embodied in the classic Marvel heroes. This is done not only by placing the counterargument in the mouths of Marvel's most popular heroes—Spider-Man, Daredevil, and Wolverine, all led by Captain America—but also in the aftermath of the victory of registration forces. The Thunderbolts are turned over to the most vicious of villains—Green Goblin, Bullseye, Venom. Nonregistered heroes are forced to accept a biological implant that renders them powerless. The government creates a series of new superhero groups for the entire country, but in each case political manipulation serves some insidious goal rather than the noble service one expects of heroes. In short, while the Civil War series offers debate between the pro- and antiregistration positions, it is unclear which side is given the privileged moral position. The architects of this act, of its tools—the biological implants, the Negative Zone prison—are the scientist-heroes of the 1960s who were the moral core of the progressive, liberal individual consensus of Marvel stories. Now the inner-directed moral code they follow has led them to the hubris of registration, the regulation of their fellow heroes, and the rendering of heroism impossible. Their opponents only stop fighting when the level of destruction they are causing becomes extreme; they are, in fact, guilty of exactly the uncontrolled violence that gave rise to the Registration Act in the first place. The liberal consensus has come undone, broken into pieces represented by the hubristic, controlling righteousness of Iron Man and Mr. Fantastic and the libertarian righteousness of Captain America. Civil War is just that, but it is not only a war of superheroes; it is the final denouement in the story of the unraveling of the liberal consensus and how that unraveling undermined the effectiveness of the rhetoric of the mythic American national identity in the process.

The end of the conflict continues to leave the questions unanswered. Trying to bolster their forces, Stark, Richards, and Pym clone the now dead Thor. His power, however, is untempered by any sense of responsibility, and in a melee he kills the superhero Goliath.[17] This extreme action is recalled at the end, when on the verge of victory, Captain America realizes that the battle between the two sides is destroying Manhattan. As he is about to deliver the final blow in his battle with Iron Man, Captain America is tackled by a group of civilians. "Let me go," he calls. "I don't want to hurt you," to which they reply, "Don't want to hurt us? Are you trying to be funny?" The next panel offers a view of the destruction in the city from Captain America's point of view. Realizing

the level of destruction, he stops. "They're right. We're not fighting for the people anymore. Look at us, we're just fighting." "We
were winning back there," protests Spider-Man. "Everything but
the argument," replies Captain America, offering his wrists to the
police for handcuffs.[18]

Captain America's argument may be a comment on the
U.S. government's position in the War on Terror at home and
abroad. Perhaps terrorism is being halted, perhaps greater
security is being achieved, but at what cost? Has the argument
been lost because of hubristic actions, because of an unwillingness to seek out a common ground of compromise? The Civil
War series raises this question, suggesting specifically that the
weakened rhetoric of American national identity has been a
source of the uncompromising hubris that has come to characterize the contemporary political economy. The very need for
a Superhero Registration Act implies that society cannot trust
the heroes to serve its needs simply because they share a set of
values; any assertion of some higher moral duty must be viewed
with suspicion.

Fallen Son: The Death of Captain America

The culmination of the Civil War series is the death of Captain
America.[19] Having surrendered to Iron Man out of his higher
sense of moral duty, Captain America is being led into a courthouse to be arraigned when he uses his body to absorb a sniper's
bullet targeting one of his police escorts. Wounded amid the
resultant pandemonium, Captain America lies on the courthouse
steps. His dying breath, a plea to protect innocents (innocence?),
is a testimony to his commitment to his moral duty. His longtime
girlfriend, Sharon Carter, is his murderer; under the mental control of the evil Dr. Faustus, she shoots him three times and kills
him. Dr. Faustus is in league with the Red Skull, and the Skull's
plan for world domination includes creating chaos in the United
States, a plan that will play out over the next several years.

Captain America's death at the hands of his love, even though
her mind is not her own, continues the theme of betrayal that so
dominated the comics of the 1980s and early 1990s. The impli-
cation is that without intention, and without reasoned control,

Figure 7.1. The Death of the Dream
From "The Death of a Dream" *Captain America* 25
(April 2007), 17.

Americans have destroyed the myth of the American self. With
the death of Captain America, the "death of the dream" as Marvel has called it, the myth of American virtue and progress must
also die.

This does not mean that the rhetoric of American national
identity has been rendered powerless. While the consensual myth
of American identity that dominated the early Cold War is gone,
and the rhetorical elements that were used to construct it have
lost their descriptive power, they remain an ideal to be achieved.
Captain America's longtime ally Sam Wilson (the Falcon) speaks
to this at a memorial for Captain America. He tells the crowd,

> We usually see the difference between us, separated by nation-
> ality, by color, by religion, and yet here we are, all connected.
> Steve Rogers, that skinny blond-haired kid who grew up on
> the streets of New York showed us the ideals of the American
> dream, the great melting pot that can bring out the best in
> each of us and bind us all together actually works! And he can
> keep teaching us that long after he's gone. . . . This doesn't
> have to be a day of sadness. We can accept it as a gift of unity
> and hope, the kind of day Captain America lived for.[20]

After a year of eulogies and conspiracies, Captain America returned in March 2008. It was not, however, Steve Rogers but Bucky Barnes who assumed the mantle.

Having spent a year underground, trying to come to terms with the new world in which he dwelt and his new reality as a blend of Soviet brainwashing and American dreaming, Bucky reemerges to confront Iron Man, whom he deems responsible for Captain America's death. Reluctantly assuming the role of Captain America, Bucky offers a different definition of the American icon. Carrying not only the shield but also a gun, he is more willing to take fatal action than was Steve Rogers. Such violence generates no major remorse from the new Captain America as there was from Steve Rogers in the mid-1980s or in the killing of terrorists in 2002. Where Steve Rogers had become increasingly a paragon of American virtue, an ideal to emulate but impossible to replicate, Bucky as Captain America offers a more flawed, less virtuous ideal. Where Rogers had slept through the deepest dark of the Cold War, Bucky is an agent of America's enemy. Rogers brought World War II values to the late twentieth century; Bucky upholds these ideals, tempered by the reality of four decades of Cold War transformations. Where Steve Rogers stood as an example of the best America could be and a condemnation of the failure of others to be that (although he himself never was one to condemn), Bucky is one of the people, an everyman trying to do his best. Where Steve Rogers's constantly questioned whether his values still mattered in a changed world, Bucky assumes that those values matter wholeheartedly but also knows he will probably never live up to them. His constant question is whether he is worthy of the shoes of Steve Rogers.

The dream has not died with Steve Rogers, but it has indeed been revealed to be a dream, an aspiration rather than a description. With irony and cynicism we note that Steve Rogers is dead, if he ever lived. But if he never lived, he still matters, the most stolid of individuals, representing the hope of American virtue and progress. Like President Bill Clinton, we see the collapse of the myth of consensus as both frightening and an exciting opportunity to engage the reality of a multicultural America. Like President Bush, we aspire to promote progress around the world in "hope and human rights . . . the non-negotiable demands of human freedom." Like Sharon Carter, we continue to be American dreamers, even in the face of our cynicism. Like Sam Wilson, we continue to celebrate our national community through rituals of hope. Like Bucky, we aspire to regain the belief that living the ideal is possible, that the American self can be found, identified, touched, and felt. We mourn the dying fire of that faith but nurture an ember of hope that we can reignite the flame to burn more brightly, free of the blinders of myth, and open to the faith that "out of the many, one."

Notes

Comic books are products of collaborative efforts between writers and artists, and thus have multiple authors, not all credited. In the notes and bibliography I have tried to follow the conventions of the Comic Art and Comics Area of the Popular Culture Association, "Comic Art in Scholarly Writing: A Citation Guide," by Ellis and Allen (1998), available at http://www.comicsreasearch.org/CAC/cite.html. Following this format, these abbreviations are used:

- (w) writer
- (p) penciller
- (i) inker
- (a) artist (when penciller and inker are not distinguished)

Introduction

1. Stan Lee and George Mair, *Excelsior: The Amazing Life of Stan Lee* (New York: Fireside Books, 2002), 167–68.
2. Godfrey Hodgson, *America in Our Time* (New York: Doubleday, 1976).
3. For a history of the emergence of the comic book industry that emphasizes the exuberance of this period, see Gerard Jones, *Men of Tomorrow: Geeks, Gangsters, and the Birth of the Comic Book* (New York: Basic Books, 2004).
4. Ibid., 233.
5. Bradford Wright, *Comic Book Nation: The Transformation of Youth Culture in America* (Baltimore: Johns Hopkins University Press, 2001), 75.
6. William Savage Jr., *Commies, Cowboys, and Jungle Queens: Comic Books and America, 1945–1954* (Hanover, NH: Wesleyan University Press, 1990), 74.
7. David Gaines, quoted in David Hajdu, *The Ten-Cent Plague: The Great Comic Book Scare and How It Changed America* (New York: Farrar, Straus and Giroux, 2008), 183.
8. Amy Kiste Nyberg, *Seal of Approval: The History of the Comics Code* (Jackson: University Press of Mississippi, 1998), 26–27. See also Hadju, *The Ten-Cent Plague.*
9. Fredric Wertham, *Seduction of the Innocent* (New York: Rinehart, 1954).
10. "Testimony of William E. Gaines before the Senate Subcommittee to Investigate Juvenile Delinquency, 21 April 1954," reprinted in Fred von Bernewitz and Grant Geissman, *Tales of Terror: The EC Companion* (Seattle: Fantagraphic Books, 2000), 24.

11. On the events surrounding Werthem's crusade and the Kefauver hearings, see Hadju, *Ten-Cent Plague.* On the Comics Code, see Nyberg, *Seal of Approval.*

12. Savage sees the impact of the Comics Code as so profound that he concludes there is no significant cultural commentary in the medium after 1956. See Savage, *Cowboys, Commies,* 102.

13. This story has been recounted numerous times in both academic and popular histories. Reliable versions can be found in Peter Sanderson, *Marvel Universe* (New York: Abradale Press, 1996); and Les Daniels, *Marvel: Five Fabulous Decades of the World's Greatest Comics* (New York: Henry Abrams, 1991). See also Ronin Ro, *Tales to Astonish: Jack Kirby, Stan Lee, and the American Comic Book Revolution* (New York: Bloomsbury Press, 2004); and Jordan Raphael and Tom Spurgeon, *Stan Lee and the Rise and Fall of the American Comic Book* (Chicago: Chicago Review Press, 2003).

14. For a visual examination of the process, see Daniels, *Marvel,* 226–31.

15. For an application of Cold War cultural history constructs to Marvel characters, see Robert Genter, "'With Great Power Comes Great Responsibility': Cold War Culture and the Birth of Marvel Comics," *Journal of Popular Culture* 40 (2007): 953–78.

16. DC, publishers of Superman, Batman, and Wonder Woman, among others, did not adopt such a close continuity until the 1970s, and it always remained much looser.

17. Richard Reynolds, *Superheroes: A Modern Mythology* (Jackson: University Press of Mississippi, 1992), 44–45.

18. Thanks are due to Judith Hiltner for this comparison.

19. The superhero comics of the mid-1980s have received much critical attention because of this. See Reynolds, *Superheroes,* 84–118; and Geof Klock, *How to Read Superhero Comics and Why* (New York: Continuum, 2002).

20. Reynolds, *Superheroes.*

21. Peter Coogan, *Superhero: The Secret Origin of a Genre* (Austin, TX: Monkeybrain Books, 2006); Thomas Inge, *Comics as Culture* (Jackson: University Press of Mississippi, 1990).

22. John Shelton Lawrence and Thomas Jewitt, *The Myth of the American Superhero* (New York: Eerdmans, 2002).

23. Ariel Dorfman and Armand Mattelart, *How to Read Donald Duck: Imperialist Ideology in the Disney Comic* (London: IG Editions, 1975).

24. Gary Engel, "What Makes Superman So Darned American?" in *Superman at 50: The Persistence of a Legend,* edited by Dennis Dooley and Gary Engel (Cleveland, OH: Octavia Press, 1987), 79–88.

25. Will Brooker, *Batman Unmasked: Analyzing a Cultural Icon* (New York: Continuum, 2000).

26. Reynolds, *Superheroes,* 77.

27. Mike Alsford, *Heroes and Villains* (Waco, TX: Baylor University Press, 2006), 22; emphasis in the original.

28. Ibid., 124.

29. Jewitt and Lawrence, *Myth.*

30. Brooker, *Batman Unmasked*, 35.

31. Umberto Eco, "The Myth of Superman," in *The Role of the Reader*, translated by Natalie Chilton (Bloomington: Indiana University Press, 1979), 124.

32. This is contra Reynolds, who unlike most analysts from a mythic perspective, sees the embeddedness in continuity as the source of the mythic narrative; see Reynolds, in *Superheroes*, particularly 44–45.

33. Jones, *Men of Tomorrow*, 29.

34. Reynolds, *Superheroes*, 29.

35. Ibid., 37.

36. Danny Fingeroth, *Superman on the Couch: What Superheroes Really Tells Us About Ourselves and Our Society* (New York: Continuum, 2004), 60. A similar argument is developed in Tom Morris, "What's Behind the Mask? The Secret of Secret Identities," in *Superheroes and Philosophy: Truth, Justice and the Socratic Way*, edited by Tom Morris and Matt Morris (Chicago: Open Court Press, 2005), 250–66.

37. Fingeroth, *Superman on the Couch*, 57–58; emphasis in the original.

38. Both Marvel and DC ran significant story lines involving secret identity that crossed through all of their hero titles in 2005 and 2006. See Brad Meltzer (w), Rags Morales (p), and Mike Bair (i), *Identity Crisis* 1–7, (April 2004–February 2005); and Mark Millar (w), Steve McNiven (p), and Dexter Vines (i), *Civil War* 1–7 (July 2006–January 2007).

39. See Reyolds, *Superheroes*, especially 50–51.

40. See Jesse T. Moore, "The Education of Green Lantern: Culture and Ideology," *Journal of American Culture* 26, no. 2 (2003): 263–78.

41. Thierry Groensten, *The System of Comics*, translated by Bart Beaty and Nick Nguyen (Jackson: University Press of Mississippi, 2007) offers a similar argument, noting that the first moment of analysis of the comic book page is to determine if the organization of the page varies from the expected norm.

42. While underdeveloped, the subject is widely discussed. The seminal works in the field continue to be largely produced by comics artists, such as Will Eisner. See his two significant works *Comics and Sequential Art* (Tamarac, FL: Poorhouse Press, 1985); and *Graphic Storytelling and Visual Narrative* (Tamarac, FL: Poorhouse Press, 1996). One of the most useful works is Scott McCloud, *Understanding Comics: The Invisible Art* (New York: Harper, 1994). More academic works include Joseph Witek, *Comic Books as History: The Narrative Art of Jack Jackson, Art Spiegelman, and Harvey Pekar* (Jackson: University Press of Mississippi, 1989); Robert C. Harvey, *The Art of the Comic Book: An Aesthetic History* (Jackson: University Press of Mississippi, 1996); Eric Smoodlin, "Cartoon and Comic Classicism: High-Art Histories of Lowbrow Culture," *American Literary History* 4 (1992): 129–40; and Groensteen, *The System of Comics.*

43. See Allen Ellis, "Comic Art in Scholarly Writing: A Citation Guide," 1998; *http://www.comiresearch.org/CAC/cite.html* (accessed May 4, 2008).

Chapter One

1. Derek Leebaert, *The Fifty-Year Wound: The True Price of America's Cold War Victory* (Boston: Little, Brown, 2002); see especially 3–84.

2. There is a vast literature on hegemonic stability theory. See, especially, Charles Kindleberger, *The World in Depression, 1929–1939* (Berkeley and Los Angeles: University of California Press, 1986); and Robert Keohane, *After Hegemony* (Princeton, NJ: Princeton University Press, 1985).

3. The literature on the Cold War and bipolarity is extensive. Some important works include John Lewis Gaddis, *The Cold War: A New History* (New York: Penguin, 2005); Martin Walker, *The Cold War: A History* (New York: Holt, 1995); and Vlasilav Zubok and Constantine Pleshakov, *Inside the Kremlin's Cold War* (Cambridge, MA: Harvard University Press, 1997).

4. Leebaert, *Fifty-Year Wound*, 49.

5. James Patterson, *Grand Expectations: The United States, 1945–1974* (New York: Oxford University Press, 1996), 143.

6. Aaron L. Friedberg, *In the Shadow of the Garrison State: America's Anti-Statism and Its Cold War Grand Strategy* (Princeton, NJ: Princeton University Press, 2000).

7. Terrence Ball, "The Politics of Social Science in Postwar America," in *Recasting America*, edited by Lary May (Chicago: University of Chicago Press, 1989), 76–92; Ron Robin, *The Making of the Cold War Enemy* (Princeton, NJ: Princeton University Press, 2001).

8. The sociologist on the cover of *Time*, September 27, 1954, was David Reisman; the two Kinsey reports are discussed in Stephen Whitfield, *The Culture of the Cold War*, 2nd ed. (Baltimore: Johns Hopkins University Press, 1996), 184–87; the 1957 study is discussed in Elaine Tyler May, "Explosive Issues: Sex, Women and the Bomb," in Lary May, ed., *Recasting America*, 156.

9. Alfred Chandler, *Strategy and Structure: Chapters in the History of the American Industrial Enterprise* (Cambridge, MA: MIT Press, 1962).

10. Warren Sussman, "Did Success Spoil the United States? Dual Representation in Postwar America" in May, ed., *Recasting America*, 19–38.

11. Michael Dukakis, "Speech Accepting the Presidential Nomination from the 1988 Democratic National Convention," 21 July 1988; *http://www.transcripts.cnn.com/TRANSCRIPTS/0006/04/sm.11.html* (accessed April 14, 2008).

12. David Reisman, "The Nylon War," in *Abundance for What?* (New York: Doubleday, 1964), 67–79.

13. Allan Carlson, *The "American Way": Family and Community in the Shaping of the American Identity* (Washington: ISI Books, 2003), 110.

14. Warren Sussman, *Culture as History: Transformations in American Society in the Twentieth Century* (New York: Pantheon Books, 1984), 150–84.

15. Richard Hofstadter, *The American Political Tradition and the Men Who Made It* (New York: Vintage, 1948).

16. Eric Hoffer, *The True Believer* (New York: Harper and Brothers, 1951).

17. See, for instance, Robert Dahl, *A Preface to Democratic Theory* (Chicago: University of Chicago Press, 1956); and Seymour Martin Lipset, *Political Man: The Social Bases of Politics* (New York: Doubleday, 1960).

18. See, for instance, Daniel Lerner, *The Passing of Traditional Society: Modernizing the Middle East* (Glencoe, IL: Free Press, 1958); and Walt Whitman Rostow, *The Stages of Economic Growth: Non-Communist Manifesto* (New York: Cambridge, 1960).

19. Daniel Bell, *The End of Ideology: On the Exhaustion of Political Ideas in the Fifties* (New York: Crowell Collier and MacMillan, 1961).

20. Lary May, "Introduction," in May, ed., *Recasting America*, 8, 5.

21. Ibid., 2. See also Richard Noble, *Death of a Nation: American Culture and the End of Exceptionalism* (Minneapolis: University of Minnesota Press, 2002).

22. John Winthrop, "A Modell of Christian Charity," in *American Sermons*, edited by Michael Warner (New York: Library of America, 1999), 39–40.

23. Ibid., 41–42.

24. This notion of a rhetoric of American identity is very similar to that described by Sacvan Bercovitch in *The Rites of Assent* (New York: Routledge, 1993), 29–67. See also Whitfield, *The Culture of the Cold War*, 53–54. This argument is also developed in slightly different form in Matthew J. Costello, "The Pilgrimage and Progress of George Bailey: Puritanism, *It's a Wonderful Life*, and the Language of Community in America," *American Studies* 40, no. 3 (1999): 31–52.

25. Benjamin Franklin, *Autobiography and Other Writings* (New York: Penguin: 1986). On the progressivism of postrevolutionary thinkers, see Michael Lienisch, *A New Order for the Ages: Time, the Constitution, and the Making of Modern American Political Thought* (Princeton, NJ: Princeton University Press, 1988).

26. Ralph Waldo Emerson. "The Young American," in *Essays and Lectures*, edited by Joel Porte (New York: Library of America, 1983), 211–30.

27. Abraham Lincoln, "Annual Message to Congress, 3 December 1861," in *Speeches and Writings*, 1859–1865, edited by Don E. Fehrenbacher (New York: Library of America, 1989), 296–97.

28. On Southern slaveholders, see James M. MacPherson, *Battle Cry of Freedom: The Civil War Era* (New York: Oxford University Press, 1988), 50, 196–98. See also John Crowe Ransom. "Reconstructed but Unregenerate," in *I'll Take My Stand: The South and the Agrarian Tradition*, edited by John Crowe Ransom, et al. (New York: Harper Torchbooks, 1962).

29. Alan Nadel, *Containment Culture: American Narratives, Postmodernism, and the Atomic Age* (Durham, NC: Duke University Press, 1995), 92.

30. George Kennan [writing as X], "The Sources of Soviet Conduct," *Foreign Affairs* 25 (1947): 566–82.

31. "National Security Council Memorandum 68: United States Objectives and Programs for National Security (14 April 1950)," in *American Cold War Strategy: Interpreting NSC 68*, edited by Ernest May (Boston: Bedford, 1993), 43, 68, 54.

32. Jackson, Lears, "A Matter of Taste: Corporate Cultural Hegemony in a Mass-Consumption Society," In May, ed., *Recasting America*, 50.

33. Leerom Medovoi, "Democracy, Capitalism, and American Literature: The Cold War Construction of J. D. Salinger's Paperback Hero," in *The Other Fifties: Interrogating Midcentury Icons*, edited by Joel Foreman (Urbana: University of Illinois Press, 1997), 256.

34. William Whyte, *The Organizational Man* (New York: Simon and Schuster, 1956); David Reisman, *The Lonely Crowd: A Study of Changing American Character* (New Haven, CT: Yale University Press, 1950).

35. John Kenneth Galbraith, *The Affluent Society*, 3rd ed. (New York: New American Library, 1976).

36. John F. Kennedy, speaking in Salt Lake City, September 1960, quoted in Patterson, *Grand Expectations*, 486.

37. Thomas Borstelman, *The Cold War and the Color Line: American Race Relations in the Global Arena* (Cambridge, MA: Harvard University Press, 2001); Mary L. Dudziak, *Cold War Civil Rights: Race and the Image of American Democracy* (Princeton, NJ: Princeton University Press, 2000); Nelson Hathcock, "A Spy in the Enemy's Country: *Black Like Me* as Cold War Narrative," American Studies 44, no. 3 (2003): 99–120.

38. Dwight Eisenhower, "Inaugural Address 20 January 1953," Avalon Project at Yale Law School; *http://www.yale.edu/lawweb/avalon/presiden/inaug/eisen1.htm* (accessed January 23, 2008).

39. Ibid.

40. Ibid.

41. John Kenneth White, *Still Seeing Red: How the Cold War Shapes the New American Politics* (Boulder, CO: Westview Press, 1998).

42. Victor S. Navasky, *Naming Names*, 3rd ed. (New York: Hill and Wang, 2003), 7.

43. For an insightful reading of Cold War film, see Michael Rogin, "*Kiss Me Deadly*: Communism, Motherhood and the Cold War," in *Ronald Reagan, the Movie and Other Studies in Political Demonology* (Berkeley and Los Angeles: University of California Press, 1987), 236–71.

44. Carlson, *The "American" Way*, 108–48; Elaine Tyler May, *Homeward Bound: American Families in the Cold War Era* (New York: Basic Books, 1988); Joanne Meyerowitz, "Sex, Gender, and the Cold War Language of Reform," in *Rethinking Cold War Culture*, edited by Peter J. Kuznick and James Gilbert (Washington, DC: Smithsonian Institution Press, 2001), 106–23.

45. James Gilbert, *A Cycle of Outrage* (New York: Oxford University Press, 1986).

46. Whitfield, *The Culture of the Cold War*, 164–65.

47. "NSC Memorandum 68," 32.

48. Tom Engelhardt, *The End of Victory Culture: Cold War America and the Disillusioning of a Generation* (Amherst: University of Massachusetts Press, 1998), 184.

49. See, for instance, Lisa McGirr, *Suburban Warriors: The Origins of the New American Right* (Princeton, NJ: Princeton University Press, 2001); and Rick Perlstein, *Before the Storm: Barry Goldwater and the Unmaking of the American Consensus* (New York: Hill and Wang, 2001).

50. Lary May, "Introduction," 5.

51. Elaine Tyler May, *Homeward Bound*.

52. Gilbert, *Cycle of Violence*.

53. Carlson, *The "American" Way*, 109–40.

54. Amy Kiste Nyberg, *Seal of Approval: The History of the Comics Code* (Jackson: University Press of Mississippi, 1998); David Hajdu, *The Ten-Cent Plague: The Great Comic Book Scare and How It Changed America* (New York: Farrar, Straus and Giroux, 2008), 116–19, 148–50.

55. Barbara Ehrenreich, *The Hearts of Men: American Dreams and the Flight from Commitment* (New York: Doubleday, 1983).

56. K. A. Courdileone, "Politics in the Age of Anxiety: The Cold War and the 'Crisis of Masculinity,'" *Journal of American History* 87 (2000): 515–45; Phillip Wylie, *Generation of Vipers* (Normal, IL: Dalkey Archive Press, 1996); Arthur Schlesinger Jr., *The Vital Center Our Purpose and Perils on the Tightrope of American Liberalism* (Boston: Houghton Mifflin, 1949).

57. Betty Friedan, *The Feminine Mystique* (New York: W. W. Norton, 1963).

58. Martha L. Crowner, "Review of John Michel Metzel, Prozac on the Couch," *Psychiatric Services* 5 (2004): 200–201.

59. On the development of the civil rights movement see Gary Gerstle, *American Crucible: Race and Nation in the Twentieth Century* (Princeton, NJ: Princeton University Press, 2001), 238–310.

Chapter Two

1. Godfrey Hodgson, *America in Our Time* (New York: Doubleday, 1976), 7

2. Todd Gitlin, *The Sixties: Years of Hope, Days of Rage*, rev. ed. (New York: Bantam Books, 1993), 62.

3. See, for instance, Rebecca Klatch, *A Generation Divided: The New Left, The New Right and the 1960s* (Berkeley and Los Angeles: University of California Press, 1999), especially 30–31; and Rick Perlstein, *Before the Storm: Barry Goldwater and the Unmaking of the American Consensus* (New York: Hill and Wang, 2001).

4. Todd Gitlin sees in this protest—and the anti-HUAC sit-in in San Francisco in May—the end of the 1950s, as direct action galvanized enclaves of opposition to the liberal consensus across the country. Gitlin, *The Sixties*, 81–84.

5. Howard Brick, *Age of Contradiction: American Thought and Culture in the 1960s* (Ithaca, NY: Cornell University Press, 1985), xii.

6. On the rise the conservative movement and its power, with particular reference to California, see Lisa McGirr, *Suburban Warriors: The Origins of the New American Right* (Princeton, NJ: Princeton University Press, 2001). On the Goldwater crusade, see Perlstein, *Before the Storm.*

7. See Gitlin, *The Sixties*, 45–80.

8. Klatch, *A Generation Divided*, 66–70, notes that the works of Camus, particularly *The Rebel*, were widely cited by both members of the Students for a Democratic Society and of Young Americans for Freedom as major influences on their thought.

9. John F. Kennedy, quoted in James Patterson, *Grand Expectations: The United States, 1945–1974* (New York: Oxford University Press, 1996), 486.

10. Stan Lee, Larry Lieber (w), Jack Kirby (p), and Dick Ayers (i), "The Mighty Thor: Prisoner of the Reds," *Journey into Mystery* 87 (December 1962), Marvel Comics.

11. Stan Lee (w), Robert Bernstein (p), and Don Heck (i), "Iron Man: Trapped by the Red Barbarian," *Tales of Suspense* 42 (June 1963), Marvel Comics.

12. Stan Lee and George Mair, *Excelsior: The Amazing Life of Stan Lee* (New York: Fireside Books, 2002), 121.

13. Stan Lee (w) and Jack Kirby (a), "Enter the Gargoyle," *Incredible Hulk* 1 (May 1962), Marvel Comics.

14. The conflict between private heroes and public authorities would, however, become increasingly relevant by the mid-1970s.

15. Stan Lee (w), Gil Kane (p), and Joe Sinnott (i), "Captain America: The Last Defeat," *Tales of Suspense* 91 (July 1967), Marvel Comics.

16. Stan Lee (w) and Don Heck (p), "To Smash a Serpent," *Mighty Avengers* 33 (October 1966), Marvel Comics.

17. Stan Lee (w), Robert Bernstein (p) and Don Heck (i), "Iron Man Faces the Crimson Dynamo," *Tales of Suspense* 46 (October 1963), Marvel Comics. The irony that this death threat is a piece of disinformation planted by the democratic hero Iron Man seemed to have been completely lost on both the readers and writers of the Iron Man books.

18. See, particularly, *Tales of Suspense* 60 and 64 (December 1965 and April 1966), Marvel Comics.

19. *Tales of Suspense*, 92–94, (August–October 1967), Marvel Comics.

20. He similarly argues that modernization theory, the dominant paradigm of development studies into the 1970s that claimed that all cultures move inevitably from a simple and stagnant tradition to a dynamic and progressive modernity, justified as morally superior Western political economies. Totalitarianism would arise in those states undergoing rapid modernization (read: Germany and Russia) as the breakdown of traditional structures created social upheaval that required centralized authority, armed with newly modernized industry, to assert total control over their societies. See Ron Robin, *The Making of the Cold War Enemy* (Princeton, NJ: Princeton University Press, 2001).

21. Harry S. Truman, "Address Before a Joint Session of Congress, 12 March 1947." Avalon Project, Yale University Law School; *www.yale.edu/lawweb/avalon/trudoc.htm* (accessed April 1, 2008).

22. In 1948 Bucky, considered a liability to the Captain America comic, was shot and thus disappeared from the series. This new story, however, would create a couple of problems for Marvel's continuity. First, Captain America must constantly lament the loss of his young sidekick and feel guilt over it. More significantly, how will Marvel explain the reappearance of Captain America in the 1950s since he was supposedly frozen in ice during that time?

23. Stan Lee (w), Jack Kirby (p), and Chic Stone (i), "Captain America: The Strength of the Sumo," *Tales of Suspense* 61 (January 1965), Marvel Comics.

24. Stan Lee (w), Jack Kirby and Don Heck (p), and Mike Esposito (i), "Now, by My Hand, Shall Die a Villain," *Mighty Avengers* 15 (April 1965), Marvel Comics.

25. Stan Lee (w), Jack Kirby and Dick Ayers (a), and J. Tartaglione (i), "Captain America: Thirty Minutes to Live," *Tales of Suspense* 75 (March 1966), Marvel Comics.

26. Stan Lee (w) and Steve Ditko (a), "Just a Guy Named Joe," *Amazing Spider-Man* 38 (July 1965), Marvel Comics.

27. See William Savage Jr., *Commies, Cowboys and Jungle Queens: Comic Books and America, 1945–1954.* (Hanover, NH: Wesleyan University Press, 1990), 14–23.

28. Stan Lee (w), Adam Austin (p), and Gary Michaels (i), "The Invincible Iron Man: If This Guilt Be Mine," *Tales of Suspense* 74 (February 1966), Marvel Comics.

29. The investigation is ordered by Senator Byrd in Stan Lee (w), Don Heck (a), and Mickey Demeo (i), "Hoorah for the Conquering Hero!" *Tales of Suspense* 72 (December 1965), Marvel Comics.

30. Stan Lee (w), Gene Colan (p), and Frank Giacoia (i), "The Other Iron Man," *Tales of Suspense* 84 (December 1966), Marvel Comics.

31. Stan Lee (w), Gene Colan (a), and Frank Giacoia (i), "Into the Jaws of Death," *Tales of Suspense* 85 (January 1967), Marvel Comics.

32. Stan Lee (w), Gene Colan (p), and Gary Michaels (i), "Victory," *Tales of Suspense* 83 (November 1966), Marvel Comics.

33. Gitlin, *The Sixties*, 66–67. The quest for authentic experience is the major theme of Doug Rossinow. *The Politics of Authenticity: Liberalism, Christianity and the New Left in America* (New York: Columbia University Press, 1998).

34. Sharon Jeffrey, quoted in James Miller, *Democracy Is in the Streets: From Port Huron to the Siege of Chicago* (New York: Touchstone Books, 1995), 205.

35. Brick, *Age of Contradiction*, 68–72.

36. Stan Lee (w), Jack Kirby (p), and Frank Giacoia (i), "The Maddening Mystery of the Inconceivable Adaptoid," *Tales of Suspense* 82 (October 1966), Marvel Comics.

37. Lee, Colan, and Giacoia, "Into the Jaws of Death"; and Stan Lee (w), Gene Colan (p), and Frank Giacoia (i), "Death Duel for the Life of Happy Hogan," *Tales of Suspense* 86 (February, 1967), Marvel Comics.

38. Sharon Carter first appeared in *Tales of Suspense* 75 (March 1966). Captain America's attraction to her was that she bore a striking resemblance to a girl he loved during World War II. It would be revealed later that her older sister, Peggy, had been Captain America's World War II love.

39. Stan Lee (w), Jack Kirby (p), and Joe Sinnott (i), "Captain America: A Time to Die—A Time to Live," *Tales of Suspense* 95 (November 1967), Marvel Comics.

40. These stories have been collected in Stan Lee, Roy Thomas, and Jim Steranko (w), Jack Kirby, and John Buscema (a), *Nick Fury, Agent of S.H.I.E.L.D.* (New York: Marvel Comics, 2000), 138–221.

41. Jim Steranko (w) and Joe Sinnott (a), "Today the Earth Died," *Strange Tales* 168 (May 1968), Marvel Comics.

42. Stan Lee (w), Gene Colan (p), and Dan Adkins (i), "The Tragedy and the Triumph," *Tales of Suspense* 94 (October 1967), Marvel Comics.

43. Ibid.

44. As it turns out, it is not really Zemo who had died in *Avengers* 15, but his former aid who assumes the role to try to re-create the Nazi regime.

45. Stan Lee (w) and Jack Kirby (a), "Cap Goes Wild," *Captain America* 106 (October 1968), Marvel Comics.

46. Archie Goodwin (w), George Tuska (p), and Johnny Craig (i), "A Duel Must End," *Invincible Iron Man* 8 (December 1968), Marvel Comics.

47. Stan Lee, "Stan Lee's Soapbox," *Tales of Suspense* 90 (June 1967), Marvel Comics.

Chapter Three

1. See Bruce Schulman. *The Seventies: The Great Shift in American Culture, Society, and Politics* (New York: Free Press, 2001), introduction.

2. William Graebner, "America's *Poseidon Adventure:* A Nation in Existential Despair," in *America in the 1970s*, edited by Beth Bailey and David Farber (Lawrence: University Press of Kansas, 2004), 157–80.

3. Jimmy Carter, *Why Not the Best?* (Nashville: Broadman, 1975), dustjacket.

4. Kenneth Morris, *Jimmy Carter: American Moralist* (Athens: University of Georgia Press, 1996), 89.

5. On Western conservatives see Lisa McGirr, *Suburban Warriors: The Origins of the New American Right* (Princeton, NJ: Princeton University Press, 2001). Southern conservatism is treated in Dan Carter, *From George Wallace to Newt Gingrich: Race in the Conservative Revolution, 1963–1994* (Baton Rouge: Lousiana State University Press, 1996) and in Matthew Lassiter, *The Silent Majority: Suburban Politics in the Sunbelt South* (Princeton, NJ: Princeton University Press, 2006).

6. Eric Porter, "Affirming and Disaffirming Actions: Remaking Race in the 1970s," in Bailey and Farber, eds., *America in the 1970s*, 50–74.

7. Jefferson Cowie, "'Vigorously Left, Right, and Center': The Crosscurrents of Working-Class American in the 1970s," in Bailey and Farber, eds., *America in the 1970s*, 75–106.

8. Beth Bailey, "She 'Can Bring Home the Bacon': Negotiating Gender in the 1970s," in Bailey and Farber, eds., *America in the 1970s*, 107–28.

9. At DC Comics, only Batman and Superman outsold Marvel titles in 1968. Paid circulation figures for Marvel titles can be gleaned from annual statements of ownership for most of this period; DC circulation figures are less clear. Figures can be found in John J. Miller, Maggie Thompson, Peter Bickford, and Brent Frankenhoff, *The Comic Buyer's Guide Standard Catalogue of Comic Books*, 4th ed. (Iola, WI: KP Books, 2005).

10. Thomas had been a very active comic book fan, publishing one of the first fanzines, *Alterego*. He was one of the first fans to move into the professional ranks, and brought with him an appreciation for the history of comics as well as a specific interest in the new Marvel style.

11. The letters column in the Captain America books was titled "Let's Rap with Cap." See issues 127 (July), 128 (August), and 132 (December) 1970, Marvel Comics.

12. "Let's Rap with Cap," *Captain America* 100 (February 1968), Marvel Comics.

13. Roy Thomas (w), John Buscema (p), and Tom Palmer (i), "Come on in, The Revolution's Fine," *Mighty Avengers* 83 (December 1970), Marvel Comics; Roy Thomas (w), Herb Trimpe (p), and John Severin (i), "They Shoot Hulks Don't They?" *Incredible Hulk* 142 (August 1971), Marvel Comics.

14. The Femme Force first appears in Gary Friedrich (w), Gil Kane (a), and John Romita (i), "Skyjacked," *Captain America and the Falcon* 145 (January 1972), Marvel Comics. The Femme Force story continued for three issues.

15. Stan Lee (w), Gene Colan (a), and Joe Sinnott (i), "Cracked on Campus," *Captain America* 120 (December 1969), Marvel Comics.

16. Amy Kiste Nyberg, *Seal of Approval: The History of the Comics Code* (Jackson: University Press of Mississippi, 1998), 139–42.

17. The O'Neil/Adams run on *Green Lantern/Green Arrow* (76–89) and in *The Flash* (217–219) from 1970 to 1972 is the start of a relevance movement in comic books, reflecting the influence of New Left ideas on writers and artists. It is the subject of much critical scrutiny and was frequently offered as evidence of the sophistication of superhero comic books. See Max S. Skidmore and Joey Skidmore, "More Than Mere Fantasy: Political Themes in Contemporary Comic Books," *Journal of Popular Culture* 17, no. 1 (1983): 83–92; Jesse T. Moore, "The Education of Green Lantern: Culture and Ideology," *Journal of American Culture* 26, no. 2 (2003): 263–78; and Bradford Wright, *Comic Book Nation: The Transformation of Youth Culture in America* (Baltimore: Johns

Hopkins University Press, 2001), 226–27. The stories have been collected in Dennis O'Neil and Neal Adams, *Green Lantern/Green Arrow*, 2 vols. (New York: DC Comics, 2004).

18. See especially Harlan Ellison, Roy Thomas (w), Herb Trimpe, (a) and Sam Grainger (i), "The Brute That Shouted Love at the Heart of the Atom," *Incredible Hulk* 140 (June 1971), Marvel Comics.

19. The Black Panther was the first black superhero created by Marvel, but he was an African king of the mythical nation of Wakanda, introduced in Stan Lee (w) and Jack Kirby (a), *Fantastic Four* 52 (July 1966), Marvel Comics.

20. Jim Steranko (w/p) and Joe Sinnott (i), "Who Is Scorpio?" *Nick Fury, Agent of SHIELD* 1 (June 1968), Marvel Comics.

21. While the magazine ran for eighteen issues, the last three issues reprinted earlier stories.

22. Stan Lee (w), Gene Colan (p), and Dick Ayers (i), "Bucky Reborn," *Captain America* 131 (November 1970), Marvel Comics.

23. M. Gold (w), Don Heck (p), and Chic Stone (i), "Save the People . . . Save the Country," *Invincible Iron Man* 29 (September 1970), Marvel Comics.

24. Over the years, several other products of the "supersoldier" formula would emerge, ranging from the swamp beast Man-Thing; to Victorious, a foe of jungle-lord, Kazar; to the Captain America of the 1950s, and finally a black Captain America.

25. Stan Lee (w), Jack Kirby (p), and Syd Shores (i), "The Hero That Was," *Captain America* 109 (January 1969), Marvel Comics.

26. See especially Jim Steranko (w/p) and Tom Palmer (i), "The Strange Death of Captain America," *Captain America* 113 (May 1969), Marvel Comics.

27. Stan Lee (w), John Romita (p), and Sal Buscema (i), "The Man Behind the Mask," *Captain America* 114 (June 1969), Marvel Comics.

28. Ibid.

29. Stan Lee (w), Gene Colan (p), and Joe Sinnot (i), "The Sting of the Scorpion," *Captain America* 122 (February 1970), Marvel Comics.

30. Stan Lee (w) and Gene Colan (p), "Captured in Vietnam," *Captain America* 125 (May 1970), Marvel Comics.

31. Archie Goodwin (w), Geroge Tuska (p), and Johnny Craig (i), "There Lives a Green Goliath," *Invincible Iron Man* 9 (January 1969), Marvel Comics.

32. Archie Goodwin (w), George Tuska (p), and Johnny Craig (i), "What Price Life?" *Invincible Iron Man* 19 (November 1969), Marvel Comics.

33. Archie Goodwin (w), George Tuska (p), and Joe Gaudioso (i), "From This Conflict, Death!" *Invincible Iron Man* 22 (February 1969), Marvel Comics.

34. Gerry Conway (w), Sal Buscema (p), and Jim Mooney (i), "All the Colors of Evil," *Captain America and the Falcon* 149 (May 1972), Marvel Comics.

35. Steve Engelhart (w), Sal Buscema (p), and Jim Mooney (i), "Captain America: Hero or Hoax?" *Captain America and the Falcon* 153 (September 1972), Marvel Comics.

36. Steve Engelhart (w), Sal Buscema (p), and John Verpooten (i), "The Falcon Fights Alone," *Captain America and the Falcon* 154 (October 1972), Marvel Comics.

37. Ibid.

38. This is not the same origin as told in *Young Men* 24, although several pages from that issue are reproduced in *Captain America* 155 to suggest that there is continuity between the tales. In the 1950s book, this was the same Captain America and Bucky as in World War II. The incorporation of older, precontinuity stories onto the new continuity is often referred to as "retrospective continuity," and made into the verb "to retcon." Most people aficionados attribute the term to Roy Thomas.

39. Steve Engelhart (w), Sal Buscema (p), and Frank McGlaughlin (i), "The Incredible Origin of the Other Captain America," *Captain America and the Falcon* 155 (November 1972), Marvel Comics.

40. Steve Engelhart (w), Sal Buscema (p), and Frank McGlaughlin (i), "Two into One Won't Go," *Captain America and the Falcon* 15 (December 1972), Marvel Comics.

41. Ibid.

42. For a similar interpretation see Jason Dittmer, "Retconning America: Captain America in the Wake of World War II and the McCarthy Hearings," in *The Amazing, Transforming Superhero!* edited by Terrence Wandtke (Jefferson, NC: McFarland, 2007), 33–51.

43. Steve Engelhart (w), Sal Buscema (p), and John Verpooten (i), "Beware of Serpents!" *Captain America and the Falcon* 163 (July 1973), Marvel Comics.

44. Steve Engelhart (w), Sal Buscema (p), and Vinnie Colletta (i), ". . . Before the Dawn," *Captain America and the Falcon* 175 (July 1974), Marvel Comics.

45. Steve Engelhart claims that he wanted to identify Number One as Nixon, but stopped himself for fear of being censored. In retrospect, he suggests that this was a mistake, because he believes Marvel would have accepted it. This suggests how deeply the Comics Code had been gutted by the mid-1970s. See *http://www.steveengelhart.com* (accessed December 12, 2007).

46. Steve Engelhart (w), Sal Buscema (p), and Vinnie Colletta (i), "Captain America Must Die," *Captain America and the Falcon* 176 (August 1974), Marvel Comics.

47. Ibid.

48. Ibid.

49. Steve Engelhart (w), Frank Robbins (p), and Frank Giacoia (i), "Nomad: No More!" *Captain America and the Falcon* 183 (March 1975), Marvel Comics.

50. "Let's Rap with Cap," *Captain America and the Falcon* 179 (November 1974), Marvel Comics.

51. "Let's Rap with Cap," *Captain America and the Falcon* 177 (September 1974), Marvel Comics.

52. "Let's Rap with Cap," *Captain America and the Falcon* 180 (December 1974), Marvel Comics.

53. "Let's Rap with Cap," *Captain America and the Falcon* 185 (May 1975), Marvel Comics.

54. "Let's Rap with Cap," *Captain America and the Falcon* 187 (July 1975), Marvel Comics.

55. Ibid.

56. Roy Thomas (w), Barry Smith (a), and Jim Mooney (i), "Why Must There Be an Iron Man?" *Invincible Iron Man* 47 (June 1972), Marvel Comics.

57. Bill Mantlo (w), George Tuska (a), and Vinnie Colletta (i), "Long Time Gone," *Invincible Iron Man* 78 (September 1975), Marvel Comics.

58. Ibid.

59. Ibid.

60. Archie Goodwin (w), Don Heck (a), and John Craig (i), "The Fury of Firebrand," *Invincible Iron Man* 27 (July 1970), Marvel Comics.

61. Ibid.

62. James Patterson, *Grand Expectations: The United States, 1945–1974* (New York: Oxford University Press, 1996).

63. Jeffrey A. Brown, *Black Superheroes, Milestone Comics, and Their Fans* (Jackson: University Press of Mississippi, 2001), 20–23.

64. Race is also a prominent issue in the O'Neil/Adams *Green Lantern/ Green Arrow* series; the first story (issue 76) has the Green Lantern confronted by a black man who castigates him for his neglect of racial issues in the United States and a later story (issue 87) has the Green Lantern confront his own prejudices when a black man, John Stewart, is selected as a Green Lantern.

65. Gary Friedrich (w) and John Romita (i), "Power to the People," *Captain America and the Falcon* 143 (November 1971), Marvel Comics.

66. Gary Friedrich (w) and John Romita (a), "Hydra over All," *Captain America and the Falcon* 144 (December 1971), Marvel Comics.

67. Steve Engelhart (w), Frank Robbins (a), and Frank Giacoia (i), "Scream the Scarlet Skull," *Captain America and the Falcon* 185 (May 1975), Marvel Comics.

68. See Richard Reynolds, *Superheroes: A Modern Mythology* (Jackson: University Press of Mississippi, 1992), chapter 3.

69. Stan Lee, "Stan Lee's Soapbox," *Captain America* 108 (December 1968), Marvel Comics.

70. Stan Lee, "Stan Lee's Soapbox," *Captain America* 135 (March 1971), Marvel Comics.

71. "Let's Rap with Cap," *Captain America* 118 (October 1969), Marvel Comics.

Chapter Four

1. Archie Goodwin (w), George Tuska (p), and Vinnie Collette (i) "Fear Wears Two Faces," *Invincible Iron Man* 88 (July 1976), Marvel Comics.

2. Jimmy Carter, "Address to the Nation, 15 July 1979"; *http://miller center.org/scripps/archive/speeches/detail/3402* (accessed November 11, 2007).

3. Ibid.

4. Ibid.

5. Bruce Schulman, *The Seventies: The Great Shift in American Culture, Society, and Politics* (New York: Free Press, 2001).

6. Christopher Lasch, *The Culture of Narcissism* (New York: Signet Books, 1979).

7. For a similar argument see David Farber, "'The Torch Had Fallen," in *America in the '70s*, edited by Beth Bailey and David Farber (Lawrence: University Press of Kansas, 2004), 22; Kenneth Morris goes further, seeing in the tax revolt a rejection of economic liberalism, but similarly notes it as evidence of declining faith in governmental efficacy; see Morris, *Jimmy Carter: American Moralist* (Athens: University of Georgia Press, 1996), 210–13.

8. Schulman, *The Seventies*, 102–20.

9. Farber, "The Torch Had Fallen," 24–25.

10. The "New Hollywood" is generally dated from the success of *Bonnie and Clyde* (1967) to the release of *Star Wars* (1978). See, for instance, Peter Biskind, *Easy Riders, Raging Bulls: How the Sex-Drugs-And-Rock 'n' Roll Generation Saved Hollywood* (New York: Simon and Schuster, 1998); and Mark Harris, *Pictures at a Revolution: Five Movies and the Birth of the New Hollywood* (New York: Penguin, 2008).

11. For references to television ratings, see David Wallechinsky and Irving Wallace, *The People's Almanac*, 3rd ed. (New York: Bantam Books, 1981).

12. Les Daniels, *DC Comics: Sixty Years of the World's Favorite Comic Book Heroes* (Boston: Bulfinch Press, 1995), 172.

13. Peter Carroll, *It Seemed Like Nothing Happened: America in the 1970s* (New Brunswick, NJ: Rutgers University Press, 2000), 168–71; Philip Agee, *Inside the Company* (Middlesex, England: Penguin, 1975). Reports from the House of Representatives and Senate were also released in 1975.

14. As reported in Carroll, *Nothing Happened*, 235.

15. Jim Shooter (w), George Perez (p), and Pablo Marcos (i), "First Blood," *Avengers* 168 (February 1978), Marvel Comics.

16. David Micheline (w), John Byrne and Gene Day (a), "On the Matter of Heroes," *Avengers* 181 (March 1979), Marvel Comics.

17. David Michelinie (w), George Perez (p), and Josef Rubinstein (i), "Interlude," *Avengers* 194 (April 1980), Marvel Comics.

18. David Michelinie (w), John Byrne and Dan Green (a), "Back to the Stone Age," *Avengers* 191 (January 1980), Marvel Comics.

19. Peter Gallis (w), Jerry Bingham (p), and Alan Gordon (i), "The Sins of the Father," *Captain America* 246 (June 1980), Marvel Comics.

20. Roger Stern (w), John Byrne and Josef Rubinstein (a), "Cap for President," *Captain America* 250 (October 1980), Marvel Comics.

21. J. M. DeMatteis (w), Mike Zeck (p), and John Beatty (i), "The Man Who Made a Difference," *Captain America* 267 (March 1982), Marvel Comics.

22. Christopher Lasch, *Haven in a Heartless World: The Family Besieged* (New York: Basic Books, 1978).

23. Carroll, *Nothing Happened*, 298.

24. Carroll, *Nothing Happened*.

25. Jim Shooter and David Michilinie (w), and Mike Zeck (a), "Rite of Passage," *Captain America* 259 (July 1981), Marvel Comics.

26. DeMatteis, et al., "The Man Who Made a Difference."

27. J. M. DeMatteis (w), Sal Buscema (p), and Kim DeMulder (i), "Diverging . . ." *Captain America* 284 (August 1983), Marvel Comics.

28. Steve Gerber (w), Sal Buscema (p), and Esposito and Tartag (i), "Devastation," *Captain America* 225 (September 1978), Marvel Comics.

29. Bill Mantlo (w), Geroge Tuska (p), and Mike Esposito (i), "Every Hand Against Him," *Iron Man* 105 (December 1977), Marvel Comics.

30. David Michelinie (w), John Romita, Jr. (p), and BobLayton (i), "Demon in a Bottle," *Invincible Iron Man* 128 (November 1979), Marvel Comics.

31. Steve Engelhart, the writer for the Captain America Watergate allegory (see chapter 3), makes a similar journey. By the early 1980s he is writing *The Vision and Scarlet Witch* miniseries, which focuses on the problems faced by an unconventional couple in love and seeking marriage (the Vision is an android, the Scarlet Witch is a mutant). Again, the retreat into privacy is clearly evident.

32. Doc Samson first appears in Roy Thomas (w) and Herb Trimpe and John Severin (a), "His Name Is Samson," *Incredible Hulk* 141 (July 1971), Marvel Comics.

33. Bill Mantlo (w), Sal Busema (p), and Jim Novak (i), "Now Somewhere in the Black Holes of Sirius Major There Lived a Young Boy Name of Rocket Racoon," *Incredible Hulk* 276 (May 1982), Marvel Comics.

34. Bill Mantlo (w), Mark Gruenwald and Greg LaRocque (a), "Acceptance," *Incredible Hulk* 279 (January 1983), Marvel Comics.

35. Steve Engelhart (w), and Sal Buscema (p), and Jim Verpooten (i), "Beware of Serpents," *Captain America and the Falcon* 163 (July 1973), Marvel Comics.

36. J. M. DeMatteis (w), Paul Neary (p), and Josef Rubinstein (i), "The Measure of a Man," *Captain America*, 294 (June 1984), Marvel Comics.

37. J. M. DeMatteis (w), Paul Neary (p), and Roy Richardson (i), "All My Sins Remembered," *Captain America* 297 (September 1984), Marvel Comics.

38. J. M. DeMatteis (w), Paul Neary (p), and Roy Richardson (i), "Sturm and Drang: The Life and Times of the Red Skull," *Captain America* 298 (October 1984), Marvel Comics.

39. J. M. DeMatteis and Michael Ellis (w), Paul Neary (p), and Denis Janke (i), "Das Ende," *Captain America* 300 (December 1984), Marvel Comics.

40. Dennis O'Neil (w), Luke McDonnell (p), and Ian Akin and Brian Garvey (i), "The Choice and the Challenge," *Invincible Iron Man* 193 (April 1985), Marvel Comics.

41. Dennis O'Neil (w), Luke McDonnell (p), and Ian Akin and Brian Garvey (i), "A Duel of Iron," *Invincible Iron Man* 192 (March 1985), Marvel Comics.

42. Dennis O'Neil (w), Luke McDonnell (p), and Ian Akin and Brian Garvey (i), "The Most Precious Thing," *Invincible Iron Man* 195 (June 1985), Marvel Comics.

43. Dennis O'Neil (w), Mark Bright (a), and Ian Akin and Brian Garvey (i), "Resolutions," *Invincible Iron Man* 200 (November 1985), Marvel Comics.

44. Ronald Reagan, "Address to Members of the British Parliament," June 8, 1982; *http://www.reagan.utexas.edu/archives/speeches/publicpapers.html* (accessed March 14, 2008).

45. Ronald Reagan, "Remarks to American Troops at Camp Liberty Bell, Republic of Korea," November 13, 1983; *http://www.reagan.utexas.edu/archives/speeches/publicpapers.html* (accessed March 14, 2008).

46. Ronald Reagan. "Inaugural Address, 20 January 1981"; *http://www.reaganlibrary.com/reagan/speeches/first.asp* (accessed April 2, 2008).

47. Ronald Reagan, "National Address on the Economy," October 13, 1982; *http://www.reagan.utexas.edu/archives/speeches/publicpapers.html* (accessed April 2, 2008)

48. Ronald Reagan, "Address at Bitburg Airbase, Federal Republic of Germany," May 5, 1985; *http://www.reagan.utexas.edu/archives/speeches/publicpapers.html* (accessed April 2, 2008).

49. Ronald Reagan, "Address to the National Association of Evangelicals," March 8, 1983, Orlando Florida; *http://www.reagan.utexas.edu/archives/speeches/publicpapers.html* (accessed April 2, 2008).

50. Ronald Reagan. "State of the Union Address," January 27, 1984; *http://www.reagan.utexas.edu/archives/speeches/publicpapers.html* (accessed April 2, 2008).

51. Ibid.

52. "Letters to the Living Legend," *Captain America* 246 (June 1980), Marvel Comics.

53. "Letters to the Living Legend," *Captain America* 267 (December 1983), Marvel Comics.

54. J. M. DeMatteis (w), Mike Zeck (p), and John Beatty (i), "Sermon of Straw," *Captain America* 280 (April 1983), Marvel Comics.

Chapter Five

1. Benjamin Ginsberg and Martin Shefter, *Politics by Other Means: The Declining Importance of Elections in America* (New York: Basic Books, 1990).

2. Paul Kennedy, *The Rise and Fall of the Great Powers* (New York: Random House, 1987).

3. See Kennedy, *Rise and Fall;* and also Robert Keohane, *After Hegemony* (Princeton, NJ: Princeton University Press, 1985).

4. Allan Bloom, *The Closing of the American Mind* (New York: Simon and Schuster, 1988); E. D. Hirsch Jr., *Cultural Literacy: What Every American Needs to Know* (New York: Vintage, 1988).

5. Robert Bellah, Richard Madsen, William Sullivan, Ann Swidler, and Steven Tipton, *Habits of the Heart: Individualism and Commitment in American Life* (New York: Harper, 1985), vi.

6. Al Milgrom (w/p) and Dennis Janke (i), "The More Things Change," *Incredible Hulk* 324 (October 1986), Marvel Comics.

7. Peter David (w), Jeff Purves (p), and Mike Gustovich (i), "Crap Shoot," *Incredible Hulk* 347 (September 1988), Marvel Comics.

8. Peter David (w), Dale Keown (p), and Bob McLeod (i), "Honey, I Shrunk the Hulk," *Incredible Hulk* 377 (January 1991), Marvel Comics.

9. Mark Gruenwald (w), Paul Neary (p), and Dennis Janke (i), "The Little Bang Theory," *Captain America* 320 (August 1986), Marvel Comics.

10. Ibid.

11. Mark Gruenwald (w), Paul Neary (p), and John Beatty (i), "Ultimatum," *Captain America* 321 (September 1986), Marvel Comics.

12. This is very similar to the famous cover of *Daredevil* 182 by Frank Miller, signaling the newer, more vicious character that would become his hallmark.

13. Mark Gruenwald (w), Tom Morgan (p), and Bob McLeod (i), "The Choice," *Captain America* 332 (August 1987), Marvel Comics.

14. Mark Gruenwald (w), Kieron Dwyer (p), and Al Milgrom (i), "Don't Tread on Me," *Captain America* 344 (August 1988), Marvel Comics.

15. Mark Gruenwald (w), Kieron Dwyer (p), and Allen Milgrom (i), "Surrender," *Captain America* 345 (September 1988), Marvel Comics.

16. Mark Gruenwald (w), Kieron Dwyer (p), and Allen Milgrom (i), "Seeing Red," *Captain America* 350 (February 1989), Marvel Comics.

17. David Michelinie (w), Mark Bright (p), and Bob Layton (i), "Stark Wars," *Iron Man* 225 (December 1987), Marvel Comics.

18. David Michelinie (w), Mark Bright (p), and Bob Layton (i), "Stark Wars: Glitch," *Iron Man* 226 (January 1988), Marvel Comics.

19. David Michelinie (w), Mark Bright (p), and Bob Layton (i), "Red Snow," *Iron Man* 229 (April 1988), Marvel Comics.

20. John Byrne (w), John Romita Jr. (p), and Bob Wiacek (i), "Armor Wars II," *Iron Man* 258–66 (July 1990–March 1991), Marvel Comics.

21. John Byrne (w), Paul Ryan (p), and Bob Wiacek (i), "The Dragon Seed Saga," *Iron Man* 267–75 (April–December 1991), Marvel Comics.

22. See, especially, John Byrne (w), Paul Ryan (p), and Bob Wiacek (i), "The Persistence of Memory," *Iron Man* 267 (April 1991), Marvel Comics.

23. Fabian Nicieza (w), Rick Mays and Pete Garcia (a), and Greg Adams (i), "American Dreamers," *Nomad* 22–25 (February–May 1994), Marvel Comics.

24. Mark Gruenwald (w), Ron Lim (p), and Danny Bulanadi (i), "Streets of Poison," *Captain America* 372–78 (July 1990–October 1990), Marvel Comics.

25. The story begins in Mark Gruenwald (w), Dave Hoover (p), and Danny Bulanadi (i), "Superpatriot Games," *Captain America* 425 (March 1994), Marvel Comics.

26. Mark Waid (w), Ron Garney (p), and Denis Rodier (i), "Operation Rebirth," *Captain America* 445 (November 1995), Marvel Comics.

27. Mark Waid (w), Ron Garney (p), and Scott Koblish (i), "Man Without a Country," *Captain America* 450–53 (April–July 1996), Marvel Comics.

28. This was a six-issue series. Bob Harras (w), Paul Neary (p), and Kim DeMulder (i), *Nick Fury vs. S.H.I.E.L.D.* 1–6 (June–November 1988), Marvel Comics.

29. D. G. Chichester (w), Keith Pollard (p), and Kim DeMulder (i), "The Chaos Serpent," *Nicky Fury, Agent of SHIELD* 2, nos. 7–10 (January–April 1990), Marvel Comics.

30. This series actually spread across several titles, but the core is Bob Harras and Terry Kavanagh (w), Mike Deodato (p), and Tom Palmer (i), "The Crossing," *Avengers* 390–395 (September 1995–February 1996), Marvel Comics; Bob Harras and Terry Kavanagh (w) and Mike Deodato (a), *Avengers: The Crossing* (September 1995), Marvel Comics; and Bob Harras and Terry Kavanagh (w), Roger Cruz, Luke Ross, and Fabio Laguna (p), and Scott Koblish and Rene Micheleti (i), *Avengers: Timeslide* (February 1996), Marvel Comics.

31. Dan Raviv, *Comic Wars: How Two Tycoons Battled over the Marvel Comics Empire and Both Lost* (New York: Random House, 2002).

Chapter Six

1. William Jefferson Clinton, "Remarks by the President on Responsible Citizenship and the American Community," Georgetown University, Washington, DC, July 6, 1995; *http://www.clintonfoundation.org/legacy/070695-speech-bt-president-at-georgetown.htm* (accessed April 15, 2008).

2. See U.S. Deprtment of Commerce, Census Bureau, *U.S. Historical Statistics and Statistical Abstract of the United States* (Washington, DC: GPO, various years). On the growing level of income inequality and the validity of Census Bureau data, see Alan Reynolds, "Policy Analysis: Has U.S. Income Inequality Really Increased?" Cato Institute Policy Analysis No. 586, January 8, 2007; *http://www.cato.org/pub_display.php?*

pub_id6880 (accessed April 15, 2008). See also Gary Burtless, "Comments on 'Has U.S. Income Inequality Really Increased?'" Brookings Institute, January 11, 2007; *http://www3.brookings.edu/views/papers/burtless/20070111.pdf* (accessed April 15, 2008).

3. Clinton, "Remarks on Responsible Citizenship."

4. American National Election Studies, "The ANES Guide to Public Opinion and Electoral Behavior"; *http://www.electionstudies.org/nesguide/toptable/tab5a_5.htm* (accessed April 15, 2008.

5. See, for example, Gertrude Himmelfarb, *One Nation, Two Cultures* (New York: Vintage, 2001); Robert Samuelson, *The Good Life and Its Discontents: The American Dream in the Age of Entitlement* (New York: Vintage, 1997); and Gregg Easterbrook, *The Progress Paradox* (New York: Random House, 2004).

6. See, for example, Thomas Frank, *What's the Matter with Kansas: How Conservatives Won the Heart of America* (New York: Henry Holt, 2004).

7. See, for instance, Morris Fiorina, *Culture War? The Myth of a Polarized America* (New York: Pearson, Longman, 2005); and Allan Wolfe, *One Nation After All: What Middle-Class Americans Really Think About* (New York: Penguin, 1998).

8. The index reached 36 percent in 2000 and climbed farther, to 43 percent in 2002 after the attacks of 9/11. It soon headed back down, though, to 37 percent in 2004; American National Election Survey.

9. Dan Raviv, *Comic Wars: How Two Tycoons Battled over the Marvel Comics Empire and Both Lost* (New York: Random House, 2002).

10. Ibid., 65–72.

11. Mark Waid (w), Ron Garney (p), and Beatty and Smith (i), "The Power and the Glory," *Captain America* 2, nos. 5–7 (May–July 1998), Marvel Comics.

12. Mark Waid (w), Andy Kubert (p), and Jesse Delperdang (i), "American Nightmare," *Captain America* 2, nos. 9–12 (September–December 1998), Marvel Comics.

13. Jeffrey S. Lang and Patrick Trimble, "Whatever Happened to the Man of Tomorrow? An Examination of the American Monomyth and the Comic Book Superhero," *Journal of Popular Culture* 22, no. 3 (1988): 157–73.

14. Paul Jenkins (w) and Ron Garney (p), "The Dogs of War," *Incredible Hulk* 13–20 (April–November 2000), Marvel Comics.

15. Jenkins and Garney, "The Dogs of War," *Incredible Hulk* 16 (July 2000).

16. Jenkins and Garney, "The Dogs of War," *Incredible Hulk* 19 (October 2000).

17. Kurt Busiek (w), Mark Bagley (p), and Vince Russell (i), "Justice, Like Lightening," *Thunderbolts* 1 (April 1997), Marvel Comics.

18. Stan Lee (w), Jack Kirby (p), and Dick Ayers (i), "The Old Order Changeth," *Avengers* 16 (May 1965), Marvel Comics.

19. Kurt Busiek (w), Mark Bagley (p), and Scott Hanna (i), "Trust," *Thunderbolts* 21 (December 1998), Marvel Comics.

20. Fabian Nicieza (w), Mark Bagley (p), and Scott Hanna (i), "Blackhearts," *Thunderbolts* 39 (June 2000), Marvel Comics.

21. Fabian Nicieza (w), Patrick Zircher (p), and Al Vey (i), "Explanations: The End of the Beginning," *Thunderbolts* 49 (April 2001), Marvel Comics.

22. Fabian Nicieza (w), Mark Bagley (p), Greg Adams, Al Vey, and Scott Hanna (i), "Redemption?" *Thunderbolts* 50 (May 2001), Marvel Comics.

23. A three-issue filler series, *Captain America: Dead Man Walking*, served as volume 3.

24. Jeff Bartle, "John Ney Rieber Interview," *Comics Journal* 241 (February 2002): 88.

25. John Ney Rieber (w) and John Cassady (a), "Enemy," *Captain America* 4, nos. 1–6 (June–December 2002), Marvel Comics.

26. John Ney Rieber (w) and John Cassady (a), "Liberty and Justice for All," *Captain America* vol. 4, no. 6 (December 2002), Marvel Comics.

27. Ibid.

28. John Ney Rieber (w) and John Cassady (a), "Never Give Up," *Captain America* 4, no. 4 (September 2002), Marvel Comics.

29. John Ney Rieber (w) and John Cassady (a), "Warlords," *Captain America* 4, no. 5 (October 2002), Marvel Comics.

30. It is this note of complicity in the origins of terrorism that so enflamed conservative film critic Michael Medved that he published an article titled "Captain America: Traitor?" *National Review Online*, April 4, 2003; *www.nationalreview.com/comment/comment-medved040403. asp* (accessed June 15, 2007).

31. George W. Bush, "Remarks by the President," Cincinnati Museum Center, Cincinnati, OH, October 7, 2002; *www.whitehouse.gov/news/ releases/2002/10/20021007-8.html* (accessed 5 May 2008).

32. National Security Council, "National Security Strategy" 2006, section 1; *www.whitehouse.gov/nsc/nss/2006* (accessed 5 May 2008).

33. This position is summarized in National Secrity Council, "National Security Strategy" 2006, section 5A.

34. For advocates of a new "imperial" thinking see, for example, Charles Krauthammer, "The Bush Doctrine," *Time*, March 5, 2001; and Max Boot, "The Case for American Empire," *Weekly Standard*, October 15, 2001. For the critics of such thought, see, among others, Andrew Bacevich, *American Empire* (Cambridge, MA: Harvard University Press, 2002); Chalmers Johnson, *The Sorrows of Empire* (New York: Metropolitan Books, 2002); and Michael Mann, *Incoherent Empire* (London: Verso, 2003).

35. John J. Miller (w) and Jorge Lucas (a), "The Best Defense," *Invincible Iron Man* 3, nos. 73–78 (December 2003–May 2004).

36. John J. Miller (w) and Jorge Lucas (a), "Best Defense, Part 1: Acquisition," *Invincible Iron Man* 3, no. 73 (December 2003), Marvel Comics.

37. John J. Miller (w) and Jorge Lucas(a), "Best Defense, Part 4: Advice and Consent," *Invincible Iron Man* 3, no. 76 (March 2004), Marvel Comics.

38. Dan Jurgens (w), Alan Davis (p), and Robin Riggs (i), "Standoff, Part 1" *Mighty Thor* 2, no. 58 (March 2003), Marvel Comics.

39. Dan Jurgens (w), Tom Mandrake (p), and Brian Reber (i), "Cometh the End," *Mighty Thor* 2, no. 66 (September 2003), Marvel Comics.

40. Dan Jurgens (w), Max Fumara (p), and Carl Smith and Rich Perrotta (i), "The Gates of Hell," *Mighty Thor* 2, no. 67 (October 2003).

41. Dan Jurgens (w), Scott Eaton (p), and Drew Geraci (i), "Letting Go," *Mighty Thor*, 2, no. 79 (July 2004), Marvel Comics.

42. John Ney Rieber (w) and John Cassady (a), "The Extremists," *Captain America* 4, nos. 7–11 (January–May, 2003) Marvel Comics.

43. John Ney Rieber (w), Trevor Hairsine (p), and Danny Miki (i), "The Extremists Part 4," *Captain America* 4, no. 10 (April 2003), Marvel Comics.

44. John Ney Rieber (w), Trevor Hairsine (p), and Danny Miki (i), "The Extremists Part 5," *Captain America* 4, no. 11 (May 2003), Marvel Comics.

45. Geoff Johns (w), Oliver Coipel (p), and Andy Laning (i), "Red Zone, Part 5" *Avengers* 3, no. 69 (September 2003), Marvel Comics; quotation marks in the original.

Chapter Seven

1. George Gene Gustines, "Captain American Is Dead: National Hero since 1941," New York Times Online, March 8, 2007; *http://www. nytimes.com/2007/03/08/books/08capt.html* (accessed May 10, 2008).

2. Larry Holmes, Jonathan O'Beirne, and Glenn Perreira, "Shocking Event for Captain America," CNN.com, March 7, 2007; *http://www. cnn.com/2007/SHOWBIZ/books/03/07/captain.america/index.html* (accessed May 10, 2008).

3. Bill Schneider, "Poll: GOP Support for Iraq War Beginning to Wane," CNN.com, June 26, 2007; *http://www.cnn.com/2007/POLITICS/06/26/ poll.iraq.schneider/index.html* (accessed May 1, 2008).

4. Brian Michael Bendis (w), Oliver Coipel (p), and Tim Townsend (i), *House of M*, 1–8 (August–December 2005), Marvel Comics.

5. Warren Ellis (w) and Adi Granov (a), "Extremis, Part 1," *Invincible Iron Man* 1 (January 2005), Marvel Comics. This is not offered as an origin story, although the parallel to Iron Man's origin is clear. It does occur in the text prior to the first emergence of Iron Man in the story, with no reference to a Vietnam War origin. This places the origin of Iron Man narratively in the War on Terror rather than in Vietnam.

6. Warren Ellis (w) and Adi Granov (a), "Extremis," *Invincible Iron Man* 1–6 (January 2005–May 2006), Marvel Comics.

7. Daniel Knauf and Charles Knauf (w), Patrick Zircher (p), and Scott Hanna (i), "Execute Program," *Invincible Iron Man* 7–12 (June–December 2006), Marvel Comics.

8. Daniel Knauf and Charles Knauf (w), Patrick Zircher (p), and Scott Hanna (i), "Execute Program, Part 1," *Invincible Iron Man* 6 (June 2006), Marvel Comics.

9. Ed Brubaker (w), and Steve Epting and Michael Lark(a), "Out of Time," *Captain America* 1–6 (January–June 2005), Marvel Comics.

10. Ed Brubaker (w), and Steve Epting and Michael Lark (a), "Out of Time, Part 2," *Captain America* 2 (February 2006), Marvel Comics.

11. Ed Brubaker (w), and Steve Epting and Michael Lark (a), "The Winter Soldier," *Captain America* 8–9, 11–14 (September–October 2005, November 2005–April 2006), Marvel Comics.

12. Brian Michael Bendis (w) and Gabrielle Dell'otto (a), Secret War. (New York: Marvel, 2006). Reprint of *Secret War* 1–5, originally published in 2005.

13. Mark Millar (w), Steve McNiven (p), and Dexter Vines (i), *Civil War* 1–7 (July 2006–January 2007), Marvel Comics.

14. Christos Gage (w), Jeremy Haun (p), and Mark Morales (i), "Rubicon," *Iron Man/Captain America: Casualties of War* 1 (February 2007), Marvel Comics.

15. Brian Michael Bendis and Brian Reed (w), Jim Cheung (p), and Mark Morales (i), *New Avengers: Illuminati* 1–5 (February 2007–January 2008), Marvel Comics.

16. Greg Pak (w), Carlo Pagulayan (p), and Jeffrey Huet (i), "Planet Hulk," *Incredible Hulk* 92–105 (April 2006–June 2007), Marvel Comics; "World War Hulk" runs through several titles, but the main story is contained in Greg Pak (w) and John Romita Jr. (a), *World War Hulk* 1–5 (August 2007–January 2008), Marvel Comics.

17. Mark Millar (w), Steve McNiven (p), and Dexter Vines (i), *Civil War* 4 (October 2006), Marvel Comics.

18. Mark Millar (w), Steve McNiven (p), and Dexter Vines (i), *Civil War* 7 (January 2007), Marvel Comics.

19. Ed Brubaker (w) and Steve Epting (a), "Death of a Dream," *Captain America* 25 (March 2007), Marvel Comics. The aftermath of his death is treated in subsequent issues of *Captain America*, and in Jeph Loeb (w) and John Cassady (a), *Fallen Son: The Death of Captain America* 1–5 (July–August 2007), Marvel Comics.

20. Jeph Loeb (w) and John Cassady (a), *Fallen Son: The Death of Captain America* 5 (August 2007), Marvel Comics.

Bibliography

Agee, Philip. *Inside the Company: A CIA Diary*. Middlesex, England: Penguin, 1975.

Alsford, Mike. *Heroes and Villains*. Waco, TX: Baylor University Press, 2006.

American National Election Studies, "The ANES Guide to Public Opinion and Electoral Behavior"; *http://www.electionstudies.org/nesguide/toptable/tab5a_5.htm* (accessed April 15, 2008).

Bacevich, Andres. *American Empire*. Cambridge, MA: Harvard University Press, 2002.

Bailey, Beth. "She 'Can Bring Home the Bacon': Negotiating Gender in the 1970s." In *America in the 1970s*, edited by Beth Bailey and David Farber, 107–28. Lawrence: University Press of Kansas, 2004.

Ball, Terrence. "The Politics of Social Science in Postwar America." In *Recasting America*, edited by Lary May, 76–92. Chicago: University of Chicago Press, 1989.

Barthes, Roland. *Image—Music—Text*. Translated by Stephen Heath. New York: Hill and Wang, 1977.

Bartle, Jeff. "John Ney Rieber Interview." *Comics Journal* 241 (February 2002).

Bell, Daniel. *The End of Ideology: On the Exhaustion of Political Ideas in the Fifties*. New York: Free Press, 1962.

Bellah, Robert, Richard Marsden, William Sullivan, Ann Swidler, and Steven Tipton. *Habits of the Heart: Individualism and Commitment in American Life*. New York: Harper, 1985.

Bendis, Brian Michael (w), Oliver Coipel (p), and Tim Townsend (i) *House of M* 1–8 (August–December 2005), Marvel Comics.

Bendis, Brian Michael (w), and Gabriele Dell'otto (a). *Secret War*. (New York: Marvel, 2006). Reprint of *Secret War* 1–5, originally published in 2005.

Bendis, Brian Michael, and Brian Reed (w), Jim Cheung (p), and Mark Morales (i). *New Avengers: Illuminati* 1–5 (February 2007–January 2008), Marvel Comics.

Bercovitch, Sacvan. *The Rites of Assent*. New York: Routledge, 1993.

Berkowitz, Edward D. *Something Happened: A Political and Cultural Overview of the Seventies*. New York: Columbia University Press, 2006.

Biskind, Peter. *Easy Riders and Raging Bulls: How the Sex–Drugs–and–Rock 'n' Roll Generation Saved Hollywood*. New York: Simon and Schuster, 1998.

Bloom, Allan. *The Closing of the American Mind.* New York: Simon and Schuster, 1988.

Boot, Max. "The Case for American Empire." *Weekly Standard,* October 2001.

Borstelmann, Thomas. *The Cold War and the Color Line: American Race Relations in the Global Arena.* Cambridge, MA: Harvard University Press, 2001.

Brick, Howard. *Age of Contradiction: American Thought and Culture in the 1960s.* Ithaca, NY: Cornell University Press, 1998.

Brooker, Will. *Batman Unmasked: Analyzing a Cultural Icon.* New York: Continuum, 2000.

Brown, Jeffrey A. *Black Superheroes, Milestone Comics, and Their Fans.* Jackson: University Press of Mississippi, 2001.

Brubaker, Ed (w), and Steve Epting (a). "Death of a Dream." *Captain America* 25 (March 2007), Marvel Comics.

Brubaker, Ed (w), and Steve Epting and Michael Lark (a). "Out of Time." *Captain America* 1–6 (January–June 2005), Marvel Comics.

———. "The Winter Soldier." *Captain America* 8–9, 11–14 (September–October 2005, November 2005–April 2006), Marvel Comics.

Burtless, Gary. "Comments on 'Has U.S. Income Inequality Really Increased?'" Brookings Institute, January 11, 2007; *http://www3.brookings.edu/views/papers/burtless/20070111.pdf* (accessed April 15, 2008).

Bush, George W. "Remarks by the President." Cincinnati Museum Center, Cincinnati, OH, October 7, 2002; *www.whitehouse.gov/news/releases/2002/10/20021007-8.htm* (accessed May 5, 2008).

Busiek, Kurt (w), Mark Bagley (a), and Scott Hanna (i). "Trust." *Thunderbolts* 21 (December 1998), Marvel Comics.

Busiek, Kurt (w), Mark Bagley (p), and Vince Russell (i). "Justice, Like Lightening." *Thunderbolts* 1 (April 1997), Marvel Comics.

Byrne, John (w), John Romita Jr. (p), and Bob Wiacek (i). "Armor Wars II." *Iron Man* 258–266 (July 1990–March 1991), Marvel Comics.

Byrne, John (w), Paul Ryan (p), and Bob Wiacek (i). "The Persistence of Memory." *Iron Man* 267 (April 1991), Marvel Comics.

———. "The Dragon Seed Saga." *Iron Man* 267–275 (April 1991–December 1991), Marvel Comics.

Carlson, Allan. *The "American Way": Family and Community in the Shaping of the American Identity.* Washington, DC: ISI Books, 2003.

Carroll, Peter N. *It Seemed Like Nothing Happened: America in the 1970s.* New Brunswick, NJ: Rutgers University Press, 1982.

Carter, Dan. *From George Wallace to Newt Gingrich: Race in the Conservative Counterrevolution, 1963–1994.* Baton Rouge: Louisiana State University Press, 1996.

Carter, Jimmy. *Why Not the Best?* Nashville, TN: Broadman, 1975.

———. "Address to the Nation, 15 July 1979"; *http://millercenter.org/scripps/archive/speeches/detail/3402* (accessed April 2, 2008).

Chandler, Alfred. *Strategy and Structure Chapters in the History of the American Industrial Enterprise* (Cambridge, MA: MIT Press, 1962).

Chichester, D. G. (w), Keith Pollard (p), and Kim DeMulder (i). "The Chaos Serpent." *Nicky Fury, Agent of SHIELD* 2, nos. 7–10 (January 1990–April 1990), Marvel Comics.

Clinton, William Jefferson. "Remarks by the President on Responsible Citizenship and the American Community." Georgetown University, Washington, DC, 6 July 1995; *http://www.clintonofundation.org/legacy/070695-speech-bt-president-at-georgetown.htm* (accessed April 15, 2008).

Conway, Gerry (w), Sal Buscema (p), and Jim Mooney (i). "All the Colors of Evil." *Captain America and the Falcon* 149 (May 1972), Marvel Comics.

Conway, Gerry, and Bill Mantlo (w), Geroge Tuska (p), and Don Perlin (i). "Showdown with the Guardsman." *Invincible Iron Man* 97 (April 1977), Marvel Comics.

Coogan, Peter. *Superhero: The Secret Origin of a Genre.* Austin, TX: Monkeybrain Books, 2006.

Costello, Matthew J. "The Pilgrimage and Progress of George Bailey: Puritanism, *It's a Wonderful Life*, and the Language of Community in America." *American Studies* 40, no. 3 (1999): 31–52.

Courdileone, K. A. "Politics in the Age of Anxiety: The Cold War and the 'Crisis of Masculinity.'" *Journal of American History* 87 (2000) 515–45.

Cowie, Jefferson. "Vigorously Left, Right, and Center': The Crosscurrents of Working-Class America in the 1970s." In *America in the 1970s*, edited by Beth Bailey and David Farber, 75–106. Lawrence: University Press of Kansas, 2004.

Crowner, Martha L. "Review of John Michael Metzel, *Prozac on the Couch*." *Psychiatric Services* 5 (2004) 200–201.

Dahl, Robert. *A Preface to Democratic Theory.* Chicago: University of Chicago Press, 1956.

Daniels, Les. *DC Comics: Sixty Years of the World's Favorite Comic Book Heroes.* Boston: Bulfinch Press, 1995.

———. *Marvel: Five Fabulous Decades of the World's Greatest Comics.* New York: Harry N. Abrams, 1991.

De Hart, Jane Sherron. "Containment at Home: Gender, Sexuality and National Identity in Cold War America." In *Rethinking Cold War Culture*, edited by Peter Kuznick and James Gilbert, 124–55. Washington, DC: Smithsonian Institution Press, 2001.

DeMatteis, J. M. (w), Sal Buscema (p), and Kim DeMulder (i). "Diverging . . ." *Captain America* 284 (August 1983), Marvel Comics.

DeMatteis, J. M., and Michael Ellis (w), Paul Neary (p), and Denis Janke (i). "Das Ende." *Captain America* 300 (December 1984), Marvel Comics.

DeMatteis, J. M. (w), Paul Neary (p), and Roy Richardson (i). "All My Sins Remembered." *Captain America* 297 (September 1984), Marvel Comics.

———. "Sturm and Drang: The Life and Times of the Red Skull." *Captain America* 298 (October 1984), Marvel Comics.

DeMatteis, J. M. (w), Paul Neary (p), and Josef Rubinstein (i). "The Measure of a Man." *Captain America* 294 (June 1984), Marvel Comics.

DeMatteis, J. M. (w), Mike Zeck (p), and John Beatty (i). "The Man Who Made a Difference." *Captain America* 267 (March 1982), Marvel Comics.

———. "Sermon of Straw." *Captain America* 280 (April 1983), Marvel Comics.

Dittmer, Jason. "Captain America's Empire: Reflections on Identity, Popular Culture, and Post-9/11 Geopolitics." *Annals of the Association of American Geographers* 95, no. 3 (2005): 626–43.

———. "Retconning America: Captain America in the Wake of World War II and the McCarthy Hearings." In *The Amazing, Transforming Superhero!* edited by Terrence Wandtke, 33–51. Jefferson, NC: McFarland, 2007.

Dorfman, Ariel, and Armand Mattelart. *How to Read Donald Duck: Imperialist Ideology in the Disney Comic.* London: IG Editions, 1975.

DuBose, Mike. "Holding Out for a Hero: Reaganism, Comic Book Vigilantes, and Captain America." *Journal of Popular Culture* 40 (2007): 915–35.

Dudziak, Mary L. *Cold War Civil Rights: Race and the Image of American Democracy.* Princeton, NJ: Princeton University Press, 2000.

Dukakis, Michael. "Speech Accepting the Presidential Nomination from the 1988 Democratic National Convention." July 21, 1988; *http://www.transcripts.cnn.com/TRANSCRIPTS/0006/04/sm.11.html* (accessed January 28, 2008).

Easterbrook, Gregg. *The Progress Paradox.* New York: Random House, 2004.

Eco, Umberto. "The Myth of Superman." In *The Role of the Reader*, translated by Natalie Chilton, 107–25. Bloomington: Indiana University Press, 1979.

Ehrenreich, Barbara. *The Hearts of Men: American Dreams and the Flight from Commitment.* New York: Doubleday, 1983.

Ehrman, John. *The Eighties: America in the Age of Reagan.* New Haven, CT: Yale University Press, 2005.

Eisenhower, Dwight D. "Inaugural Address, 20 January 1953." Avalon Project at Yale Law School; *http://www.yale.edu/lawweb/avalon/presiden/inaug/eisen1.htm* (accessed May 9, 2008).

Eisner, Will. *Comics and Sequential Art.* Tamarac, FL: Poorhouse Press, 1985.

———. *Graphic Storytelling and Visual Narrative.* Tamarac, FL: Poorhouse Press, 1996.

Ellis, Allen. "Comic Art in Scholarly Writing: A Citation Guide"; *http://www.comicresearch.org/CAC/cite.html* (accessed May 15, 2007).

Ellis, Warren (w), and Adi Granov (a). "Extremis." *Invincible Iron Man* 1–6 (January 2005–May 2006), Marvel Comics.

Ellison, Harlan, and Roy Thomas (w), Herb Trimpe (p), and Sam Grainger (i). "The Brute That Shouted Love at the Heart of the Atom." *Incredible Hulk* 140 (June 1971), Marvel Comics.

Emad, Mitra C. "Reading Wonder Woman's Body: Mythologies of Gender and Nation." *Journal of Popular Culture* 39 (2006) 954–84.

Emerson, Ralph Waldo. "The Young American." In *Essays and Lectures*, edited by Joel Porte, 211–30. New York: Library of America, 1983.

Engel, Gary. "What Makes Superman So Darned American?" In *Superman at 50: The Persistence of a Legend*, edited by Dennis Dooley and Gary Engel, 79–88. Cleveland, OH: Octavia Press, 1987.

Engelhart, Steve (w), Sal Buscema (p), and Vinnie Colletta (i). ". . . Before the Dawn." *Captain America and the Falcon* 175 (July 1974), Marvel Comics.

———. "Captain America Must Die." *Captain America and the Falcon* 176 (August 1974), Marvel Comics.

Engelhart, Steve (w), Sal Buscema (p), and Frank McGlaughlin (i). "The Incredible Origin of the Other Captain America." *Captain America and the Falcon* 155 (November 1972), Marvel Comics.

———. "Two into One Won't Go." *Captain America and the Falcon* 156 (December 1972), Marvel Comics.

Engelhart, Steve (w), Sal Buscema (p), and Jim Mooney (i). "Captain America: Hero or Hoax?" *Captain America* 153 (September 1972), Marvel Comics.

Engelhart, Steve (w), Sal Buscema (p), and John Verpooten (i). "The Falcon Fights Alone." *Captain America and the Falcon* 154 (October 1972), Marvel Comics.

———. "Beware of Serpents!" *Captain America and the Falcon* 163 (July 1973), Marvel Comics.

Engelhart, Steve (w), Frank Robbins (p), and Frank Giacoia (i). "Nomad: No More!" *Captain America and the Falcon* 183 (March 1975), Marvel Comics.

———. "Scream the Scarlet Skull." *Captain America and the Falcon* 185 (May 1975), Marvel Comics.

Engelhardt, Tom. *The End of Victory Culture: Cold War America and the Disillusioning of a Generation.* New York: Basic Books, 1995.

Farber, David. "The Torch Had Fallen." In *America in the 1970s*, edited by Beth Bailey and David Farber, 9–28. Lawrence: University Press of Kansas, 2004.

Fingeroth, Danny. *Superman on the Couch: What Superheroes Really Tell Us About Ourselves and Our Society.* New York: Continuum, 2004.

Fiorina, Morris. *Culture War? The Myth of a Polarized America.* New York: Pearson, Longman, 2005.

Foreman, Joel. "Introduction." In *The Other Fifties: Interrogating Midcentury American Icons*, edited by Joel Foreman, 1–23. Urbana: University of Illinois Press, 1997.

Frank, Thomas. *What's the Matter with Kansas: How Conservatives Won the Heart of America.* New York: Henry Holt, 2004.

Franklin, Benjamin. *Autobiography and Other Writings.* New York: Penguin, 1986.

Friday, Nancy. *My Mother/My Self: The Daughter's Search for Identity.* 20th anniversary edition. New York: Delta, 1997.

Friedberg, Aaron L. *In the Shadow of the Garrison State: America's Anti-Statism and Its Cold War Grand Strategy.* Princeton, NJ: Princeton University Press, 2000.

Frieden, Betty. *The Feminine Mystique.* New York: W. W. Norton, 1963.

Friedrich, Gary (w), Gil Kane (p), and John Romita (i). "Skyjacked!" *Captain America and the Falcon* 145 (January 1972), Marvel Comics.

Friedrich, Gary (w), and John Romita (a). "Hydra over All." *Captain America and the Falcon* 144 (December 1971), Marvel Comics.

———. "Power to the People." *Captain America and the Falcon* 143 (November 1971), Marvel Comics.

Frum, David. *The 70's: How We Got Here.* New York: Basic Books, 2000.

Gaddis, John Lewis. *The Cold War: A New History.* New York: Penguin, 2005.

Gage, Christos (w), Jeremy Haun (p), and Mark Morales (i). "Rubicon." *Iron Man/Captain America: Casualties of War* 1 (February 2007), Marvel Comics.

Galbraith, John Kenneth. *The Affluent Society.* 3rd edition. New York: New American Library, 1976.

Gallis, Peter (w), Jerry Bingham (p), and Alan Gordon (i). "The Sins of the Father." *Captain America* 246 (June 1980), Marvel Comics.

Genter, Robert. "'With Great Power Comes Great Responsibility': Cold War Culture and the Birth of Marvel Comics." *Journal of Popular Culture* 40 (2007): 953–78.

Gerber, Steve (w), Sal Buscema (p), and Mike Esposito and John Tartagioni (i). "Devastation." *Captain America* 225 (September 1978), Marvel Comics.

Gerstle, Gary. *American Crucible: Race and Nation in the Twentieth Century.* Princeton, NJ: Princeton University Press, 2001.

Gilbert, James. *A Cycle of Outrage.* New York: Oxford University Press, 1986.

Ginsberg, Benjamin, and Martin Shefter. *Politics by Other Means: The Declining Importance of Elections in America.* New York: Basic Books, 1990.

Gitlin, Todd. *The Sixties: Years of Hope, Days of Rage.* Revised edition. New York: Bantam Books, 1993.

Gold, Mimi (w), Don Heck (p), and Chic Stone (i). "Save the People . . . Save the Country!" *Invincible Iron Man* 29 (September 1970), Marvel Comics.

Goldberg, Robert Alan. *Enemies Within: The Culture of Conspiracy in Modern America.* New Haven, CT: Yale University Press, 2001.

Goodwin, Archie (w), Don Heck (p), and John Craig (i). "The Fury of Firebrand." *Invincible Iron Man* 27 (July 1970), Marvel Comics.

Goodwin, Archie (w), George Tuska (p), and Vinnie Collette(i). "Fear Wears Two Faces." *Invincible Iron Man* 88 (July 1976), Marvel Comics.

Goodwin, Archie (w), George Tuska (p), and Johnny Craig (i). "A Duel Must End." *Invincible Iron Man* 8 (December 1968), Marvel Comics.

———. "There Lives a Green Goliath." *Invincible Iron Man* 9 (January 1969), Marvel Comics.

. "What Price Life?" *Invincible Iron Man* 19 (November 1969), Marvel Comics.

Goodwin, Archie (w), George Tuska (p), and Joe Gaudioso (i). "The Replacement." *Invincible Iron Man* 21 (January 1970), Marvel Comics.

———. "From This Conflict, Death!" *Invincible Iron Man* 22 (February 1969), Marvel Comics.

Graebner, William. "America's Poseidon Adventure: A Nation in Existential Despair." In *America in the 1970s*, edited by Beth Bailey and David Farber, 157–80. Lawrence: University Press of Kansas, 2004.

Groensteen, Thierry. *The System of Comics*. Translated by Bart Beaty and Nick Nguyen. Jackson: University Press of Mississippi, 2007.

Gruenwald, Mark (w), Kieron Dwyer (p), and Al Milgrom (i). "Don't Tread on Me." *Captain America* 344 (August 1988), Marvel Comics.

Gruenwald, Mark (w), Kieron Dwyer (p), and Allen Milgrom (i). "Seeing Red." *Captain America* 350 (February 1989), Marvel Comics.

———. "Surrender." *Captain America* 345 (September 1988), Marvel Comics.

Gruenwald, Mark (w), Dave Hoover (p), and Danny Bulanadi (i). "Superpatriot Games." *Captain America* 425 (March 1994), Marvel Comics.

Gruenwald, Mark (w), Ron Lim (p), and Danny Bulanadi (i). "Streets of Poison." *Captain America* 372–78 (July 1990–October 1990), Marvel Comics.

Gruenwald, Mark (w), Tom Morgan (p), and Bob McLeod (i). "The Choice." *Captain America* 332 (August 1987), Marvel Comics.

Gruenwald, Mark (w), Paul Neary (p), and John Beatty (i). "Ultimatum." *Captain America* 321 (September 1986), Marvel Comics.

Gruenwald, Mark (w), Paul Neary (p), and Dennis Janke (i). "The Little Bang Theory." *Captain America* 320 (August 1986), Marvel Comics.

Hadju, David. *The Ten-Cent Plague: The Great Comic Book Scare and How It Changed America.* New York: Farrar, Straus and Giroux, 2008.

Harras, Bob, and Terry Kavanagh (w), Roger Cruz, Luke Ross, and Fabio Laguna (p), and Scott Koblish and Rene Micheleti (i). *Avengers: Timeslide* (February 1996), Marvel Comics.

Harras, Bob, and Terry Kavanagh (w), and Mike Deodato (p). *Avengers: The Crossing* (September 1995), Marvel Comics.

Harras, Bob, and Terry Kavanagh (w), Mike Deodato (p), and Tom Palmer (i). "The Crossing." *Avengers* 390–95 (September 1995–February1996), Marvel Comics.

Harras, Bob (w), Paul Neary (p), and Kim DeMulder (i). *Nick Fury vs. S.H.I.E.L.D.* 1–6 (June 1988–November 1988), Marvel Comics.

Harris, Mark. *Pictures at a Revolution: Five Movies and the Birth of the New Hollywood.* New York: Penguin, 2008.

Harris, Thomas. *I'm OK, You're OK.* New York: Harper, 2004.

Harvey, Robert C. *The Art of the Comic Book: An Aesthetic History.* Jackson: University Press of Mississippi, 1996.

Hatch, Rebecca. *A Generation Divided: The New Left, The New Right, and the 1960s.* Berkeley and Los Angeles: University of California Press, 1999.

Hathcock, Nelson. "A Spy in the Enemy's Country": *Black Like Me* as Cold War Narrative." *American Studies* 44, no. 3 (2003): 99–120.

Himmelfarb, Gertrude. *One Nation, Two Cultures.* New York: Vintage, 2001.

Hirsch, E. D., Jr. *Cultural Literacy: What Every American Needs to Know.* New York: Vintage, 1988.

Hodgson, Godfrey. *America in Our Time.* New York: Doubleday, 1976.

Hoffer, Eric. *The True Believer: Thoughts on the Nature of Mass Movements.* New York: Harper and Brothers, 1951.

Hofstadter, Richard. *The American Political Tradition and the Men Who Made It.* New York: Vintage, 1948.

Hughes, Jamie A. "'Who Watches the Watchmen?' Ideology and 'Real World' Superheroes." *Journal of Popular Culture* 39, no. 4 (2006): 546–57.

Inge, Thomas. *Comics as Culture.* Jackson: University Press of Mississippi, 1990.

Jenkins, Paul (p), and Ron Garney (p). "The Dogs of War." *Incredible Hulk* 13–20 (April–November 2000), Marvel Comics.

Jenkins, Philip. *Decade of Nightmares: The End of the Sixties and the Making of Eighties America.* New York: Oxford University Press, 2006.

Johnson, Chalmers. *The Sorrows of Empire* (New York: Metropolitan Books, 2002).

Jones, Gerard. *Men of Tomorrow: Geeks, Gangsters, and the Birth of the Comic Book.* New York: Basic Books, 2004.

Jurgens, Dan (w), Alan Davis (p), and Robin Riggs (i). "Standoff, Part 1." *Mighty Thor* 2, no. 58 (March 2003), Marvel Comics.

Jurgens, Dan (w), Scott Eaton (p), and Drew Geraci (i). "Letting Go." *Mighty Thor* 2, no. 79 (July 2004), Marvel Comics.

Jurgens, Dan (w), Max Fumara (p), and Carl Smith and Rich Perrotta (i). "The Gates of Hell." *Mighty Thor* 2, no. 67 (October 2003), Marvel Comics.

Jurgens, Dan (w), and Ben Lai and Ray Lai (a). "Frenzy." *Mighty Thor* 2, no. 65 (August 2003), Marvel Comics.

Jurgens, Dan (w), Tom Mandrake (p), and Brian Reber (i). "Cometh the End." *Mighty Thor* 2, no. 66 (September 2003), Marvel Comics.

Kennan, George. "The Sources of Soviet Conduct." *Foreign Affairs* 25 (1947): 566–82.

Kennedy, Paul. *The Rise and Fall of the Great Powers.* New York: Random House, 1987.

Keohane, Robert. *After Hegemony: Cooperation and Discord in the World Political Economy*. Princeton, NJ: Princeton University Press, 1985.

Kindleberger, Charles. *The World in Depression, 1929–1939*. Berkeley and Los Angeles: University of California Press, 1986.

Klatch, Rebecca E. *A Generation Divided: The New Left, the New Right, and the 1960s*. Berkeley and Los Angeles: University of California Press, 1999.

Klock, Geoff. *How to Read Superhero Comics and Why*. New York: Continuum, 2002.

Knauf, Daniel, and Charles Knauf (w), Patrick Zircher (p), and Scott Hanna (i). "Execute Program." *Invincible Iron Man* 7–12 (June–December 2006), Marvel Comics.

Krauthhammer, Charles. "The Bush Doctrine." *Time*, March 5, 2001.

Lang, Jeffrey S., and Patrick Trimble. "Whatever Happened to the Man of Tomorrow? An Examination of the American Monomyth and the Comic Book Superhero." *Journal of Popular Culture* 22, no. 3 (1988): 157–73.

Lasch, Christopher. *The Culture of Narcissism*. New York: Signet Books, 1979.

———. *Haven in a Heartless World: The Family Besieged*. New York: Basic Books, 1978.

Lassiter, Matthew D. *The Silent Majority: Suburban Politics in the Sunbelt South*. Princeton, NJ: Princeton University Press, 2006.

Lawrence, John Shelton, and Thomas Jewitt. *The Myth of the American Superhero*. New York: William B. Eerdman's, 2002.

Lears, Jackson. "A Matter of Taste: Corporate Cultural Hegemony in a Mass-Consumption Society." In *Recasting America*, edited by Lary May, 38–60. Chicago: University of Chicago Press.

Lee, Stan. "Stan Lee's Soapbox." Marvel Comics, various issues.

Lee, Stan (w), Adam Austin (p), and Gary Michaels (i). "Invincible Iron Man: If This Guilt Be Mine!" *Tales of Suspense* 74 (February 1966), Marvel Comics.

Lee, Stan (w), Robert Bernstein (p), and Don Heck (i). "Iron Man Faces the Crimson Dynamo." *Tales of Suspense* 46 (October 1963), Marvel Comics.

———. "Iron Man: Trapped by the Red Barbarian." *Tales of Suspense* 42 (June 1963), Marvel Comics.

Lee, Stan (w), Gene Colan (p), and Dan Adkins(i). "The Tragedy and the Triumph." *Tales of Suspense* 94 (October 1967), Marvel Comics.

Lee, Stan (w), Gene Colan (p), and Dick Ayers (i). "Bucky Reborn." *Captain America* 131 (November 1970), Marvel Comics.

———. "Madness in the Slums." *Captain America* 133 (January 1971), Marvel Comics.

Lee, Stan (w) and Gene Colan (p), and Frank Giacoia (i). "Into the Jaws of Death." *Tales of Suspense* 85 (January 1967), Marvel Comics.

Lee, Stan (w), Gene Colan (p), and Frank Giacoia (i). "Captured in Vietnam!" *Captain America* 125 (May 1970), Marvel Comics.

————. "Death Duel for the Life of Happy Hogan." *Tales of Suspense* 86 (February 1967), Marvel Comics.

————. "The Other Iron Man." *Tales of Suspense* 84 (December 1966), Marvel Comics.

Lee, Stan (w), Gene Colan (p), and Gary Michaels (i). "Victory." *Tales of Suspense* 83 (November 1966), Marvel Comics.

Lee, Stan (w), Gene Colan (p), and Joe Sinnott (i). "The Coming of the Falcon." *Captain America* 117 (September 1969), Marvel Comics.

————. "Cracked on Campus." *Captain America* 120 (December 1969), Marvel Comics.

————. "The Sting of the Scorpion." *Captain America* 122 (February 1970), Marvel Comics.

Lee, Stan (w), and Steve Ditko (p). "Just a Guy Named Joe." *Amazing Spider-Man* 38 (July 1965), Marvel Comics.

Lee, Stan (w), and Don Heck (p). "To Smash a Serpent." *Mighty Avengers* 33 (October 1966), Marvel Comics.

Lee, Stan (w), Gil Kane (p), and Joe Sinnott (i). "Captain America: The Last Defeat." *Tales of Suspense* 91 (July 1967), Marvel Comics.

Lee, Stan (w), and Jack Kirby (a). "Enter the Gargoyle." *Incredible Hulk* 1 (May 1962), Marvel Comics.

Lee, Stan (w), Jack Kirby (a), and Dick Ayers (i). "The Old Order Changeth." *Avengers* 16 (May 1965), Marvel Comics.

Lee, Stan (w), Jack Kirby (p), and Dick Ayers and J. Tartaglione (i). "Captain America: Thirty Minutes to Live." *Tales of Suspense* 75 (March 1966), Marvel Comics.

Lee, Stan (w), Jack Kirby (p), and Frank Giacoia (i). "Cap Goes Wild." *Captain America* 106 (October 1968), Marvel Comics.

————. "Captain America: The Maddening Mystery of the Inconceivable Adaptoid!" *Tales of Suspense* 82 (October 1966), Marvel Comics.

Lee, Stan (w), Jack Kirby, and Don Heck (p), and Mike Esposito (i). "Now, by My Hand, Shall Die a Villain." *Mighty Avengers* 15 (April 1965), Marvel Comics.

Lee, Stan (w), Jack Kirby (p), and Syd Shores (i). "The Hero That Was." *Captain America* 109 (January 1969), Marvel Comics.

Lee, Stan (w), Jack Kirby (p), and Joe Sinnott (i). "Captain America: A Time to Die—A Time To Live!" *Tales of Suspense* 95 (November 1967), Marvel Comics.

————. "Captain America: To Be Reborn!" *Tales of Suspense* 96. (December 1967), Marvel Comics.

Lee, Stan (w), Jack Kirby (p), and Chic Stone (i). "Captain America: The Strength of the Sumo." *Tales of Suspense* 61 (January 1965), Marvel Comics.

Lee, Stan (w), Jack Kirby (p), and George Tuska (i). "Captain America: The Sleeper Awake!" *Tales of Suspense* 72 (December 1965), Marvel Comics.

Lee, Stan, and Larry Lieber (w), Jack Kirby (p), and Dick Ayers (i). "The Mighty Thor: A Prisoner of the Reds." *Journey into Mystery* 87 (December 1962), Marvel Comics.

Lee, Stan, and George Mair. *Excelsior: The Amazing Life of Stan Lee.* New York: Fireside Books, 2002.

Lee, Stan (w), John Romita (p), and Sal Buscema (i). "The Man Behind the Mask." *Captain America* 114 (June 1969), Marvel Comics.

Lee, Stan, Roy Thomas and Jim Steranko (w), and Jack Kirby and John Buscema (p). *Nick Fury, Agent of S.H.I.E.L.D.* (New York: Marvel Comics, 2000).

Leebaert, Derek. *The Fifty-Year Wound: The True Price of America's Cold War Victory.* Boston: Little, Brown, 2002.

Lerner, Daniel. *The Passing of Traditional Society: Modernizing the Middle East.* Glencoe, IL: Free Press, 1958.

"Let's Rap with Cap!" *Captain America,* Marvel Comics, various issues.

"Letters to the Living Legend." *Captain America,* Marvel Comics, various issues.

Lewis, A. David. "Graphic Responses: Comic Book Superheroes' Militarism Post 9/11." *Magazine Americana,* January 2008; *http://americanpopularculture.com/emerging.htm* (accessed January 18, 2008).

Lienisch, Michael. *A New Order for the Ages: Time, the Constitution, and the Making of Modern American Political Thought.* Princeton, NJ: Princeton University Press, 1988.

Lincoln, Abraham. "Annual Message to Congress, 3 December 1861." In *Speeches and Writings, 1859–1865,* edited by Don E. Fehrenbacher, 279–97. New York: Library of America, 1989.

Lindsay, Hal. *The Late, Great Planet Earth.* New York: Zondervan Books, 1973.

Lipset, Seymour Martin. *Political Man: The Social Bases of Politics.* New York: Doubleday, 1960.

Loeb, Jeph (w), and John Cassady (a). *Fallen Son: The Death of Captain America* 1–5 (July–August 2007), Marvel Comics.

MacPherson, James. *Battle Cry of Freedom.* New York: Oxford University Press, 1988.

Maland, Charles. "*Dr. Strangelove* (1964): Nightmare Comedy and the Ideology of Liberal Consensus." In *Hollywood as Historian,* edited by Peter Rollins, 190–210. Lexington: University Press of Kentucky, 1983.

Mann, Michael. *Incoherent Empire* (London: Verso, 2003).

Mantlo, Bill (w), George Tuska (p), and Vinnie Colletta (i). "Long Time Gone." *Invincible Iron Man* 78 (September 1975), Marvel Comics.

Mantlo, Bill (w), Geroge Tuska (p), and Mike Esposito (i). "Every Hand Against Him." *Iron Man* 105 (December 1977), Marvel Comics.

May, Elaine Tyler. "Explosive Issues: Sex, Women and the Bomb." In *Recasting America,* edited by Lary May, 154–70. Chicago: University of Chicago Press, 1988.

———. *Homeward Bound: American Families in the Cold War Era.* Revised edition. New York: Basic Books, 1999.

May, Ernest, ed. *American Cold War Strategy: Interpreting NSC 68.* Boston: Bedford/St. Martin's, 1993.

May, Lary. "Introduction." In *Recasting America*, edited by Lary May, 1–18. Chicago: University of Chicago Press, 1988.

McAllister, Matthew P., Edward Sewall Jr., and Ian Gordan, eds. *Comics and Ideology.* New York: Peter Lang, 2001.

McCloud, Scott. *Understanding Comics: The Invisible Art.* New York: Harper. 1994.

McGirr, Lisa. *Suburban Warriors: The Origins of the New American Right.* Princeton, NJ: Princeton University Press, 2001.

Medovoi, Leerom. "Democracy, Capitalism, and American Literature: The Cold War Construction of J. D. Salinger's Paperback Hero." In *The Other Fifties: Interrogating Midcentury Icons*, edited by Joel Foreman, 255–87. Urbana: University of Illinois Press, 1997.

Medved, Michael. "Captain America, Traitor?" *National Review Online*, April 4, 2003; *www.nationalreview.com/comment/comment-medved040403. asp* (accessed June 15, 2007).

Meltzer, Brad (w), Rags Morales (p), and Mike Bair (i). *Identity Crisis* 1–7 (April 2004–February 2005), DC Comics.

Meyerowitz, Joanne. "Sex, Gender, and the Cold War Language of Reform." In *Rethinking Cold War Culture*, edited by Peter J. Kuznick and James Gilbert, 106–23. Washington, DC: Smithsonian Institution Press, 2001.

Michelinie, David (w), Mark Bright (p), and Bob Layton (i). "Red Snow." *Iron Man* 229 (April 1988), Marvel Comics.

———. "Stark Wars." *Iron Man* 225 (December 1987), Marvel Comics.

———. "Stark Wars: Glitch." *Iron Man* 226 (January 1988), Marvel Comics.

Michelinie, David (w), and John Byrne and Dan Green (p). "Back to the Stone Age." *Avengers* 191 (January 1980), Marvel Comics.

———. "On the Matter of Heroes." *Avengers* 181 (March 1979), Marvel Comics.

Michelinie, David (w), George Perez (p), and Josef Rubinstein (i). "Interlude." *Avengers* 194 April 1980), Marvel Comics.

Michelinie, David (w), John Romita Jr. (p), and Bob Layton (i). "Demon in a Bottle." *Invincible Iron Man* 128 (November 1979), Marvel Comics.

Millar, Mark (w), Steve McNiven (p), and Dexter Vines (i). *Civil War* 1–7 (July 2006–January 2007), Marvel Comics.

Miller, Frank (w/a), and Klaus Jansen and Lynn Varley (i). *Batman: The Dark Knight Returns.* Tenth anniversary edition. New York: DC Comics, 1996.

Miller, James. *Democracy Is in the Streets: From Port Huron to the Siege of Chicago.* New York: Touchstone Books, 1987.

Miller, John. J. (w), and Jorge Lucas (a). "The Best Defense." *Invincible Iron Man* 3, nos. 73–78 (December 2003–May 2004), Marvel Comics.

Miller, John J., Maggie Thompson, Peter Bickford, and Brent Frankenhoff. *The Comic Buyer's Guide Standard Catalog of Comic Books.* 4th edition. Iola, WI: KP Books, 2005.

Moore, Alan (w), and Dave Gibbons (p). *Watchmen.* New York: Warner Books, 1986.

Moore, Jesse T. "The Education of Green Lantern: Culture and Ideology." *Journal of American Culture* 26, no. 2 (2003): 263–78.

Morgan, Ted. *Reds: McCarthyism in Twentieth Century America.* New York: Random House, 2004.

Morris, Kenneth. *Jimmy Carter: American Moralist.* Athens: University of Georgia Press, 1996.

Morris, Tom. "What's Behind the Mask? The Secret of Secret Identities." In *Superheroes and Philosophy: Truth, Justice, and the Socratic Way,* edited by Tom Morris and Matt Morris, 250–266. Chicago: Open Court Press, 2005.

Nadel, Alan. *Containment Culture: American Narratives, Postmodernism, and the Atomic Age.* Durham, NC: Duke University Press, 1995.

Naional Security Council, "National Security Strategy 2006"; *www.white house.gov/nsc/nss/2006* (accessed May 5, 2008).

Navasky, Victor S. *Naming Names.* 3rd edition. New York: Hill and Wang, 2003.

Nicieza, Fabian (w), Mark Bagley (p), and Greg Adams, Al Vey, and Scott Hanna (i). "Redemption?" *Thunderbolts* 50 (May 2001), Marvel Comics.

Nicieza, Fabian (w), Mark Bagley (p), and Scott Hanna (i). "Blackhearts." *Thunderbolts* 39 (June 2000), Marvel Comics.

Nicieza, Fabian (w), Rick Mays and Pete Garcia (p), and Greg Adams (i). "American Dreamers." *Nomad* 22–25 (February–May 1994), Marvel Comics.

Nicieza, Fabian (w), Patrick Zircher (p), and Al Vey (i). "Explanations: The End of the Beginning." *Thunderbolts* 49 (April 2001), Marvel Comics.

Noble, Richard. *Death of a Nation: American Culture and the End of Exceptionalism.* Minneapolis: University of Minnesota Press, 2002.

Nyberg, Amy Kiste. *Seal of Approval: The History of the Comics Code.* Jackson: University Press of Mississippi, 1998.

O'Neil, Dennis, and Neal Adams. *Green Lantern/Green Arrow.* 2 vols. New York: DC Comics, 2004.

O'Neil, Dennis (w), Mark Bright (p), and Ian Akin and Brian Garvey (i). "Resolutions." *Invincible Iron Man* 200 (November 1985), Marvel Comics.

O'Neil, Dennis (w), Luke McDonnell (p), and Ian Akin and Brian Garvey (i). "A Duel of Iron." *Invincible Iron Man* 192 (March 1985), Marvel Comics.

———. "The Choice and the Challenge." *Invincible Iron Man* 193 (April 1985), Marvel Comics.

———. "The Most Precious Thing." *Invincible Iron Man* 195 (June 1985), Marvel Comics.

Pak, Greg (w), Carlo Pagulayan (p), and Jeffrey Huet (i). "Planet Hulk" *Incredible Hulk* 92–105 (April 2006–June 2007), Marvel Comics.

Pak, Greg (w), and John Romita Jr. (a). *World War Hulk* 1–5 (August 2007–January 2008), Marvel Comics.

Patterson, James. *Grand Expectations: The United States, 1945–1974.* New York: Oxford University Press, 1996.

———. Restless Giant: *The United States from Watergate to Bush v. Gore.* New York: Oxford University Press. 2005.

Perlstein, Rick. *Before the Storm: Barry Goldwater and the Unmaking of the American Consensus.* New York: Hill and Wang, 2001.

Porter, Eric. "Affirming and Disaffirming Actions: Remaking Race in the 1970s." In *America in the 1970s,* edited by Beth Bailey and David Farber, 50–74. Lawrence: University Press of Kansas, 2004.

Putnam, Robert. *Bowling Alone: The Collapse and Revival of American Community.* New York: Touchstone Books, 2000.

Ransom, John Crowe. "Reconstructed but Unregenerate." In *I'll Take My Stand: The South and the Agrarian Traidition,* edited by John Crowe Ransom. New York: Harper Torchbooks, 1962.

Raphael, Jordan, and Tom Spurgeon. *Stan Lee and the Rise and Fall of the American Comic Book.* Chicago: Chicago Review Press, 2003.

Raviv, Dan. *Comic Wars: How Two Tycoons Battled over the Marvel Comics Empire and Both Lost.* New York: Random House, 2002.

Reagan, Ronald. "Address at Bittburg Airbase, Federal Republic of Germany," May 5, 1985; *http://www.reagan.utexas.edu/archives/speeches/publicpapers.html* (accessed April 2, 2008).

———. "Address to the National Association of Evangelicals," March 8, 1983, Orlando FL; *http://www.reagan.utexas.edu/archives/speeches/publicpapers.html* (accessed April 2, 2008).

———. "Inaugural Address," January 20, 1981; *http://www.reaganlibrary.com/reagan/speeches/first.asp* (accessed April 2, 2008).

———. "National Address on the Economy." October 13, 1982; *http://www.reagan.utexas.edu/archives/speeches/publicpapers.html* (accessed April 2, 2008).

———. "State of the Union Address," January 27, 1984; *http://www.reagan.utexas.edu/archives/speeches/publicpapers.html* (accessed April 2, 2008).

Regaldo, Aldo. "Modernity, Race and the American Superhero." In *Comics as Philosophy,* edited by Jeff McLaughlin, 84–99. Jackson: University Press of Mississippi, 2005.

Reisman, David. *The Lonely Crowd: A Study of Changing American Character.* New Haven, CT: Yale University Press, 1950.

Reisman, David. "The Nylon War." *In Abundance for What? And Other Essays* 67–79. New York: Doubleday, 1964.

Reynolds, Alan. "Policy Analysis: Has U.S. Income Inequality Really Increased?" Cato Institute Policy Analysis No. 586 (January 8, 2007); *http://www.cato.org/pub_display.php?pub_id6880* (accessed April 15, 2008).

Reynolds, Richard. *Superheroes: A Modern Mythology.* Jackson: University Press of Mississippi, 1992.

Rieber, John Ney (w), and John Cassady (a). "Enemy." *Captain America* 4, nos. 1–6, (June–December 2002), Marvel Comics.

Rieber, John Ney (w), Trevor Hairsine (p), and Danny Miki (i). "The Extremists." *Captain America* 4, nos. 7–11 (February–May 2003), Marvel Comics.

Ro, Ronin. *Tales to Astonish: Jack Kirby, Stan Lee, and the American Comic Book Revolution.* New York: Bloomsbury Press, 2004.

Robin, Ron. *The Making of the Cold War Enemy.* Princeton, NJ: Princeton University Press, 2001.

Rogin, Michael. *"Kiss Me Deadly*: Communism, Motherhood and Cold War Movies." In *Ronald Reagan the Movie: And Other Episodes in Political Demonology,* 236–71. Berkeley and Los Angeles: University of California Press, 1987.

Rossinow, Doug. *The Politics of Authenticity: Liberalism, Christianity and the New Left in America.* New York: Columbia University Press, 1998.

Rossiter, Clinton, ed. *The Federalist Papers.* New York: Mentor Books, 1961.

Rostow, Walt Whitman. *The Stages of Economic Growth: A Non-Communist Manifesto.* New York: Cambridge University Press, 1960.

Samuelson, Robert. *The Good Life and Its Discontents: The American Dream in the Age of Entitlement.* New York: Vintage, 1997.

Sanchez, Julian. "The Revolt of the Comic Books." *American Prospect,* November 9, 2007; *http://www.prospect.org/cs/articles?article=the_revolt_of_the_comic_books* (accessed April 15, 2008).

Sanderson, Peter. *Marvel Universe.* New York: Abradale Press, 1996.

Savage, William, Jr. *Commies, Cowboys, and Jungle Queens: Comic Books and America, 1945–1954.* Hanover, NH: Wesleyan University Press, 1990.

Schlessinger, Arthur, Jr. *The Vital Center: Our Purpose and Perils on the Tightrope of American Liberalism.* Boston: Houghton Mifflin, 1949.

Schulman, Bruce. *The Seventies: The Great Shift in American Culture, Society, and Politics.* New York: Free Press, 2001.

Shooter, Jim, and David Michilinie (w), and Mike Zeck (p). "Rite of Passage." *Captain America* 259 (July 1981), Marvel Comics.

Shooter, Jim (w), George Perez (p), and Pablo Marcos (i). "First Blood." *Avengers* 168 (February 1978), Marvel Comics.

Skidmore, Max S., and Joey Skidmore. "More Than Mere Fantasy: Political Themes in Contemporary Comic Books." *Journal of Popular Culture* 17, no. 1 (1983): 83–92.

Smoodlin, Eric. "Cartoon and Comic Classicism: High-Art Histories of Lowbrow Culture." *American Literary History* 4 (1992): 129–40.

Steranko, Jim (w/a), and Tom Palmer (i). "The Strange Death of Captain America." *Captain America* 113 (May 1969), Marvel Comics.

Steranko, Jim (w/a), and Joe Sinott (i). "Today Earth Died." *Strange Tales* 168 (May 1968), Marvel Comics.

———. "Who Is Scorpio?" *Nick Fury, Agent of SHIELD* 1 (June 1968), Marvel Comics.

Stern, Roger (w), and John Byrne and Josef Rubinstein (a). "Cap for President." *Captain America* 250 (October 1980), Marvel Comics.

Sussman, Warren. *Culture as History: Transformations in American Society in the Twentieth Century.* New York: Pantheon Books, 1984.

Sussman, Warren, and Edward Griffen. "Did Success Spoil the United States? Dual Representations in Postwar America." In *Recasting America,* edited by Lary May, 19–37. Chicago: University of Chicago Press, 1988.

Thomas, Roy. "Writing Comics Turned Out to Be What I Really Wanted to Do with My Life." *Alter Ego* 3, no. 70 (2007) 3–62.

Thomas, Roy (w), John Buscema (p), and Tom Palmer (i). "Come on in, the Revolution's Fine." *Mighty Avengers* 83 (December 1970), Marvel Comics.

Thomas, Roy (w), Barry Smith (p), and Jim Mooney (i). "Why Must There Be an Iron Man?" *Invincible Iron Man* 47 (June 1972), Marvel Comics.

Thomas, Roy (w), Herb Trimpe (p), and John Severin (i). "They Shoot Hulks, Don't They?" *Incredible Hulk* 142 (August 1971), Marvel Comics.

Truman, Harry S. "Address Before a Joint Session of Congress, 12 March 1947." Avalon Project at Yale University Law School; *http://www.yale.edu/lawweb/avalon/trudoc.htm* (accessed April 1, 2008).

U.S. Department of Commerce, Census Bureau. *U.S. Historical Statistics.* Washington DC: GPO, various years.

———. *Statistical Abstract of the United States.* Washington DC: GPO, various years.

Von Bernewitz, Fred, and Grant Geissman. *Tales of Terror: The EC Companion.* Seattle, WA: Fantagraphic Books, 2000.

Von Eschen, Penny. "Who's the Real Ambassador? Exploding Cold War Racial Ideology." In *Cold War Constructions,* edited by Christian Appy, 110–31. Amherst: University of Massachusetts Press, 2000.

Waid, Mark (w), Ron Garney (p), and Scott Koblish (i). "Man Without a Country." *Captain America* 450–53 (April 1996–July 1996), Marvel Comics.

Waid, Mark (w), Ron Garney (p), and Denis Rodier (i). "Operation Rebirth." *Captain America* 445 (November 1995), Marvel Comics.

Waid, Mark (w), Ron Garney (p), and John Beatty and Andy Smith (i). "The Power and the Glory." *Captain America* 2, nos. 5–7 (May–July 1998), Marvel Comics.

Waid, Mark (w), Andy Kubert (p), and Jesse Delperdang (i). "American Nightmare." *Captain America* 2, nos. 9–12 (September–December 1998), Marvel Comics.

Walker, Martin. *The Cold War: A History.* New York: Henry Holt, 1995.

Wallechinsky, David, and Irving Wallace. *The People's Almanac.* 3rd edition. New York: Bantam Books, 1981.

Werthem, Frederick. *Seduction of the Innocent.* New York: Rinehart, 1954.

White, John Kenneth. *Still Seeing Red: How the Cold War Shapes the New American Politics.* Boulder, CO: Westview Press, 1998.

Whitfield, Stephen. *The Culture of the Cold War*. 2nd edition. Baltimore: Johns Hopkins University Press, 1996.

Whyte, William. *The Organizational Man*. New York: Simon and Schuster, 1956.

Willard, Michael Nevin. "Skate and Punk at the Far End of the Century." In *America in the 1970s*, edited by Beth Bailey and David Farber, 181–207. Lawrence: University Press of Kansas, 2004.

Wills, Garry. *Reagan's America: Innocents at Home*. New York: Penguin, 1985.

Winthrop, John. "A Modell of Christian Charity." In *American Sermons*, edited by Michael Warner, 28–43. New York: Library of America, 1999.

Witek, Joseph. *Comic Books as History: The Narrative Art of Jack Jackson, Art Spiegelman and Harvey Pekar*. Jackson: University Press of Mississippi, 1989.

Wolfe, Alan. *One Nation, After All: What Middle-Class Americans Really Think About*. New York: Penguin, 1998.

Wright, Bradford. *Comic Book Nation: The Transformation of Youth Culture in America*. Baltimore: Johns Hopkins University Press, 2001.

Wylie, Philip. *Generation of Vipers*. Normal, IL: Dalkey Archive Press, 1996.

Zimmerman, David A. *Comic Book Character: Unleashing the Hero in Us All*. Downers Grove, IL: InterVarsity Press, 2004.

Zubok, Vlasila, and Constantine Pleshakov. *Inside the Kremlin's Cold War*. Cambridge, MA: Harvard University Press.

Index